Better The Devil

*An account of the perceived rivalry between
two, three, or should it be four, clubs
in the lower echelons of the EFL,
alongside an account of three of the most
dramatic seasons in Crawley Town's existence*

Steve Leake

Copyright © 2025 Steve Leake

Cover by Matthew Leake

All rights reserved, including the right to reproduce this book, or portions thereof in any form. No part of this text may be reproduced, transmitted, downloaded, decompiled, reverse engineered, or stored, in any form or introduced into any information storage and retrieval system, in any form or by any means, whether electronic or mechanical without the express written permission of the author.

ISBN: 978-1-918264-18-0

*With many thanks to all who contributed
to this book, either through your memories
or by jogging mine.*

*Thanks also to all those who have ever played
for or supported Crawley Town FC.
This book is for you..*

CONTENTS

PREFACE vii

PART ONE: HISTORY LESSON
   Chapter 1 Etymology 1
   Chapter 2 PRE THE GREAT WAR 3
   Chapter 3 BETWEEN THE WARS 5
   Chapter 4 POST WORLD WAR 2 6
   Chapter 5 THE 60s 7
   Chapter 6 THE 70s 9
   Chapter 7 THE 80s 10
   Chapter 8 THE 90s 13
   Chapter 9 THE NEW MILLENIUM
   THE NOUGHTIES 17
   Chapter 10 THE TEENS 21
   Chapter 11 THE ROARING TWENTIES 45

PART TWO: YEARS v YEARS
THE BEST YEAR EVER (OR WAS IT?)
   Chapter 1 1968/1969, 1969/1970
   Promotion to Tier 5
   followed by relegation to Tier 6 49
   Chapter 2 1983/1984, 1984/1985
   Promotion to Tier 6 52

Chapter 3 2003/2004, 2004/2005
Promotion to Tier 5 55
Chapter 4 2010/2011, 2011/2012
Promotion to Tier 4
followed by promotion to Tier 3 57
Chapter 5 2023/2024
Promotion to Tier 3 61
Chapter 6 2024/2025
Relegation to Tier 4 154
Chapter 7 Back to the Future
and wherever that may lead us 238

PART THREE: EPILOGUE 266
PART FOUR: APPENDIX 267
PART FIVE: PHOTO GALLERY 273

PREFACE

When I first started writing this book, it was to look at perceived rivalries between clubs, primarily involving Crawley Town FC and AFC Wimbledon. Alongside this book I was also starting to write my first novel, involving the dream of taking Crawley Town to Wembley for the first time. Needless to say, that idea was scrapped because of the events of 2023/2024 concerning the Red Devils. This book will now look at Rivalries, in different contexts and will also feature the historical significance of the 2023/2024 EFL Two season and the aftermath of it, comparing it with other historical seasons in the Crawley Town supporting life of yours truly. Unlike previous books which ended between seasons, this book, because of reasons known to all true Red Devil fans, will continue until the end of the 2024/2025 season and the run up to the 2025/2026 "We'll be back season".

The book has had several titles whilst I have been writing it, and I finally settled on "Better the Devil" when Scott Lindsey "left" MK and a few weeks later he returned to the Broadfield after Robbie Elliott had "left" us.

PART ONE
HISTORY LESSON

Chapter 1
Etymology

Let's start by looking at rivalries, whether that be between clubs or in a more abstract sense, between different years in the life of a football club.

Where do the words rivals, rivalry, rivalries etc. come from?

A long, long time ago in a world before football had been invented, two creatures came down to the same river to drink. Well, that is what etymologists would have you believe was where the term "to be a rival" started. The origin of the word rival comes from the Middle French and Latin "Rivalis", and the Old French "Rivus". It simply means "a person or creature who drinks from, or uses, the same brook, stream, river or water source as another". What they don't explain is whether this means a passive rivalry, where two like animals use it for the same purpose, either drinking or micturition, or whether it be the type of rivalry where one-party drinks, whilst the other takes the mick, so to speak.

Even worse than that, one of the rivals might be a carnivore who simply uses the river to eat those who simply want to drink, like Lions or Alligators picking off the thirsty wildebeest or antelope.

In our world, away from needing to stop at a river to drink, rivalry comes in a variety of forms, and across a whole range of backgrounds, but surprise, surprise, the one that I want to write about is one where one football team tries to match or beat another football team, and where it goes beyond the desire to win matches. There are many examples of rivalries like these in sport of all kinds, England V Australia in cricket, Europe V USA in golf, Manchester United v Liverpool in the Premier League. Not all of them feature teams of the same stature, and sometimes the rivalry starts between the towns involved, first over something as far away from football as you can get, like the building of a canal taking trade from one town to another.

Where rivalries exist because of the near proximity of the participants, the matches that bring such rivalry to a climax are often called derby games, but why? It all goes back to the Earl of Derby, who owned Stanley Park which separates the current home of Liverpool FC and Everton FC. Thus, matches between the two clubs were referred to as Derby matches. This game is probably the epitome of a local derby, but nowadays the word Derby can be used to identify clubs which may have something that connects them or sits between them. For example, the dockyard derby could be used to describe a game between Pompey and Plymouth Argyle, the M23 derby, between Brighton and Crystal Palace. There are also derbies that have a darker more sinister origin, such as that which describes the Old Firm derby in Glasgow, a rivalry that was borne out of the Irish troubles and allegiance to two different ways of worshipping the same God.

Before we get on to a look at our current closest rivalry, it is also good to understand that events can rival one another in the minds of supporters, they can also change over the years as clubs become distanced due to the successes or failures of either team. I will cover some of these instances after the history lesson about our current rivalry with one or is it two of our nearest neighbours.

The rivalry that exists between Crawley Town and our closest rivals was borne, I believe, out of the other party in this saga becoming, or appearing to become, pretentious in the eyes and minds of all that are of a Red Devil persuasion.

This is the story of that rivalry. Ladies and Gentlemen, girls and boys. I give you Crawley Town versus Wimbledon FC, AFC Wimbledon or Wimbledon AFC with a little bit thrown in about MK Dons.

First, though, we must look at the clubs involved, their individual histories, so we can see why the rivalry between three of the clubs exists, and to what level of antagonism it has evolved to. However, this is not an in-depth history of Crawley Town or any of the clubs who have claimed the history of Wimbledon FC. It is meant simply to show how CTFC and our rivals from Wimbledon, Kingston, Merton and/or Milton Keynes, have got to where they are today and where they have crossed paths, or not, over the course of three centuries.

PART ONE
HISTORY LESSON

Chapter 2
PRE THE GREAT WAR

In 1890, some boys were playing football under the supervision of the Reverand John Barrett-Lennard, vicar of St. John the Baptist in the small town of Crawley in Sussex. The session was probably taking place in Rectory Field, now long since gone. From that sacred beginning Crawley FC became reality, playing friendlies for six years alongside other Crawley sides, Crawley Athletic and Rangers. In 1896, Crawley FC joined the West Sussex League, changed their colours from navy blue to red and started, unknowingly perhaps, the climb to the Football League.

One year before our religious beginnings, Wimbledon Old Central Football Club was formed in 1889. They took their name from the Old Central School on Wimbledon Common where the players had been pupils. Their first match was a 1–0 victory over Westminster, whereas Crawley's was a four two victory against Lingfield. Success was quick to come for the south Londoners and by the time we were just starting our first competitive season they had won the Clapham League, and the Herald League.

After winning the Clapham League again as well as two minor trophies, a club meeting on the 1st of May 1905 decided to drop "Old Central" from the club's name – the club became Wimbledon Football Club and won the South London Charity Cup the same year. As successful as they were on the pitch, excessive debts caused the club to fold in 1910. Whether or not their three one friendly victory over Crawley FC in 1907 contributed to this is uncertain. They restarted just a year after going bust under the name Wimbledon Borough but dropped the "Borough" after barely a year. The club played on Wimbledon Common and at various other locations in the Wimbledon area until 1912, when the side settled at Plough Lane.

Meanwhile, Crawley Town was still a long way from getting its name but Crawley FC had played on several pitches including Mr. Stone's Field (now Stonefield Close, Southgate), Goffs Hill, Malthouse Farm and even Town Meadow in the West Sussex League and the Mid Sussex League, winning promotion to the Senior division of the West Sussex League and the Mid Sussex League Challenge Shield in 1903, just three days after the wedding of one of the CFC founders, Bill Denman, who played in that game. Please note that unlike our rivals, Crawley had not yet changed their name and so far, had not had any financial problems.

PART ONE
HISTORY LESSON

Chapter 3
BETWEEN THE WARS

After the Great War (not called the First World War at this time) Wimbledon joined the Athenian League and in the 1920/21 season they finished as runners up. They then joined the Isthmian League and won four titles during the thirties and reached the FA Amateur Cup final in 1934/1935, losing by two goals to one to Bishop Aukland in a replay at Stamford Bridge, after drawing at Ayresome Park, Middlesbrough in the first game.

Crawley FC, during the interwar years, lost out on winning a title because of fielding an unregistered player in two matches in 1929, and then it all seemed to go downhill, not just for Crawley FC but for Crawley football in general. Crawley FC folded in 1935, followed by Crawley Athletic in 1937 and John Penfold's Rangers a year later. The three clubs then amalgamated to form Crawley FC for the start of the 1938/1939 season and finished a respectable third place in the Brighton and District Division 2. The reason for the name being Crawley FC was that the people running the new club were mostly old Crawley FC officials.

PART ONE
HISTORY LESSON

Chapter 4
POST WORLD WAR 2

In 1946–47 Wimbledon appeared in another FA Amateur cup final, this time against Leytonstone at Highbury, losing again, this time by two goals to one and finished as runners-up in the league twice over the next few seasons.

Crawley were, by then, playing on Yetman's field, behind the Embassy Cinema (ask your mum or dad if you are that young) and in 1948 added the suffix "Town" to the name, as two years earlier The New Town Act had selected us, along with other places, such as Stevenage, to be the place of dreams for those bombed out of their London homes. The Football Club, on the move yet again, moved to Town Meadow, now known as the Multiplex car park.

Wimbledon were a cut above us going through the fifties, winning the Isthmian League for the fifth time in 1958–59 before starting a period that saw them win three successive championships, between 1961 and 1964, whilst also winning the FA Amateur Cup in 1962–63, beating our other local rivals, Sutton United by four Eddie Reynolds headed goals to two in the final, which was by then being played at the old Wembley Stadium.

Meanwhile back in the New Town, Crawley Town had progressed from local Sussex football to the Metropolitan league, a league which was a mixture of small-town clubs in and around London and Football League reserve sides, such as West Ham, Arsenal and Spurs etc. Our last season in this league being the same season as Wimbledon's triumph at Wembley. The 1963/64 season saw us enter the Southern League, a year ahead of Wimbledon, already having turned semi-professional a whole two years before them as well.

PART ONE
HISTORY LESSON

Chapter 5
THE 60s

Following Wimbledon's run of success in the Isthmian League and the FA Amateur Cup they joined the Southern League Division 1 in 1964/65 and that is where the rivalry began. Division 1 was in fact level 6 in what was to be the English football pyramid structure, with the Premier Division and the Northern Premier League being at level 5, the equivalent of today's National League. Their success continued, with them winning promotion in their first season as runner up to Hereford United. Corby Town and Poole Town also went up, with Stevenage and Crawley missing out by four and six points respectively. Our consolation was that we beat Wimbledon by two goals to nil at Town Meadow in front of 2400 people, 900 above our season's average. The goals in that match, came from Ernie Healer and one of Roy Jennings' 38 penalties. We lost the return by one goal to nil on April 10th and the rivalry had started and almost finished in the one season, because of their promotion, but luckily for us Hastings United were relegated to take their place and another potential rivalry was in the making (but that might have to wait for another book).

The Red Devils would not meet Wimbledon again until the 1966/67 season when we gained a creditable three all draw in the Premier Midweek Floodlit League at Plough Lane, with goals from Bobby Finch to level it at one-one, Dave Hannam to put us two one up and a late equaliser from Brian Knight against a team from the division above, but lost the return by three goals to nil on the 22nd April 1967.

We met again in the 1969/70 season, the year after we had won promotion ourselves to tier 5, the Southern League Premier Division.

That season we were to play Wimbledon five times, three times in the 4th qualifying round of the FA Cup and twice in the League, scoring one goal against their eleven. The cup matches featured two nil-nil draws at Plough Lane and Town Meadow. In those days clubs would normally toss up for the right to play the second replay at their ground but the Wimbledon manager didn't fancy another game in front of 3000 plus baying hostile Red Devils, and opted for the neutral venue of Guildford City where the Dons sneaked a two-nil victory to send them into the first round of the FA Cup. The League games saw us annihilated by nine goals to nil at Plough Lane, with Phil Patrick in goal, in December, and draw at home one all, with our goal coming from CTFC legend Dave Haining.

PART ONE
HISTORY LESSON

Chapter 6
THE 70s

The seventies for Crawley Town featured two re-elections to the Southern League First Division, but generally we managed to survive, and even featured in the first-round proper of the FA Cup, under Stan Markham, for the first time in our history whilst Wimbledon went from strength to strength. They won the Southern League for three years running from 1974/75 to 1976/77 and also became the first non-league side in the twentieth century to defeat a top-flight club, Burnley, away from home in the FA Cup. They eventually went out to Damned United, Leeds that is, after holding the then League champions to a nil-nil draw at Elland Road before succumbing by one goal to nil in front of 40,000 spectators at Selhurst Park. They were eventually elected to the Football League at the end of the 1976/77 season, at the expense of Workington Town, who are at the moment competing in the Northern Premier League.

In their first season in the Football League, they finished in a very respectable 13th place, but Alan Batsford resigned as manager, to be replaced by Dario Gradi (pre his Crewe days) who was to take them up the following year into the 3rd Division. (League 1 as it is now known)

PART ONE
HISTORY LESSON

Chapter 7
THE 80s

The 1980s saw some success for both clubs, albeit in larger doses for Wimbledon than for Crawley.

Wimbledon's first stay in the Third Division was not a successful one and they were relegated, finishing bottom after winning just 10 league games. It was at this time that relocation to Milton Keynes was first considered by the then chairman Ron Noades. He entered talks with Milton Keynes Development Corporation about the possibility of moving the club to the new town, but the plan was not executed at that time.

Remaining at Plough Lane, Wimbledon regained Third Division status at the first attempt and behind the scenes, chairman Ron Noades walked out of the club to take over Crystal Palace, taking manager Dario Gradi with him. This led to Dave Bassett being promoted from assistant manager to manager, but once again Wimbledon were relegated in 22nd place. It was indeed a sad time for our rivals, as just before the survival battle was lost, the injured defender Dave Clement committed suicide.

The next season they repeated their impression of a yo-yo by regaining their Third Division status at the first time of asking, going up as Fourth Division champions. They continued their excellent form in the next season and were promoted to the Second division as high scoring runners up.

There was seemingly to be no end to their meteoric climb to the top level of English football, whereas in North Sussex our climb to the Football League was also just starting. In the same season as Wimbledon won promotion to the Second division, Crawley Town also stepped up a rung on the ladder by winning promotion to the Southern League Premier Division, for the second time, under John Maggs. Having survived a couple of re-elections back in the 70s, the Red Devils finally made it back into the Premier Division by finishing as runners up to RS Southampton. However, the Premier Division was no longer level five in the English Football pyramid as the Conference was now the next step on the ladder to Football league nirvana. Still a way to go.

In the 1984/85 season Wimbledon finished in a more than respectable 12th position in the Second division, whilst the Red Devils missed out on the Southern Premier title by just three points. Crawley Town would remain in the Southern Premier for twenty years, moving to our present home in Broadfield in 1997. In South London, Wimbledon would rise to the very heights, in terms of divisions, in English football and then disappear in controversial clouds of franchise style bs.

Let me explain.

Their second year in the second division started well, with a three nil home defeat of Middlesbrough and on the last day of the season they clinched promotion to the First Division, winning away against Huddersfield Town. This meant that in only four years they had climbed the entire league and just nine years after having been elected to the Football League. Something which that club, who don't exist anymore, should be justifiably proud of.

They were, like we are every year, tipped to go down but, having lost their first match away at Maine Road, they won the next four on the trot and, by the first of September, sat at the very pinnacle of the Football League. They finished 6th in their first season before manager Dave Bassett moved on to take charge of Watford. His replacement, Bobby Gould, came in from Bristol Rovers, and "The Crazy Gang" era was born.

Meanwhile, Crawley Town were improving on their league form and managed to finish in 6th place, but in the same year as Wimbledon were to win the FA Cup, another thing which that club, who don't exist anymore, should be justifiably proud of, we failed to get over our first hurdle, losing at home to the mighty Chatham.

To give credit to Wimbledon, not to be confused with either of the two clubs seeking to purloin their history, they beat Liverpool in the final with a solitary goal from Lawrie Sanchez, who later went on to manage Dannie "always a Red" Bulman at

Wycombe Wanderers. Another highlight from the final, as far as the 37,000 Wimbledon fans were concerned, was Dave Beasant becoming the first goalkeeper to save a penalty in an FA Cup final, saving John Aldridge's shot. Unfortunately, for them, they were prevented from representing England in the Cup Winner's Cup because of the ban on English clubs which was in affect at the time due to the Heysel Stadium Disaster, which rather ironically involved Liverpool, their beaten opponents at Wembley.

Before the start of the 1988/89 season, in fact just days after their FA Cup triumph, the Wimbledon directors announced plans to build a new all-seater stadium in the club's home borough of Merton, whilst in Crawley we were still playing at Town Meadow, and if you wanted to go to the Cinema you would be going to the Embassy in the High street, or going out of town. In the year after the Wimbledon sides cup triumph Crawley finished 12th in the Southern Premier and almost reached the 1st round proper of the FA Cup, losing to Merthyr Tydfil, the eventual champions, in a replay in Wales, after having held them to a three all draw in Crawley in what, to most people present, will always be known as the Grant Gallagher game. (Ask someone who has read Noli Cedere to explain this to you, as unfortunately my first book is no longer in print).

For Wimbledon, Bobby Gould steered them to 12th place and 8th place in the First division over the next two seasons but despite these successes, Bobby Gould was replaced in 1990 by Luton Town's manager Ray Harford who had won the League Cup with them in the same year that Wimbledon won the FA Cup. I know what you're thinking, Luton Town, aaah yes, we later became their champions.

After almost getting to the first round of the FA Cup in 1988, we failed at the first hurdle the following year, going out to Staines Town, whilst a year later we went out just one round later, going out to Worthing.

PART ONE
HISTORY LESSON

Chapter 8
THE 90s

The nearest we would get to rivalling (there's that word again) Wimbledon's success came in the form of the Sussex cup double winning the Senior Cup in both 1990 and 1991, coupled with the Sussex Floodlit Cup in 1991.

At that time, no one would have considered us and the Crazy Gang of Wimbledon to be rivals. We had briefly crossed each other's paths around twenty years previously and since then we had largely stood still in the shadow of their meteoric rise to the First Division. Indeed, it could have been a whole lot worse if Rushden (pre adding Diamonds to their name) hadn't failed ground grading regulations and been relegated in our place. In fact, three of the four teams that thought they had been relegated were saved, by two of the clubs who thought they had won promotion failing the same ground grading regulations.

Meanwhile, in the First Division, Wimbledon under Harford's management, finished seventh in 1990/91 and because of nothing coming of the plans for a new ground the club's board decided to share with Crystal Palace at Selhurst Park as they thought Plough Lane was beyond being upgraded to meet the new regulations for all-seater stadium.

The 1991/92 season saw Wimbledon have a season like ours, yet to come in 2022/23, where three managers came and two of them went. Harford suddenly resigned in October 1991, to be replaced by Peter Withe. Withe lasted until just after the turn of the new year, when Joe Kinnear was promoted from the role of youth team coach, initially taking over as interim manager. He managed to steer them to 13th place in the First Division which meant they would be one of the founding clubs of the Premier League. Joe Kinnear's position was made permanent as a result.

Back in Crawley we were to finish 17th in a division of twenty-two teams but, as us old timers know, that was not the story of our season that year. We won through six rounds of the FA Cup, gaining a place in the 3rd round for the first time in our history, against our near neighbours, Brighton and Hove Albion. We lost, not sure what the score was, but Arsenal lost to Wrexham that same day and Wimbledon lost in the same round, to Bristol City, in a replay after having drawn at Ashton Gate. These things happen!!

1992/93 saw both Crawley Town and Wimbledon, worlds apart at this time, have varying degrees of success. Wimbledon finished 12th in the Premier League, having been third from bottom on Boxing Day, whilst the Red Devils finished 6th in the Southern League and won the Sussex Floodlit Cup for the third year running. However, we failed to capitalise on our exemption to the 4th qualifying round of the FA Cup, going out to Yeovil at home.

The next season proved to be one of Wimbledon's best ever seasons, which saw them finish 6th in the Premier League and reach the quarter finals of the League Cup, whilst Crawley finished a disappointing 5th, disappointing because in the last eight games of the season we won just two matches and slipped from the top of the league finishing nine points behind the eventual champions, Farnborough Town. We did, however, reach the second round of the FA Cup going out to Division 2 (League 1 in today's lingo) side, Barnet. Having sold Craig Whittington to Scarborough Athletic the week before, we paid the price and missed out on a potential tie with Chelsea in the third round.

Away from football Pete Winkelman, moved from his south London home to set up the Great Linford Manor residential recording studio in Milton Keynes. Watch this space!!

In the 1994/95 season, or rather in the close season before it, Wimbledon made their first venture into European competition, playing a side consisting mainly of reserves and youngsters in the Inter Toto Cup. They, along with Spurs, were banned from Europe for the following season for seemingly not paying any respect to the competition. In the League they finished a respectable 9th.

Meanwhile, back in God's own county, Crawley Town made the 1st round of the FA Cup, going out to Exeter City after having beaten Hastings United in a 4th Qualifying round replay at Town Mead, just as we had back in 1971. A mid table finish in the league was secured by an unbeaten run of nine matches, including seven wins, at the end of the season.

The next two seasons for Wimbledon saw them finish 14th and 8th, but in the second of those seasons, 1996/97, they reached, at one point, second place in the league before dropping to eighth on the last day and thus missing out on European qualification. They did, however, reach the semifinals of both the FA and League cups.

Crawley Town had reasonable league seasons, finishing 9th and 17th respectively but went out of the Cup to Sutton United and Bromley. The true story of the 1996/97 season for us though, was the upcoming move to Broadfield Stadium and Crawley managing to escape relegation by winning three out of our last four games. The story, for us, may well have been different since then if we had not had that late run of wins.

A year later in the 1997-98 season, everything appeared promising for Wimbledon, as up until Christmas they were regularly in the top five of the Premier League, whereas Crawley, having moved to Broadfield, were sitting in mid table, which was where we stayed until the end of the season. Wimbledon, however, after having their good start, fell away badly and finished in 15th place. The rivalry was still a long way off to becoming what it was to be in the not-too-distant future

The following season followed a similar pattern for Wimbledon, although the slump in form came later, as in March they were still close to qualifying for a UEFA Cup Place. They eventually finished in 16th after having been beaten by Spurs in the League Cup semi-finals, who went on to win the final. In Sussex, with the late Billy Smith in charge and Ben Abbey up front, Crawley maintained their midtable status despite having financial problems which meant no reserve team and culminated in Billy Smith being replaced by legend Cliff Cant and John Duly buying the club to stop us going into administration. Cliff only lasted until October, replaced by the man who he had replaced,

Billy Smith. In the end our final position for 1999/2000 was a creditable midtable slot, but just six points above relegation.

Wimbledon were not to be so fortunate. Joe Kinnear was replaced by Norwegian coach Egil Olsen before the season started, due to illness and, although they reached the quarterfinals of the League Cup, the Scandinavian left before the season's end as relegation threatened and was replaced by Terry Burton. He could not save them however, and on 14 May 2000, 12 years to the day after the FA Cup win, they were relegated from the topflight and the gap had started to narrow between them and us.

PART ONE
HISTORY LESSON

Chapter 9
THE NEW MILLENIUM
THE NOUGHTIES

Season 2000/2001 saw Crawley Town, once again, finish in mid table but we reached the Southern League Cup final for the first time losing four one on aggregate over a two-legged final against Worcester City. At Plough Lane, sorry, Selhurst Park, Terry Burton remained manager in the Championship until the end of the 2001/2002 season when, after missing out in the promotion play offs, he was sacked. At the beginning of his final season, Wimbledon announced its intention to relocate to Milton Keynes, which justifiably was opposed by Wimbledon fans, the Football League and the Football Association. However, an FA appointed three-person independent commission voted in favour of the move by two votes to one, and where there was one club there soon became two.

Meanwhile, Crawley Town, still under Billy Smith, finished fourth in the Southern League in 2001/2002 and despite slipping to seventh the following season, won the Southern League Cup, the Southern League Trophy and the Sussex Senior Cup. Things were on the up at Broadfield, at least on the pitch they were. Bill Smith left the club in January 2003, being replaced by centre forward Francis Vines.

In that season, a new club came into being, as AFC Wimbledon were formed and competed in the Combined Counties League finishing with 111 points, which astonishingly only earned them third place behind Withdean 2000 and AFC Wallingford. In a league where the crowds were only a little larger than the proverbial two men and a dog, their presence presented the smaller clubs with much needed finance.

Now under the management of Goalkeeping coach, Stuart Murdoch, and with most Wimbledon fans adopting AFC to watch, attendances plummeted below that which AFC were attracting in a level 9 League some seven levels below. Wimbledon, not AFC or MK just yet, finished 10th in the league during the club's last full season at Selhurst Park, but in so doing they entered administration in June 2003 and played their first match in Milton Keynes in September and even though crowds attending the club's games at its new base were bigger than those at Wimbledon, because of the machinations of administration, players who could command a transfer fee were sold, and as a result they were relegated to League 1. Coming out of administration at the end of their relegation season, that is when the franchise tag was well and truly hung round their necks and MK Dons were born.

In comparison, the two other clubs in this trilogy, us at Crawley and AFC Wimbledon, had great seasons in 2003/2004. In the last year of Doc Martens sponsoring the Southern League, Crawley Town won the championship by twelve points over nearest rivals Weymouth, (there's that word again) in a season which marked the final year of just one team being promoted from both the Southern, Northern and Isthmian leagues. In the end, only two teams were promoted, us from the Southern League and Canvey Island from the Isthmian, as neither the champions of the Northern League, Hucknall Town, or the runners up, Droylesden were deemed to meet the Conference Premier ground regulations. However, this coincided with the Conference expanding to three divisions and, in effect, the Southern, Northern and Isthmian leagues going down one rung on the football ladder. Whilst we were going up to Level 5 of the Pyramid and winning the Southern League Cup and Trophy, AFC Wimbledon were winning the Combined Counties League, at only their second attempt, remaining unbeaten throughout the entire league season and amassing a colossal 130 points.

It was during this time that the owners to be of Kingstonian FC, the Khosla family, had purchased the stricken club from administrators and opted to sell the stadium lease for £2.4m to AFC Wimbledon – who needed a medium-term venue for their phoenix club. The Khosla's, rather than the club itself, profited from this sale. Kingstonian, a very proud club, were allowed to stay on for little or no rent, and for a while very little changed, except for the colour of paint around the stadium.

The beginning of 2004/2005 saw MK and Crawley Town separated by just two divisions, with AFC a further three rungs down the ladder. The gaps were closing fast though as MK just survived their first season back in League 1, Crawley finished comfortably in mid table in the Conference, won the Sussex Senior Cup for the second time in three years whilst the phoenix club, AFC, won promotion from Isthmian One to Isthmian Premier at their first attempt.

2005/2006, up until the end of 2007/2008, saw Crawley Town finish in the lower reaches of the Conference Premier three seasons running, without really getting into relegation worries, whereas MK were relegated to League 2 only to win promotion back to League 1 two years later. AFC, finished fourth and fifth in the first two of those seasons before gaining promotion to Conference South via the playoffs at the end of 2007/2008. As a point of interest, the first match between Crawley Town and AFC Wimbledon took place on Tue, 09 Aug 2005, when the two sides played out a 9-goal 'friendly' at Broadfield Stadium in front of 921 spectators, the Red Devils winning 5-4 with Francis Vines as manager. Steve Burton scored a hattrick with our other goals coming from Marvin Brown and Stuart Douglas.

All three clubs were now within three divisions of each other, but by the end of the 2008/2009 season the spread was just two divisions, thanks to AFC's fourth promotion in just seven seasons since their formation. The Crawley Town versus AFC Wombles rivalry was just about to start in earnest.

2009/10 saw our first competitive matches with AFC Wimbledon, and in four games we beat them at home and drew away in the League but could only draw at home with them in the FA Cup, before losing an ill-tempered replay at Kingsmeadow in the borough of Kingston.

Kingston was the venue for the first competitive game between the two clubs where, on September the 22nd, a Jefferson Louis goal earned us a point in the League, in front of 3,408 spectators.

Just over a month later, in front of 2,204 spectators, the first FA Cup game saw Danny Forrest give Crawley the lead only for Sam Hatton to force a replay late on. With the second game level at one all, Jon Main put AFC one up before Jefferson Louis equalised to put Town on the front foot. AFC's Derek Duncan crudely brought down Simon Rusk, just before half time, and was promptly sent off. Terry Brown, back in charge of the Dons, reorganised his ten men at half time and it was they who came out on top, by three goals to one. The second half goals being scored by Luke Moore and Danny Kedwell. 2,469 spectators were to witness their win in a match described by AFC reporter, Stephen Crabtree, as "one of the best nights of the Dons' 18-year tenure at Kingsmeadow". For Crawley fans it was the first competitive loss against AFC Wimbledon.

Point of Order: Stephen Crabtree also wrote this in the same article.

"On the two previous occasions when the Dons have drawn Crawley in the FA Cup, replays have been required. 51 years ago, in November 1969, it took three games to separate the sides,"

Really? Wasn't that Wimbledon we played back in 1969, not AFC?

Terry Brown after the game said "For 30 minutes they battered us and then we lost Duncan, I was delighted with the response of the players. Every time I ask them to give me something extra, they stand up and deliver."

The second league game, in front of 1,569 spectators saw Crawley come out on top by two goals to one with goals from Danny Forrest and Charlie Ademeno. This match marked our first competitive victory over AFC Wimbledon, yet despite this, Charlie Ademeno left Crawley at the end of the season, to join a much bigger club, Grimsby Town. Great decision Charlie!!!

The stage was set, however, for Project Promotion and theirs and nearly everyone else's, accusations of us buying the league.

PART ONE
HISTORY LESSON

Chapter 10
THE TEENS

The season of 2010/2011 proved eventful for all three clubs, as all had fabulous seasons in their respective leagues. MK Dons finished their league fixtures in 5th place, securing them a playoff semifinal tie against 4th Placed Peterborough United. The other League 1 semifinal being between 3rd placed Huddersfield and 6th placed Bournemouth. MK, after having won the home tie by three goals to two in front of 12, 662 spectators, lost the return game by two goals to nil, and thus stayed in League 1 for another year.

In the Blue Square Premier, Crawley Town and AFC became embroiled in bitter rivalry even before the season had started. Project Promotion, financed by Bruce "The Legend" Winfield and Paul Hayward, aka Hong Kong Paul wound up all our opponents from the beginning of the most memorable season in our history. We were accused of "buying the league", whereas all we did was buy players who would go on to win the league. The two do not always go together. AFC, in particular, took umbrage with us trying to buy their forward Danny Kedwell, and when we met on the 23rd of September at Kingsmeadow in front of 4,018 paying customers, Kedwell, still their player, donned an under garment emblazoned with "Somethings money can't buy". (See Photo Gallery). Danny Kedwell in an AFC online article entitled "Catch up with Keds" had this to say about the incident.

"I remember arriving at that game and wondering where all the yellow t-shirts were coming from. It was my boy that made me realise that it was me on them! I've still got one of them now – a fan threw one to me after we beat Crawley. You couldn't write the script of it all. They'd had their bid turned down and not long later I got the winner against them."

We lost that game by two goals to one, and yes, Danny Kedwell scored the winner in a two one victory which put them top of the league table. This marked our first league defeat to AFC and saw the Red Devils given three yellow cards against two given to the Wombles.

The feelings held by their supporters are quite clear to see in the write-up on the match by an AFC Wimbledon fan whose feelings towards CTFC are quite clear (my comments are in parenthesis) :-

"If any Wimbledon fan dreamt last night how this pulsating match would finish, tonight it was played out in oh so perfect high definition. It's a poorly kept secret that these two do not get on. Little history of course, more a matter of morals. (Morals brought into question? Try telling that to the supporters of Kingstonians)

Newly rich Crawley's failed attempts to lure legend-in-the-making Danny Kedwell to the Broadfield was not well received. Defeat was far from well taken. (A legend in the making, who scored 25 goals in total, whereas our slightly smaller Legend scored forty)

Manager Steve Evans, the self-styled 'Special One' of Conference football, went public claiming Wimbledon reneged on a verbal agreement with the player to allow a transfer should a £60,000 bid be lodged. Rubbish, of course. (and then you say he was offered a £40,000 signing on fee)

In the same paper, Evans then suggested Kedwell was "desperate" to join the Crawley revolution. Something to do with an apparent £40,000 signing on fee perhaps.

Wimbledon fans and their wisely tight-lipped hierarchy were fuming at the blatant attempt to unsettle their star and their club days before the start of the season.

Tonight came closure. This was one of AFC Wimbledon's greatest evenings. (What? Another one?)

Kedwell scored the winning goal to send Wimbledon top of the Blue Square Bet Premier, overtaking the Scot's Red Devils as a sudden gust of irony swept through Kingsmeadow.

They went behind just before half-time when Ed Harris' slip, his only error on an otherwise flawless evening, allowed Matt Tubbs to score from close range.

Sam Hatton levelled things up before time stood still as Kedwell nodded the sweetest of winners ten minutes from time.

If one thing is going to keep this talented Crawley team from the championship, it could be their manager's loose lips.

Predictably this evening, Evans delivered more mind games, offered more of a stick for his critics to beat him with.

"Who played the football tonight, Wimbledon or Crawley? Who?" he demanded. "Who played long ball tonight, Wimbledon or Crawley?

"Is that the benchmark we've got to be up there, we've not got a problem. At 1-0 Brodie and Tubbs should score and kill it. They are big signings, that's what they're paid for.

"On the balance of play 3-1 to us would have been fair, it's not justice tonight," said Evans before storming out of the post-match pre-conference after a reporter questioned his defender's performance inside their own box.

Terry Brown, the Wimbledon manager, was on cloud nine as 4,000 fans saw his team return to the top in the south-west London rain.

"It was script perfect," he said. "For Danny to get the winning goal in front of what is fast becoming the Danny Kedwell End is wonderful, quite brilliant.

"If we would have sold him to Crawley, where would we be? Not top of this league let me tell you. It was a magnificent performance with a makeshift teenage defence and I couldn't be prouder."

The message, like the picture on the TV screens tonight and in the fans' dreams, is crystal clear."

Likewise, internet forums also highlighted the feeling of AFC towards CTFC:

"There has been a rivalry with them this season. We were both going for promotion for a start.':SEP:'"

"Then Fat Boy Evans tried to poach Danny Kedwell. Then when he turned them down Fat Boy tried to accuse us of holding him back."

"Behind yesterday the second-best moment of the season was Danny heading in the winner against them in a 2-1 win and seeing Fat Boy throw his toys out of the pram in the post-match interview."

"Crawley are their money. We are our fans." (That is rubbish, if you were your fans back in the day then surely AFC would not have been needed. Anyway, did not Jon Main once say that Dons players were on a £1000 a goal bonus to score against Crawley?)

"Staying up and beating Crawley home and away would be a good season for me." (Lack of ambition there!)

"Employing a convicted criminal as a manager, spending ridiculous amounts, (Could not the member teams of the Combined Counties League say that of AFC?) generally upsetting everyone. Yeah, lovely."

"Evans got done for tax evasion & received a suspended sentence I think & a fine... plus he got done by the FA for contract irregularities..." (Not while he was with us)

Moving on from that defeat, our second of only three matches lost that season, we met again on the 18th of March 2011. After the game in September, Wimbledon, AFC that is, were top of the table on 22 points ahead of Crawley Town on 20.

The return game itself was one that AFC couldn't afford to lose, but in front of a 4,054 crowd that is exactly what they did.

In a game where six yellow cards were issued (3 to CTFC), and two straight reds were also given out, one to Dannie Bulman for the Red Devils, just before half time, and one to AFC's Mulley, as injury time at 90 minutes had just started.

The real story of the game though, must be terminally ill Bruce Winfield checking himself out of the hospice to watch his beloved CTFC beat Wimbledon citing "Well, what's the worst that can happen?". He was to die just three days later, secure in the knowledge that his football club were well on the way to the EFL.

In the game itself, Crawley Town made a whirlwind start and were 2-0 up inside nine minutes thanks to Matt Tubbs 30th league goal of the season, a bullet header from Josh Simpson's cross after just five minutes and Kyle McFadzean heading home a Ben Smith corner four minutes later.

The football played by the Red Devils, in the first half hour, was outstanding and Wimbledon struggled to cope leading to McFadzean nearly extending the lead, but on 38 minutes AFC were back in the game when Brett Johnson headed home from Gareth Gwillim's in swinging free kick to make it 2-1. Indeed, with Dannie Bulman getting a straight red, just before half time for a foul on Luke Moore, many in the crowd were expecting an AFC comeback in the second half.

The much maligned (by AFC fans that is) Steve Evans brought on James Dance for Richard Brodie at the break, but it was AFC who almost equalised when Mulley and Gwillim hit the same post within a few seconds of each other on fifty minutes.

Just three minutes later the substitution paid off as Sergio Torres won the ball off Ryan Jackson, played it across the face of the area to Dance who drilled a low shot inside the left-hand post to make it 3-1.

After that, AFC never looked like getting back into the game and they ended with ten men themselves when Mulley was red carded for a foul on Josh Simpson.

After the game in March, Crawley Town, some nine points ahead of AFC as well as having four games in hand, sat at the top of the league and were only six matches away from winning the title away at Tamworth, some six games before the end of the season. Luton Town, in third place, were fourteen points off the top.

No team could keep up with the Red Devils that year, as we finished on 105 points fifteen ahead of AFC and, you may know, played in the 5th round of the FA Cup, when we almost took Manchester United to a replay. Our heaviest defeat in that season was a two-nil loss to another potential rival, Horsham, in the Sussex Senior Cup. Our other four defeats were all by the odd goal, two at home to Grimsby and Newport, and two away to Dartford and Manchester United.

AFC Wimbledon finally achieved promotion through the play offs, beating Luton Town four three on penalties after a nil-nil draw. To be fair to them, they did beat Fleetwood Town by eight goals to one in the two-legged semi-finals, and we all know how that feels, don't we?

The "Legend" Danny Kedwell did not play in the EFL for AFC and transferred to his hometown club Gillingham FC, you might have heard of them, before the start of the 2011/2012 season.

Mk Dons in 2011/2012 finished in the playoff positions for the second year running, and for the second-year running went out at the semifinal stage, this time to Huddersfield, who, like MK, had missed out in the previous season, going out in the final against MK's semifinal opponents, Peterborough. This time, despite winning the second leg by two goals to one at Stadium MK, they went out by three goals to two on aggregate, having lost two nil in the first leg. Compensation perhaps, in that the Terriers went on to win the final and gain promotion to the Championship.

2011/2012 for Crawley Town and AFC Wimbledon, marked their first season as Football League clubs. For us it marked the culmination of 115 years of effort in non-league football and for AFC it was just 10 years after their birth in 2002. Personally, I think this is the achievement that they should be proud of, the making of their own history rather than trying to claim the history of a club which still exists, albeit with a different name. My views on that other club will follow later.

The new season, for us in Crawley, proved to be another of upwards progress and it all started with a home League Cup Preliminary Round clash against AFC Wimbledon on Friday 29th July, even before we had finished with our friendlies. How very apt that they should prove to be our first opponents as a Football League club, and our first opponents in the League Cup.

The game, played in front of 3,204 spectators, proved to be as feisty as those that had gone before and was being played before the league season had started to allow Championship side Birmingham City, the holders, to start in the third round, because of their Europa League commitments.

Luke Moore fired AFC ahead but Hope Akpan, playing his first competitive game for Crawley, levelled seven minutes from the break. AFC went two one up early in the second half through their summer signing, Jack Midson, but "he's here, he's there, he's every f***ing where" Sergio Torres quickly equalised before our Legend, Matt Tubbs, scored the winner in the 64th minute., earning us a meeting with Crystal Palace in the next round, which we lost two nil. Hope, on his first competitive appearance for the club, as well as scoring our first equaliser, also received his first red card for us late on in the game.

By the time we played them again on Saturday 22nd October we had accrued 28 points from 13 games and back-to-back promotion was looking good, despite having lost two away games in that period by six goals to nil at Morecambe and by three goals to nil at Swindon. That proved to be a minor blip, as when we faced AFC at Kingsmeadow, we were attempting to win our sixth game in a row. AFC, as well as going out of the League Cup to us, had not had such a good start and sat eight points behind us, but with a game in hand.

The game itself should have been played in front of 4,550 spectators but I was helping scatter my in-laws' ashes down at Hengistbury head, so there were only 4,549 in the ground.

I missed a typical match against AFC. Crawley stormed into a two goal lead through an own goal and a Claude Davis header but a Claude Davis own goal and an equaliser from Jack Midson before half time seemed to be the prelude to a home win. However, a penalty for handball, converted by Matt Tubbs and two headers, yes headers, from Danni Bulman earned us a hard fought and well deserved five-two victory away from home and cued up the singing of "Is there a fire drill?" by the away supporters.

This result, up until the 2023/2024 season, was Crawley Town's biggest away win as a Football League Club and marked the first-ever Football League meeting between us and AFC, and our first ever League win over them.

Crawley Town maintained their unbeaten run against AFC when, on Saturday April 14th April, a one all draw between the two sides, in front of a crowd of 3,768 at Broadfield Stadium, was fought out in true derby style. Three yellow cards and one straight red were issued, Hope Akpan having the dubious honour of collecting his second red against AFC.

All Red Devils, whether old or new, should know that Steve Evans, the manager that AFC hated, had left Crawley Town just five days before our third game with them, and that coupled with forwards, Matt Tubbs and Tyrone Barnett, being transferred in the January window almost scuppered our second promotion in a row. Thankfully, Craig Brewster saw us over the line with three wins and two draws in our last six games, although we almost messed it up in our last home game, losing three nil to already relegated Hereford United. Our final game saw us win at Accrington Stanley to gain automatic promotion to League 1. Important to note that if Scott Neilson hadn't won that game for Crawley, we would have been in the play offs back in 2012, a whole 12 years ahead of it actually happening. We did progress to the 5th round of the FA Cup for the second year running, going out to my father's boyhood club, Stoke City of the Premier League, after having beaten two championship sides along the way in Bristol City and Hull City. AFC Wimbledon finished the season 30 points behind us, 10 points above Hereford United, went out of the FA Cup in the second round to Bradford City, and out of the EFL Trophy in the third round to Swindon Town.

In 2012/2013, Crawley Town finished a creditable 10th in League 1 and started our relationship with that team from the home of the concrete cows. On the 23rd of October we met MK Dons for the first time when two goals from Billy Clarke helped Crawley beat them for our fifth win in six games. Their team included Dean Lewington, ex other Red Devil Luke Chadwick and the man who helped us win promotion to the conference back in 2004, Charlie Mc Donald. The new Dons were left to rue missed chances in a game which could have ended five all.

Later in the season, Crawley Town paid their first visit to Stadium MK where they gained a creditable goalless draw, which virtually put paid to MK's playoff hopes. Their forward, Ryan Lowe, had three goals disallowed for offside, whilst Billy Clarke squandered any chances that Crawley had.

For the third year running it took a Premier League side, in Reading, to knock us out of the FA Cup. I am looking forward to playing them again this season (2024/2025) (Written before our visit to the Madejski). However, we gained two championship scalps in the League Cup, beating Millwall and Bolton Wanderers, before going out to Premier League Swansea City, who scored their winner in added on time.

Despite MK and AFC being in different divisions, the 2012/2013 season saw them compete against each other for the first time since the acrimonious move to Milton Keynes and the formation of AFC. Before the 2nd round FA Cup game, played on the 6th of December 2012, Pete Winkelman, MK's chairman, put out the following statements in the hope that it would perhaps ease tensions between the two clubs.

"I did a deal that was wrong and the owners (of Wimbledon at the time) were wrong. I'm not proud of the way football came to Milton Keynes." Perhaps he should have left it there, but he went on to say that the supporters were also wrong.

"They deserted their club; they forced it into administration, then they didn't buy it."

He then went on to argue that "The club had no other choice but to come to Milton Keynes, it was going to be liquidated."

Before we get into how the cup game went, I feel I must raise some issues here. Firstly, football did already exist in Milton Keynes, in the form of Bletchley Town, old adversaries of our club back in our Southern League days.

The developers of the New Town (as it was then) wanted a big club in residence in a modern stadium for their own business-based reasons, and Wimbledon were not the only club in the running for this dubious honour. Barnet, Crystal Palace, Queens Park Rangers, Luton and even Charlton Athletic were all either approached or mooted the idea themselves.

Needless to say, the fans of both AFC and MK see it quite differently.

Kris Stewart, the leading campaigner against the Milton Keynes move, who became AFC Wimbledon's first chairman, from 2002-06 said "We did the opposite of abandoning our club. The club died, and we did something positive, won back the Football League place stolen from us. We're proud of what we achieved. When it went into administration, I can't remember anyone considering we should buy it; it had already died for us. The whole of football now realises what was done was wrong".

I, for one, agree with that, as they proved Winkleman wrong. You can get into the Football League in ten years, and if he wanted to do that for Milton Keynes as a community, perhaps he should have bought Bletchley Town before they went out of existence.

Even John Brockwell, chair of the MK Dons supporters' association back in 2012 said "We naively thought we were saving Wimbledon, and I wish that both clubs could celebrate what they have"

John Read, who has supported MK Dons ever since they arrived, as Wimbledon, in Milton Keynes stated that "It was wrong, fundamentally, that the club was moved here. But now it feels like supporting any other club. We're used to being regarded as football's illegitimate club, people laugh at Milton Keynes, the concrete cows and roundabouts, now the franchise. We can take the stick".

No wonder then, that the fixture 10 years in the making, since AFC Wimbledon's formation by disgruntled Wimbledon FC fans in protest of their club's proposed move to Milton Keynes, turned out to be a tense affair, with both sets of fans rising to the challenge of claiming legitimacy for their two clubs. The on-field action failed, in the game's early stages, to live up to the hype and the most eye-catching moment came when a plane, chartered by AFC supporters, performed a fly past towing a banner proclaiming "We are Wimbledon"

MK struck the first blow in the 45th minute when Gleeson fired home a 25-yard shot which was uncharacteristic of the nature of the game up to that point.

The second half, though, burst into life when Jack Midson headed home, past former Wimbledon FC keeper Martin, from a Toby Ajala cross to equalise for the boys in blue, sparking a pitch invasion from some of the AFC fans, which was sorted quite quickly. They obviously were not put in the gallery back then.

Ryan Lowe thought he had won it for MK not long after that, but it was disallowed for offside earlier in the move, and just as AFC thought they had earned a replay in Kingston, Otsemobor for MK deflected a shot from Ismael over another ex-Wimbledon FC keeper, Sullivan, to win the game for the franchise illegitimates despite, after an MK Dons pitch invasion, a concerted effort by the League 2 side to secure a second equaliser.

I would imagine that the exit from the stadium was quite fraught, unlike ours in May of 2024.

AFC, after that defeat on the 2nd of December 2012, came perilously close to being relegated for the first time in their short history. With two games to go AFC were in 22nd position in

League 2 on 49 points with a worse goal difference than the two teams directly above them, Plymouth Argyle and Dagenham and Redbridge, and the two teams below them, Barnet and Aldershot. In their penultimate match they played Danny Kedwell's team Gillingham, and despite going two down, earned a point with a second half comeback. This left them in 23rd place, just above Aldershot who had 48 points, but below Plymouth (52), Daggers (51) and Barnet (51). Fortunately for AFC, on the final day of the season they beat Fleetwood in Kingston by two goals to one and all the other teams lost, which catapulted them to 20th with Barnet and Aldershot being relegated. Danny Kedwell's hometown club were champions.

In the "Catch up with Keds" article, previously referred to, this is what the "Legend" had to say about their penultimate game of the season against his ex-club, AFC Wimbledon.

"I remember playing Wimbledon in the game that Gills won the league – I told my teammates before the game that a draw would be an ideal result because it would win us the league and give Dons a point towards staying up. It was a mad day because both sets of fans were celebrating at full-time. (Sounds a bit suspicious to me.)

I have no regrets about what I've done at both clubs. I got Wimbledon back to the Football League and won a league title with my hometown club." (Oh no you didn't, you played for AFC Wimbledon, who had never been in the Football League)

The next season, 2013/2014, saw AFC finish 20th for the second year in a row, and after having lost their last two games to Morecambe and Accrington Stanley they managed to finish three points above the relegated Bristol Rovers and eight points above Torquay United. Northampton and Wycombe Wanderers being the clubs just above the dreaded drop. A final league table that clearly shows, that for some clubs, there is a very up and down life at this level. MK and Crawley Town played their last but one season together in League One, although of course they didn't realise this at the time, The home game, on Boxing Day, saw Billy Clarke sent off for a two footed tackle and Gleeson and Bamford (now what ever happened to him?) scored for MK to earn them a two nil victory. Our manager at the time was John

Gregory and theirs was Karl Robinson. On the 12th of April we gained revenge with Andy Drury scoring early on and Michael Jones adding a second in added on time at the end of the first half. The result was very welcome as we had lost our previous six games and were flirting with relegation, and another plus was that it dented their outside chances of reaching the playoffs. At the end of the season Crawley finished in fourteenth place, just three points behind MK in tenth. They were fourteen points away from their goal, whilst we were ten points above the basement four, Tranmere Rovers, Carlisle United, Shrewsbury Town and Stevenage. The next season would be one of differing fortunes for Crawley and MK.

Back in League 2, AFC Wimbledon experienced their fourth season in a row without achieving a promotion but managed to climb to 15th in the table and reached the FA Cup 3rd Round, losing in Kingston to a Steve Gerrard inspired Liverpool despite having two ex-Red Devils and one yet to be one, in their team. They were, of course, Dannie Bulman, Matt Tubbs and George Francombe.

Meanwhile, in League One, what had failed to happen the previous year occurred, sadly for Crawley but not for MK Dons. They were promoted to the Championship as runners up to Bristol City and we lost our fight to stay in League 1. In our first game against them that season, we lost by two goals to nil, a week after they had demolished Louis Van Gaal's Manchester United by four goals to nil in the League cup in front of over 26,000 spectators. Kyle McFadzean was playing for MK after his spell with Crawley and Izale Mcleod had made the opposite journey to play for the real red devils.

The hosts started well and after Dean Powell had hit the post, a 17-year-old Dele Alli forced home a rebound after Brian "The Beast" Jensen had saved from another Powell shot. Fadz was then sent off after bringing down Mcleod in the box, but unfortunately McLeod could not convert the penalty to bring us level. Arsenal loanee, Benik Afobe, scored to make the points safe for the hosts in time added on. That result put them third and was our third loss in a row.

By the time we played them again on the 10th of January 2015, we had only won three league games and looked certain favourites for relegation. Dean Saunders had taken over from John Gregory, following his illness at Christmas, and Izale McLeod had us one up from the spot early on, but when Brian Jensen, the only goalkeeper at the club at the time, went off with a dislocated finger at half time, the tallest player in the squad, Matt Harrold, had to go in goal. Just after the break Izale scored a second and an amazing result was on the cards. It wasn't to be though, as Will Grigg reduced our lead before Dele Alli struck in the sixth minute of added on to earn them a point. I thought at the time that Matt Harrold, and Brian Jensen coaching him from behind the goal, deserved medals, but don't take my word for it read what they told BBC Radio themselves after the game.

Matt Harrold "I've never played in goal before. Not even in training. I got pressured into it because everyone just looked at me and said, 'you're big'. It's a bit embarrassing because it's my first man of the match for the club. It was such a late goal to concede, and we're all devastated but we would have taken a point when I went in goal. It was a bit like playing with 10 men because we dropped deep, and they hung high balls up at me, but I did enjoy it. I felt comfortable in there in the second half after having a bit of a shocker when I first came on.

Dean Saunders. "The fourth official put the board up with five minutes extra and played 96 (I think he meant six). Eventually there're so many people in the box that one of the balls has dropped to them and it feels like we've lost two points. We've got one goalkeeper at the club which I find unbelievable really, but we have one keeper at the club, and I was hoping we could get through this game and next week I can address it. Matt Harrold has gone in goal - hero. All the players have done well today, and I can't pick any of them out. All of them have battled and done everything I asked and the reaction from the supporters tells you everything and Crawley was like Crawley again. It was hostile and they definitely got us a result, so the more I talk about it I think it's a point gained."

The BBC reported the following after the game, and whilst behaviour like this cannot be condoned, it has to be said that the cup of tea was later claimed, by the thrower, to have been empty, and that the spitting at Richie Barker must have been of the boomerang variety if it struck Charlie's Dad whilst in the dugout.

MK Dons came from 2-0 down to score a 96th-minute equaliser in an eventful game, which saw Crawley striker Matt Harrold play more than 50 minutes in goal after Brian Jensen went off injured.

Robinson alleged that Baker had a cup of tea thrown over him while retrieving the ball for a throw-in, and that former Crawley boss Barker was spat at while in the dugout.

"We have to get this right, for football as a whole," Robinson, 34, told BBC Three Counties Radio. "Football is getting an awful lot of criticism, and I thought the way we handled that was impeccable. I ran down the touchline to try and grab Carl away. My player had the red mist. You tell me any other walk of life where people can just do that and walk away scot-free. By the way, we're not criticising Dean Saunders and his players. They were sensational today."

That we are agreed on.

MK, as stated before, went on to win promotion, and Crawley finally said goodbye to League 1 after losing our last two games to Peterborough and Coventry, despite us leading in both games. It would be remiss of me to leave out the two encounters between MK and AFC this season, not in the league obviously, but in the League Cup and the League Trophy. On the day Crawley Town beat Ipswich in the League Cup, MK Dons saw off AFC in the same round with goals from Kyle "Red" Mcfadzean, Powell (not ours) and Afobe with Matt "Red" Tubbs stroking home a 94th minute penalty consolation. In the EFL Trophy, or as it was known then, The Johnstone's Paint Trophy, the tie came just short of two months later on October the 7th and marked AFC's first victory over their archrivals, winning by three goals to two. The match started brightly for MK, with Powell scoring after just two minutes and with McFadzean on the pitch for MK and Bulman and Francomb starting for AFC. Despite Azeez equalising for AFC as early as the 14th minute, by the half time break MK had regained the lead through Afobe. Neil Ardley, the AFC manager brought on Akinfenwa, Rigg and Matt Tubbs in the 65th minute and within a very short space of time Akinfenwa fed Rigg and he duly equalised. Twelve minutes later,

Akinfenwa himself scored what would turn out to be the winner to earn AFC their most wanted scalp.

2015/2016 saw Crawley Town meeting up with AFC again because of our relegation, however that reunion wasn't to last long, as AFC were destined to gain promotion via the playoffs. Before that though, there were two matches between us and them which, unfortunately for us, ended in two defeats. Following Dean Saunders leaving us at the end of the relegation season, Mark Yates had taken over as manager and we had drawn our first match of the season away to Oxford United when we met AFC at the Broadfield on August 15th and their squad included both George Francomb and Dannie Bulman. Gwion Edwards, at Morecambe in 2024, put Crawley one up after 34 minutes with a header from a Luke Rooney cross, but unfortunately, Adebayo Akinfenwa equalised in the 51st minute before Andy Barham scored their winner in the 76th after George Francomb had a shot blocked. Two points of interest were that Freddy Woodman, who played in goal for the Red Devils on loan from Newcastle United, was already a World Cup winner with England U17s, having saved a penalty in the 2014 final against Holland, and went on to repeat the achievement in 2017 with the England U20s, this time against Venezuela.

When asked about his loan spell with Crawley, Woodman said: "I'm really looking forward to it. It's a massive difference and it takes some getting used to, I'll take this experience back with me and say let's not come back here, let's play in the Premier League". Unfortunately for Crawley he was recalled by Newcastle on October 15th after their first-choice keeper Tim Krul had suffered a season ending knee injury. Woodman made 12 appearances during his spell with Crawley and kept four clean sheets in the process.

On the 9th of March 2016, Crawley Town was taken over by Ziya Eren and his Turkish conglomerate. They, not surprisingly, had a plan of Championship status in five years, and indeed we drew two and won one of their first three games in charge, however, by the time the return fixture against AFC came round in April, unbeknown to us at the time, we were in the middle of an eight-match losing streak, sitting on forty-seven points. This proved enough to keep us in the League in 20th position, above

Morecambe (47), Newport County (43) and the relegated sides, Dagenham and Redbridge (34) and York City (34), when we had finished our 46th game. The match against AFC Wimbledon was lost by a single 83rd minute goal and by the end of the season AFC were seven points above 8th, safely in the magic 7 slot, and qualified for the playoffs. They won three two on aggregate against Accrington Stanley, earning themselves a trip to Wembley where they faced Plymouth Argyle, who had disposed of Portsmouth in their semifinal. Their squad included Dannie Bulman, who played the full 101 minutes, and ex Red Devil Rhys Murphy who warmed the bench for the same amount of time. In front of nearly 58,000 spectators the result was settled late on after the introduction of Akinfenwa, who forced a corner with his first touch from which Taylor opened the scoring and who scored from the penalty spot in the 100th minute which meant that they would renew their incestuous rivalry the next year as MK Dons lasted just one season in the Championship and were relegated back to League 1. They won two and drew one of the first four games but never won two matches in a row and two five match winless streaks and one of ten games at the end of the season put paid to their Championship existence. They ended the season on 39 points and were relegated alongside Charlton Athletic and Bolton Wanderers, who we will both play in 2024/25.

Going back to November 2015, the AFC Supporters Trust voted to sell Kingsmeadow to Chelsea Women's FC, with this meaning that AFC would have the necessary funding to finance their move back to Plough Lane, but also meant that Kingstonian, come 2017, would have to leave the ground in which they had become one of the leading non-league clubs during their residence there from 1989. The sale was finalised on June 16th, 2016.

2016/2017 found both our rivals in the division above us and, as I wrote earlier, renewed their own very mixed-up rivalry. In terms of league positions, MK came out on top, finishing in 12th place, above AFC in 15th. The first game took place on the 12th of December and marked the first match in charge at MK for Robbie Neilson following the departure of Karl Robinson a few days earlier. A Dean Bowditch penalty in the second half earned a one nil win for MK, despite the presence of Bulman, Francomb,

Tyrone Barnett and Dominic Poleon in the AFC squad (he writes knowing that Red Devils will have their own views of each of those players' abilities).

When they met again in March, AFC did not include the Dons suffix in the name of their opposition in the match day programme and in front of just over 4000 spectators the Kingston side notched up their first league victory over Winkleman's usurpers to the strains of "Where were you when you were us ?" coming from the AFC fans. (perhaps from an outsider's point of view, the MK fans could have countered with "Where were you when you were needed?"). They won the game two nil through goals from Jake Reeves and Lyle Taylor. Poleon and Barnett came on in the second half for AFC but, surprisingly, there were no more goals. Please excuse me while I try and extract my tongue from my cheek.

The win for AFC put them ahead of MK in the table, but a winless streak in April, matched by MK winning four games and drawing one out of their last seven fixtures, put the Franchise team above the Phoenix club in the final table.

Meanwhile, Kingstonians played their last ever match at Kingsmeadow on the 22nd of April 2017 against a Havant and Waterlooville side managed by someone we would come to know at Crawley in the not-too-distant future, Lee Bradbury. His side needed just one point to clinch promotion to the National League, which they achieved, but this game was about far more than that. As the minutes ticked down on our final match at Town Meadow, there were tears in my eyes, but they soon dried because we were going to our own (albeit owned by Crawley Borough Council) stadium, still in the borough of Crawley. I cannot imagine how the Kingstonian's supporters were feeling as they assembled for their final game at Kingsmeadow. Some showed it by putting up crime scene tapes around the ground, others put up stickers comparing AFC Wimbledon to MK Dons, whilst about twenty fans occupied the all-seater stand at the Kingston Road end of the ground where Kingstonians supporters used to stand when it was a terrace, and the crush barriers were painted bright red.

Read below an account of Kingstonians final match at Kingsmeadow and the background to how they were the forgotten victims of other club's machinations.

"Since they had moved to Kingsmeadow in 1989, from their previous ground in Richmond, many memories had been made including being in the Conference and winning two FA Trophy finals under legendary manager Geoff Chapple, and for many those memories will stay intact despite having to move 10 miles away to share with Leatherhead for the foreseeable future. AFC Wimbledon did give them £1 million pounds to look at developing a new ground in Chessington, or to help pay rent to whatever club would host them. They did this acknow-ledging in their own words that they "recognised the position the club was in"

Opinions of officials and supporters were mixed with the former press officer saying "I'm convinced the club is going to die after this" whilst the co-chairman saw it as an opportunity saying "You have to understand that we've been paying for the sins of the past but now we have the opportunity to find and develop our own stadium." This was backed up by a comment from the AFC Wimbledon Chief executive who stated that the million pounds given to Kingstonian was "windfall money for them to get at least an equity share of their own stadium or many years' rental money". However, many Kingstonian supporters felt that AFC had in effect helped to dislodge their club, just as MK had done to them.

The contrast between the chairman of Kingstonian and others connected with the club was stark to say the least. He was quoted as saying "This has left us with unbelievable assets, so we just need to move on and get on with it, the future of this club is rosy – rosier than it's ever been, in fact. But the price we've had to pay is leaving this ground." The opposite point of view, though, was held by many who were concerned about whether the new stadium at Chessington would ever come into being, or whether they would forever have to be tenants, playing away from their true home, and what that might lead to, as it had done for other clubs in similar positions. Their crowds, which on occasions in 2016/2017, had fallen below 250 and would probably fall even further whilst sharing with Leatherhead, despite the offer from their chairman, an owner of a successful travel company to lay on free transport to and from home games. No time limit had been mooted for the ground share with the Tanners and there was growing doubt as to whether the Chessington project would ever happen.

The gate for their last game at Kingsmeadow was more than 1,200, three times their previous biggest crowd for that year and included 300 jubilant visitors from Havant and Waterlooville. That number showed a latent support that bore witness to their previous glories under Chapple and also offered some hope for the future.

One of their longtime fans, from a nearby estate, summed this up by saying "It (Kingsmeadow) was comfortable, and you just had a feeling the club was going somewhere. In the 1990s we had a team that was strong and played good, attacking football. We were there or thereabouts every year but were never quite going to win the league. In the end we were like Icarus, flying too close to the sun."

With 175,000 people living in Kingston and the level of support shown on their final day in residence seemed to provide some optimism, with their chairman saying, "I have to believe that there is hope. There would be no point carrying on otherwise. What we've seen today shows that there is still tremendous appetite for Kingstonian and for football in Kingston."

Perhaps that was why so many were deeply saddened by the club's departure. The atmosphere on the day never boiled over but chants expressing distaste for, and annoyance with, AFC Wimbledon arose with a regular frequency. One supporter said, "They're meant to have this different way of approaching things, but it doesn't feel like that to us, I can see they've been a better landlord than many might have been but that doesn't mean what they have done is right."

The complaint being, as voiced by many fans, was that AFC Wimbledon had treated Kingstonian as collateral damage in what to them (AFC) was just a business deal.

Chelsea, who now use Kingsmeadow for academy and women's fixtures, appeared to be ignored by many as to their part in this saga but their involvement in the matter says more about the David and Goliath situation that exists in modern day football than anything else.

They were perfectly entitled to take ownership of the facility that they had bought, and it was certainly time that the successful ladies' team had a home more befitting its quality than its basic accommodation in Staines. However, it has to be said that it does not sit easily that a Premier League club, based eight miles away, can extend its influence to another borough to cause the eviction of a club that has never had designs on being a competitor. Could some sort of mutually beneficial arrangement not have been made?"

From a Crawley perspective, it could also be argued that having a branch of a Premier League club's academy opposite your stadium is also wrong.

Certainly, many Kingstonian supporters' belief was that the club's board had adopted a "leaving means leaving" stance from the moment Chelsea's likely purchase had been raised as a possibility. They feared that their board had rolled over far too easily and created the crisis that existed. The chairman of Kingstonian said that earlier that year the club had asked Chelsea, via the AFC Wimbledon go-betweens, if they could continue using the stadium; the response was apparently a "flat no". AFC Wimbledon refuted this saying "it is not true Kingstonian asked for an extension to continue playing here" and perhaps that it was simply crossed wires between two clubs that, up till then had enjoyed an "excellent" relationship at boardroom level. It can be said that Wimbledon's generosity had sustained Kingstonian for well over a decade, but equally that Wimbledon had turned away from the values that used to set them apart and that the Chelsea Premier League Juggernaut had not shown any subtlety or compromise, meaning that it was inevitable that there would be only one loser.

At the final whistle, on that day in April 2017, red and white fireworks zoomed into the air from a nearby back garden, causing one lifelong female Kingstonian supporter to say "I'd been savouring the moment until then but once they went off, that was it for me, I thought I was going to cry. We've got so many memories here but that signaled the end of it". A full 45 minutes after the goalless draw, dazed Kingstonian fans and

Havant supporters in an entirely different frame of mind, shared appropriate sentiments and showed the true strength of the football community. The public address played, for the last time, its final rendition of the Tears for Fears track that had traditionally served as entry music for the club's players.

Welcome to your life
There's no turning back
Even while we sleep
We will find you

Acting on your best behaviour
Turn your back on Mother Nature
Everybody wants to rule the world

It's my own design
It's my own remorse
Help me to decide
Help me make the

Most of freedom and of pleasure
Nothing ever lasts forever
Everybody wants to rule the world

In football though, as Kingstonian have learnt the hard way, not everybody can.

Thanks must go to Nick Ames of the Guardian for his article published on 25th April 2017 which provided the information of the collateral damage caused by the whole sad story of what people can do to football clubs and communities.

As far as we were concerned at Crawley, we improved our League position by one place to finish 19th on 51 points, five points ahead of 23rd placed Hartlepool United and a whole 15 points above Leyton Orient. We also made the Sussex Senior Cup final at the Amex against Brighton but lost three nil. Our manager up to and including that defeat was Dermot Drummy, however he left the club the day after, to be replaced by Matt Harrold in temporary charge for the last league game of the season against Steve Evans' Mansfield who were on the verge of the play offs. They had to win and hope other results went their way but after going two goals up early in the first half, were pegged back to two all through goals from Dean Cox and Jordan Roberts. Needless to say, someone was not amused.

2017/2018 saw AFC and MK continue their face-to-face battles in the same division and when they faced each other at Kingsmeadow in September, both George Francomb and another future red, Kwesi Appiah were in the AFC side. They conceded after just seven minutes, with some debate as to whether it was a Ryan Seager goal or a George Francomb own goal. Despite, according to the AFC report on the match, bossing the game, they went further behind in the 27th minute when Gboly Ariyibi scored a second, followed by Qwesi Appiah having to be replaced after sustaining an injury whilst chasing a through ball. In spite of vociferous support from the locals, that was how the game ended but they did have a penalty saved in the second half. After nine games they had lost four and won twice. MK had done slightly better, having won four whilst also losing four.

By the end of the season however, the two clubs had traded places with AFC finishing in 18th place just three points above the relegation places, but with MK relegated in 22nd place with just 45 points. The turnaround happened with just seven games left of the 46-match season. Both teams were on 42 points and fighting against the drop. Before that, the return game, back in January ended in a nil nil draw. AFC won two and drew five of their last seven games, amassing a credible eleven points. MK on the other hand, could only find one win, that being on the last day of the season, having lost the preceding six matches, when they beat play off bound Shrewsbury Town. I guess that's the way to say goodbye. Shrewsbury, by the way, lost out in the final to Rotherham United. Perhaps it was no wonder MK were relegated, as they, like us in 2022/23 changed their manager a number of times, Robbie Neilson being replaced by Dan Micciche (remember him?) who was replaced by Keith Millen as caretaker, until Paul Tisdale took over in the close season.

Away from the playing side of the beautiful game, earlier in the season, on the 13th December, representatives from AFC Wimbledon, Merton council and developer GRA Acquisitions signed paperwork which meant that work could start at the site of the old Wimbledon Greyhound Stadium on Plough Lane, on the other side of the River Wandle to the old Wimbledon FC's ground. Develpment of the £25m stadium was due to start in the summer of 2018 with AFC hoping to move into the 11,000-seat ground for the start of the 2019-20 season.

Meanwhile, we appointed ex Leeds United and Liverpool player, Harry Kewell as our new manager and showed signs of improvement, finishing 14th in the league. At one point, with eleven matches to go, we were sitting just outside the playoff positions having won eleven of our last sixteen matches, but unfortunately after that we managed only one win in the last eleven games finishing on 59 points, with the plus side to the season being taking four points off Mansfield, which meant they missed out on the playoffs.

2018/2019, with Crawley Town and MK in league 2 and AFC surviving in League 1, ended with another change in the setup of the Crawley, AFC, MK trinity but before we fast forward to end of the season let's deal with AFCs League 1 season.

AFC, with neither us nor MK to worry about, continued to struggle in League 1, finishing in 20th place on 50 points, just 3 goals ahead of Plymouth Argyle in terms of goal difference. Neil Ardley was replaced by Wally Downes as manager in November and as a result, their form improved. They reached the 5th round of the FA Cup, going out to Millwall but having beaten Premier League West Ham United in the fourth round by four goals to two.

As we all know down here in God's County, MK can't win play offs, so they finished 3rd in League 2 and won outright promotion, under Paul Tisdale, by accumulating 79 points, one more than they were to in 2023/24. Coincidentally, the team they finished above in fourth place was Mansfield, who were to pip them to third place in the year we went to Wembley. Funny old game, eh Saint? We failed to score against them in their promotion year, going down four nil at Stadium MK and one nil at Broadfield. The less said the better about those games. We went through a few managers in 2018/2019, following Harry Kewell's desertion to Notts County in September. Morais and Smith as caretakers, before the flamboyant Italian Gabi Cioffi and Spaniard Edu Rubio took over and, after just fourteen games, we were 8th in the table and looking good for the playoffs, but the season deteriorated after that and with just five games to go we had only accrued 43 points and once more were flirting with relegation. However, those last five games saw us win two on the road, at Yeovil and Exeter, and one at home on the last day of the season against Tranmere Rovers. As it was, we would have been safe on 43 points as Notts County were relegated alongside Yeovil, on 41 and 40 points respectively.

2019/2020 saw the two teams known as the Dons in the same division, League 1, whereas Crawley Town were just starting to show signs of improvement in the basement division. for the fifth consecutive season. Despite the club reaching the fourth round of the EFL Cup, having beaten Norwich and Stoke along the way, manager Gabriele Cioffi left the club by mutual consent on 2 December 2019, with the club having won just once in their previous 11 league games and sitting in 17th in the League. Three days later John Yems was appointed as his successor on a deal until the end of the season. After a run of just two defeats in eleven games his contract was extended until the end of the 2022–23 season. However, in March 2020, the League Two season was postponed due to the COVID-19 pandemic. With Crawley still having a further 9 games to play, the League 2 season was curtailed leaving the Red Devils in 13th place.

MK started their first season back in League 1 reasonably well winning four of their first seven games, including a two one home win against AFC, but then twelve winless games including just two draws saw Tisdale replaced by Russell Martin, as manager. AFC started their season without a win in the first eleven games but picked up three wins on the trot to stop the rot. Manager Wally Downes was replaced at this point by Glyn Hodges. However, when the season was curtailed in March 2020 the two rival teams sat in 19th and 20th places, just above Tranmere Rovers who were top of the relegation places. The relegation places, and indeed the final placings in the league were decided on points gained per game and AFC finished just .06 of a point above Rovers, having played a game more. I know what you're thinking, what would have happened if Tranmere had played the game in hand? Well, they would have had to have won it, which would have brought them level on points per game, but for AFC to have been relegated Tranmere would have needed to win by twelve goals.

Anyway, unfortunately they were relegated and not AFC, alongside Southend United and Bolton Wanderers.

PART ONE
HISTORY LESSON

Chapter 11
THE ROARING TWENTIES

2020/2021 saw a season like no other that I have ever known. We played all our home matches, except for Barrow and Bradford City, with no spectators because of the ongoing pandemic. In front of just 625 spectators, we beat the Cumbrians by four goals to two thanks to a Max Watters hat trick and a Tom Nichols penalty and just three days later we drew against Bradford City thanks to an own goal from a Bantam. The two sad things about this season for me, apart from the obvious loss of life throughout the country and the world, was only being able to see Max Watters in the flesh twice, and of course not being able to be there when we demolished Bielsa's Premier League Leeds United in the third round of the FA Cup. We finished the season on 61 points in 12th place, but there was a general feeling that we could, and should, have done better, as in the last 13 games we dropped 27 points.

Oh, I almost forgot, we also beat AFC Wimbledon for the first time in the FA Cup, after having won by six goals to five, away to Torquay in the first round. The game against AFC marked our first victory at the new Plough Lane ground, AFC having moved in on the 3rd of November after starting the season sharing with Queens Park Rangers at Loftus Road, and their first defeat in their new stadium. We won by two goals to one, coming from behind with goals from Ashley Nadesan and Max Watters. Oh, happy days. In the League, AFC started badly and on the 30th of January, straight after MK Dons' first victory at Plough Lane, Glyn Hodges left the club and was replaced by Mark Robinson who had served the club from their first season, within the AFC Academy. The game was lost by two goals to nil, and although their form over the next thirteen games improved, they still only had 33 points with eight matches to play, and it was then that they won four on the trot and drew three to salvage their season.

MK had a mediocre season and, despite taking four points off AFC, could only finish on 65 points, nine points below the playoffs in 13th place.

Almost up to date now in what has proved to be a very interesting look at other clubs from which I have ascertained that there are more things common to all clubs than we could possibly imagine. The biggest, I believe, being the love and devotion, most fans feel for the club that God has seen fit to give them as their birthright.

The year 2021/2022 was destined to split up the stepbrothers, as that is what AFC and MK surely must be classed as, but it wasn't until the end of the season that the size of the split would become apparent. They didn't meet one another until January 2022, when a goal from Matt O'Riley in the 29th minute for MK Dons put them in the lead after 29 minutes. That was how it ended with MK moving into the playoff places and AFC remaining just two points clear off the relegation zone. At the start of the season, manager Russell Martin left the club to take over at Swansea City with Dean Lewington taking over on an interim basis before Liam Manning took over in the middle of August.

AFC's cause was not helped when left-back Nesta Guinness-Walker was sent off in the first half following two yellow cards. Ex Red Devil Max Watters was on loan at MK from Cardiff City, returning to his parent club in the winter transfer window and the current (as of June 16th, 2024) Red Devils club captain, Ben Gladwin was transferred to Swindon Town at the be-ginning of the season.

The return game on the 9th of April produced a one all draw which took MK three points clear of third-placed Rotherham in the promotion race and saw AFC narrow the gap between them and safety to three points. Having led from the 19th minute, through an Alex Woodyard mishit shot, until the 80th minute when MK equalised when Dean Lewington picked out Parrott, who crashed in a fantastic volley off the underside of the bar from a tricky angle. In the end, though, it was another two points dropped, which having not won at all since December contributed to AFC's return to League 2 at the end of the season. Perhaps they should have realised it wasn't going to be their year when, in pre-season, they lost by two goals to nil to Kingstonian at Tolworth. MK Dons, on the other hand, only lost three games in that same period, finished 3rd and earned themselves a playoff semifinal against Wycombe Wanderers, which they duly lost two one on aggregate, having lost the away game by two goals to nil. The gap between them and AFC was just one division, whereas it could have been two.

Crawley Town finished 12th for the second year running and there was great optimism when on the 7th of April 2022, it was announced that the club had been acquired by Wagmi United LLC, a group of US cryptocurrency investors. Consisting of just under 30 investors, they promised a new approach to football club ownership, talking of building a "tight-knit community" of fans "stretching from West Sussex to anywhere in the world with an internet connection" However, they quickly encountered controversy when Manager John Yems left the club in May 2022 after allegations of racist behaviour and was later banned from football until January 2026 after being found guilty of 12 charges of racist abuse towards his players. Not a great start, but not of their making. When Co-chairmen Preston Johnson and Eben Smith said they wanted to take the club to the Premier League, and in the short term to achieve promotion to League 1 within two years, there was a mixture of disbelief, excitement and incredulity, but I for one was prepared to give them the two years to reach their first target, especially as they stated that if they didn't reach that target, they would put themselves up for being voted out of their co-chairmen roles.

2022/23 was a disastrous season for MK Dons, as they were relegated back to League 2 after almost making the Championship the previous year, and almost just as bad for Crawley Town, but more of that later. Both MK, and ourselves, changed managers several times during the season, with head coach Liam Manning sacked on the 11th of December and captain Dean Lewington taking over as interim manager assisted by goalkeeper David Martin and Bradley Johnson until the announcement on the 23rd of December that Mark Jackson had been appointed as the club's new head coach. However, after just five months in charge Jackson was sacked following the club's relegation to League Two, having registered just six wins in 25 games.

Our manager employment records that year were almost as bad and were well documented in Tinpot and Proud, the third book in my chronicles of Crawley Town. Suffice it to say it went Betsy, Young, Etherington and finally and thankfully ended with the appointment of Sir Scott Lindsey. We stayed up because he instilled a belief in players and fans alike that we could do it. In the 24 games before he came, we collected just 22 points (31%), in the remaining 22 we collected 24 points (36%). Small margins make all the difference. AFC Wimbledon finished just two points above us in 21st place, albeit with a better goal difference of 11 goals and we escaped non-league football by three points over Hartlepool United, who we beat two nil away in the penultimate away game of the season. The two matches between AFC and ourselves saw away wins for both clubs. Two nil for AFC in August and one nil to Crawley in March, with "one of our own" Ashley Nadesan converting a James Tilley cross as early as the fifth minute. To be absolutely fair to our friends from South London they also beat us in the EFL Trophy by three goals to two, our goals being scored by Jack Powell and a Frimpong own goal. Mazeed Ogbungo was sent off after 28 minutes for handball which AFC took full advantage of. To close the history lesson, AFC, had just one manager through the whole season, Johnny Jackson, who came out with this quote on his appointment.

"I am extremely familiar with the AFC Wimbledon story and have total respect for what the fans have achieved - especially the marvelous new ground." Well said Johnny.

"AFC Wimbledon and The Cherry Red Records Stadium don't belong in League Two and I'll be doing everything possible to get us back up again." Oh dear, Johnny, why not? Leagues contain teams on their ability to play football, not on the work done by their supporters or the glossy finish of their stadium.

Now, why not read on and relive the season to end all seasons, and the one that followed it, preceeded by a comparison of Crawley Town seasons that I have witnessed in my 68 years of watching the Red Devils and an appendix featuring all things that unite or divide us from AFC Wimbledon, Wimbledon FC and MK Dons.

PART TWO
YEARS v YEARS
THE BEST YEAR EVER (OR WAS IT?)

Chapter 1
1968/1969, 1969/1970
Promotion to Tier 5
followed by relegation to Tier 6

This was prior to the inception of the National League (Alliance as it was when it came into being in1979) but there was no automatic promotion to the Football League back then, or indeed a way up via the play offs. You had to be elected into the then Fourth Division, with the bottom four sides having to seek re-election by clubs who probably were swayed in their voting by the thought that this could be their club in the future. No clubs failed to get re-elected at the end of the 1968/69 season, but,in the year after, Bradford Park Avenue were replaced by Cambridge United. For the record, the four clubs who survived in 1968/69 were York City, Newport County, Grimsby Town and Bradford Park Avenue, with Newport surviving a second time a year later alongside Darlington and Hartlepool but with Bradford PA, after two bottom placings in a row, finally running out of luck.

As far as Crawley Town were concerned, the success of 1968/69 in which we won 21 games, drew seventeen and lost only eight, accrued a total of 55 points, but it has to be remembered that in those days a win was only worth two points, meaning an equivalent on today's three points a win system would have given us 76 points. That was the stats of a remarkable season which included 23 clean sheets in league matches alone, nine of them coming away from home. We scored just one and a half goals per game, compared to two and a half scored by the three teams that finished above us but conversely our defence only let in a goal every 120 minutes and unsurprisingly we had the best defence in the division.

In the end though, it's not statistics that really make a season, it's the players, the characters and the memorable matches. The players; Maggs, Jennings, Sargent, Tharme, Leck, Cockell, Leedham, Bragg, Kingston, Standing, Basey, Blaber, Goodgame, Tomkys, McMullen, Haining, Patrick. Great goalkeeper, defenders, midfielders and forwards.

The characters; Brian Charlton, Malcolm Elliot (both known by politically incorrect nicknames), Paul Frisby, Brian Langridge, Mick Fox, Alan Harding, John Moon, Colin Lowes, Graham Brock, Mick Pickett, Linda Turnham, myself and many others, travelling on group save tickets all over the country, supporting a team that knew how to shut the shop and pick up points away from home, whilst never knowing they were beaten on the pristine playing surface at Town meadow. For those of you who were there at the time you will know I have painted a more than a favourable picture of the playing surface at Ifield Avenue, and that at most games from November through to March the pitch bore a close resemblance to a World War 1 battlefield, on a very rainy day. Three matches to me stand out at home, all victories in which we gained the points kicking up the slope, away from the fire station end, in the second half.

Corby Town, on September 14th, where we were two nil down at half time, but a hat trick from Phil "the Count" Basey and a Dave Sargent penalty secured the points in front of just 755 spectators.

Twenty-six games later, including twelve wins and eight draws, on the 5th of April we found ourselves two goals down again, this time against Merthyr Tydfil. Once again though, the cavalry charge up the hill proved too much for the opposition with goals from Basey (2), Goodgame, Haining and a Welsh own goal securing a five two win in front of 1190 fans.

Just seventeen days later we secured promotion against Dartford, in front of a crowd of 2,193, thanks to a Colin Blaber goal and "a hand of God" moment from Dave Haining which ended with a Kentish defender putting into his own net. It seems that in those days we did sometimes get the rub of the green.

The next season, 1969/70 started with promise, drawing the first two games and winning the third against Kings Lynn by four goals to two at home. However, by Christmas the relegation battle was one that we were deep in the middle of, and the writing was certainly on the wall when, in the space of just over a month over Christmas and the New Year, we lost nine nil and eight nil away respectively to the real Wimbledon and Cambridge United. To put those results in perspective, the Abbey Stadium outfit finished as champions, as noted earlier, with the Plough Lane lot just eight points behind in fifth place. Those of you who have read my first book, "Noli Cedere" and can remember back to the earlier pages of this tome, will know that we played Wimbledon three times in the FA Cup that season reaching the fourth qualifying round before going out at Guildford.

That season, if it had been a "three points a win" season we would have finished on just 33 points from 42 games, scoring fifty-three goals in the process but conceding one over the hundred. The only team finishing below Crawley Town was Burton Albion who would have finished on 18 points, from only 24 goals scored and 82 conceded. The results between us being two two nil home wins.

Two seasons of differing fortunes, but in my opinion, they must be talked about together as they encapsulate what supporting any club should be all about. I could include the words of Rudyard Kipling's "IF", you know the ones I mean, *"If you can meet with Triumph and Disaster and treat those two impostors just the same".*

If you can meet the ups and downs of supporting any team with equal acceptance, then take it from me, the good times can be appreciated so much more.

PART TWO
YEARS v YEARS
THE BEST YEAR EVER (OR WAS IT?)

Chapter 2
1983/1984, 1984/1985
Promotion to Tier 6

The first of these two years saw us win promotion back to Tier 6, rather than to Tier 5. (League changes, the introduction of the Alliance Premier League, had for all intents and purposes put us down a level to Tier 7 in 1979).

The two seasons 1983/84 and 1984/85 must be two of the most successful seasons for Crawley Town in terms of League results and if we hadn't lost to the eventual champions, the other CTFC, Cheltenham Town, on a cold March afternoon we might even have won the title in 1985 and won promotion to Tier 5 almost twenty years before we actually achieved that feat However, I'm jumping ahead of myself, so let's go back a year to 1983/84 when we did win promotion back to the Southern League Premier.

The season started, after a five one thrashing of Brighton and Hove Albion, with a nil-nil draw at the Crabble. Ok, it was only the Seagulls' reserves, and it was only played in front of 224 spectators, but it saw Brian Gregory score a hat trick, taking his tally to seven in seven pre-season friendlies. Our first defeat in the League came in our fifth game at home to Poole Town, but we had won two and drawn two in the League and had also beaten Gravesend and Northfleet (now Ebbsfleet United) in the Southern League Cup by four goals to two, three being scored by Gregory and the other by Jeff Wood. Sadly, FA Cup glory was to evade us as we went out in the Preliminary round away to Hornchurch in front of just 83 spectators.

The first half of the season, however, saw us win twelve league games, draw five and lose only twice. Our rivals, for the championship of the Southern League Division One South, in 1983/84 were RS Southampton and it was two defeats against them in the second half of the season that ultimately cost us the title.

We did win promotion, finishing six points ahead of Basingstoke, another team we had failed to beat in the season, completing the double over Tonbridge away on the last day of the season.

A total of 5149 spectators watched us at Town Mead that season, an average of just 275 with our last home game of the season attracting 833 against Addlestone and Weybridge.

My memory recalls crowds, that although small, got behind their team and made Town Mead a hard place for away teams to play at.

The main reasons for our success that season, in my opinion, has to be the forward line of Brian Gregory and Jeff Wood (31 and 12 league goals respectively) combined with a miserly defence featuring Ricky Collier (GK), Steve Breach, Phil Keeping, Bob Glozier and Derek McMillan. The midfield of Cant, Burtenshaw, Richards and Bryant weren't bad either.

To concede only 28 goals in 38 games whilst scoring 68 surely guarantees success and deserved to be witnessed by the size of crowds we now play against.

The next season, as mentioned earlier, saw us finish third and just miss out on promotion by three points but before we get to that lets look at the players involved.

The 31 league goals scored by Brian Gregory in the promotion season were almost replaced by the 24 scored by Terry Robbins and the additional four goals Jeff Wood added to his previous year's total of twelve but it was Dave Myers who really caught the eye, especially of the growing number of female supporters.

Our defence was not as frugal as the in the previous season, conceding fifty-two goals in the thirty-eight league games, and it was the five goals conceded at home against the other CTFC, Cheltenham Town, that ultimately cost us the League championship and promotion to Tier 5.

Played the day before I flew out to the USA for Rediffusion on a cold wintry March afternoon, we lost five one and from then on, we were playing catch up but took it till almost the last day of the season to finish just three points off the title in third place with Kings Lynn in a CTFC sandwich as runners up. Crawley, as a Town were still a long way from catching the Crawley Town bug however, as even though our home gates were up by 57% this only gave us an average gate of 426. The manager during those two seasons was, of course, John Maggs, the best goalkeeper in my opinion to ever manage the Red Devils.

PART TWO
YEARS v YEARS
THE BEST YEAR EVER (OR WAS IT?)

Chapter 3
2003/2004, 2004/2005
Promotion to Tier 5

The first of these seasons saw us promoted to Tier 5 for the first time since 1969 in the pre–National League days and also saw us retain the Southern League Cup against Moor Green (who merged with Solihull Borough in 2007 to form Solihull Moors) after having won it for the first time against Halesowen the previous season. We won the league at Welling on the 12th of April 2004 with goals from Marc Pullan, Rob Traynor and Charlie MacDonald giving us a three-nil victory whilst our closest rivals, Weymouth (Steve Claridge et al) could only draw at home against Tiverton Town. With four games left to play in the League we could even afford to lose our last two home games against Hinckley United (0-3) and Newport County (1-2) before finishing on a winning note at Weston-Super-Mare with a two goals to one victory. An incredibly remarkable season for lots of different reasons starting with the Supporters Club agreeing to pay a £1000 signing on fee for Charlie MacDonald after a four one friendly victory at Ilkeston, through the almost season long battle with Weymouth and the two remarkable victories over them, (ask Ian Payne about the away game). Although we won the league at Welling, in my opinion it was over two games previously when, thanks to a Charlie MacDonald goal, we defeated Worcester City away from home.

The season, in my opinion, was won because we had unbeaten sequences of 15, 5, 6, 6 and 5 games and only twice did we lose two games on the trot. We scored 77 goals and only conceded 43 in 42 games and, as a result, our average home attendance had risen to 1,381 with 4522 witnessing the win over Weymouth.

Apart from Charlie Mac, my favourite players that season were Ben Judge, Mo Harkin, Kevin Hemsley, Paul Armstrong and Andy Little, although Ian Payne ran Little close for the save of the season.

For my family and I personally, it will always be the year that Alex Humphrey didn't quite make it into the Red Devil family, the day when Paynie saved Claridge's penalty at the 'Muff marking Vicky and Nick's first day out since he was born asleep in the previous November.

The celebrations at Welling were emotional with the Duly family rightfully getting the credit, along with the players and manager Francis Vines for what was a tremendous achievement.

2004/2005 started with a trophy when Crawley beat Moor Green in the Southern League championship match, played between the previous year's champions and league cup winners. Moor Green taking our place as League cup representatives as you can't play yourself, can you? The League season started well with an away win at Leigh RMI followed by a home draw against Hereford United and a home win against Aldershot but our form after that was not as good but if we hadn't lost our last four league games, we might well have finished in a respectable 8th place. The season ended however with another trophy as Lewes were beaten in the Sussex Senior Cup Semifinal at Lancing, just before those four league losses, which took us to the final against Ringmer at Eastbourne Borough's ground. We won by two Alan Tait goals to nil in front of 1009 spectators and over the whole season our average home league attendance was just over 2,000 with a gate of just under 3,000 against champion select Barnet being our highest of the season and a gate of 1,237 against Tamworth being our lowest.

In the close season the Duly family sold the club to the SA group and changes galore were afoot.

PART TWO
YEARS v YEARS
THE BEST YEAR EVER (OR WAS IT?)

Chapter 4
2010/2011, 2011/2012
Promotion to Tier 4
followed by promotion to Tier 3

These two seasons, although only fourteen or so years ago, must be considered as the beginning of the time when youngsters in the town would not feel ashamed to say they supported the Red Devils. They may still have family ties to other, bigger, more famous clubs but these two seasons made it alright to talk of Crawley Town as their club.

My friend Bruce Winfield was chairman of the club as we started the 2010/11 season and Steve Evans, assisted by Paul Rayner were in charge of the playing squad. Steve and Paul were first employed by the SA Group back in 2007, probably the best move that the Majeed brothers made as far as the football club was concerned, but it wasn't until the end of the 2007/2008 season, when the club being under the ownership of Prospect Estates, in conjunction with former owner John Duly, finally seemed to put their financial worries behind them.

Despite a winding-up order on 17 February 2010; because of money being owed to HMRC, the case was later dismissed by the High Court as the club proved the debt had been paid and in a move that showed confidence in the new off field management team of Bruce Winfield and Susan Carter, on 29 March 2010 Crawley Borough Council agreed to lease the Broadfield Stadium to Crawley Town F.C. and to help secure the long-term sustainability of the club.

With Bruce and Susan as majority shareholders new investment for the club, some of which came from overseas.

allowed manager Steve Evans to start rebuilding the squad, which saw 23 players signed over a six-month period including Matt Tubbs, for £70,000, Sergio Torres for a record £100,000, and Richard Brodie for an undisclosed fee, which was rumoured to be a new Conference record of £275,000.

Not only did we win promotion that year, breaking records along the way, but we also had a fantastic FA Cup run ending at Old Trafford in the 5th Round.

Amazingly, with all the money we spent during the close season we started with a defeat at home to Grimsby Town, but by the 16th of October we had won ten, drawn two and lost just one more game, to our friends from Kingston, AFC Wimbledon, before we faced Newport at home. We lost on the 16th of October by three goals to two with our goals being scored by Richard Brodie and Scott Neilson. The following Saturday, revenge was ours as we beat the Exiles on their own ground by a Craig McAllister goal to nil in the 4th qualifying round of the FA Cup.

The only games we were to lose after that would be the one nil defeat by Manchester United and defeats to Horsham in the Sussex Senior Cup and to Dartford in an FA Trophy replay. In the Conference we finished the season at the end of a 30-match unbeaten run including twenty-one wins and nine draws whilst in the FA Cup we defeated Guiseley away, Swindon Town away in a replay, Derby County at home and Torquay away and came within a coat of paint in bringing the other Red Devils back to the Broadfield.

Bruce Winfield witnessed the complete FA Cup run but was diagnosed with cancer and died in March 2011, just after discharging himself from the hospice so he could watch his beloved Crawley Town beat AFC Wombles at home by three goals to one. Six games after that we beat Tamworth away by three goals to nil to clinch the title five games before the end of the season and we became a Football League club for the first time in our history, one hundred years after our founding in 1896. The next season proved to be a much closer encounter for the Red Devils with Crawley top of the League at the end of 2011 and also through to the 3rd round of the FA Cup after having beaten Bury of League 1 by two goals to nil away and non-league

Redbridge five nil at home. In the third round Crawley Town defeated Championship side Bristol City, with ex England player, David James, in goal with Matt Tubbs scoring the winner which was then followed by probably the most significant result in our history by us defeating another Championship side, Hull City, again by a solitary Matt Tubbs goal to nil. What could possibly go wrong? Well, despite our success in the FA Cup, our League form dipped between 17th December 2011 and 13th March 2012 with only two wins being gained in that time out of fourteen games played.

In that time span we also lost in the 5th round of the FA Cup to Premier League Stoke City by two goals to nil. Having sold both Matt Tubbs and Tyrone Barnett in the January transfer window, for £800K and £1,100,000 seemed to have contributed to our drop off in form, but we appeared to be getting back to form, winning four and drawing two of the next six games, before Steve Evans and Paul Rayner announced they were leaving the club to take charge of Rotherham United just before we were due to play Barnet away on the 9th April. Craig Brewster took the reins, and we managed a two one victory thanks to goals from John Dempster and Scott Davies.

Three matches before that, Crawley Town had won at Valley Parade against Bradford City by two goals to one, in a match that was to become known as the Battle of Bradford.

Three Crawley players were involved in a brawl as the players left the pitch on the final whistle including the then club captain Pablo Mills (suspended for six matches), fellow defender Claude Davis (suspended for four matches). They were both red carded as were two City players, resulting in Crawley being fined £18,000 and following an FA inquiry into the events that took place, Kyle McFadzean was also handed a four-game suspension after being found guilty of violent conduct. All three players released apology statements and were all fined two weeks' wages. Despite the apologies, Mills was stripped of his captaincy for behaviour not befitting the role of a club captain and he was released by the club at the conclusion of the season.

Alongside Craig Brewster, ex Manchester United player Steve Coppell was appointed as Director of Football and with just two games to play the Red Devils only needed to win against almost relegated Hereford United at the Broadfield Stadium to clinch back-to-back promotions but somewhat surprisingly lost by three goals to nil in front of 4,614 spectators.

The next week however, with Scott Shearer playing a blinder in goal and nearly 700 Crawley fans making the journey north, Crawley Town secured promotion in third place thanks to a 67th minute strike from Scott Neilson against Accrington Stanley. Simples? Not on your nelly!!

Going into that game Crawley were in the third automatic promotion spot on 81 points with a plus 21 goal difference, with Torquay in 4th place on 81 points with a plus 14 goal difference and Southend United in 5th place just one point worse off, but with a superior goal difference of 27. Torquay were due to play Hereford away with both needing victories in order to either be in the promotion mix up or secure their Football League status. If Torquay won and Crawley had lost with a swing of 7 goals in their favour, they would have pipped us for the final promotion spot. Hereford though, were not having that, and at half time they were three up and despite a two-goal comeback in the second half Torquay could not grab an equaliser and would have to make do with a playoff place. Southend, on the other hand were playing at home against the already relegated Macclesfield Town, and for approximately forty-three minutes of playing time they had climbed above Crawley into 3rd place until Scott Neilson scored in the 67th minute, which took us above them by a point. The only thing that could prevent us winning straight promotion now was if we conceded a goal and as we all know that did not happen. Swindon 93 points, Shrewsbury 88 points and the mighty Red Devils 84 points were up automatically and, rather amazingly, neither Southend nor Torquay made the playoff final, which was contested between the other CTFC, Cheltenham Town and Crewe Alexandra, with the men from Cheshire winning two nil and thus proving there is only one CTFC.

After that final game in Lancashire, both supporters and players travelled home in haste and a state of euphoria and celebrated long into the night in the Redz bar.

PART TWO
YEARS v YEARS
THE BEST YEAR EVER (OR WAS IT?)

Chapter 5
2023/2024
Promotion to Tier 3

The following part of this book includes my weekly articles published in the Crawley Observer but bolstered by appropriate information about AFC Wimbledon and MK Dons and how all three clubs stood in comparison to each other throughout the season. For those who love correct grammar, please accept my apologies for going from present tense to future and past. This part of the book was written throughout the season, and I hope you read it with that in mind.

4th June 2023

Well, the latest from the Broadfield Stadium is that there is nothing new from the Broadfield Stadium. Is that worrying, or are football fans just impatient? My new mantra is not to worry about things you have no control over and anyway, Dom Telford didn't sign up until the 24th of June 2022, did he?

Scott has said players must depart before we can bring in new players and the departure of Tony Craig, for Dorking Wanderers, whilst not earning a transfer fee, must free up some of the budget surely. We all know, I believe, who the next two are to go and hopefully this situation will be resolved soon, although I have to say I would rather it had been handled more openly.

Preston Johnson keeps things close to his chest, as have owners in our past, and I am sure that as soon as there is something to report we will hear about it. I have never been able to play cards at any level, my face doesn't allow it, but I guess our American owners are more experienced at Poker than us.

I intend to purchase my season ticket next Monday, although I should say my children are funding it for me as a combined birthday and Father's Day present, so I am almost ready for next season, as I would have been if Dom hadn't sunk Hartlepool and Corey hadn't saved that penalty at home.

When I wrote this article back in June 2023, I told you about the upcoming publication of Tinpot and Proud and accompanied that bit of news with requests for support in collecting CTFC artefacts and memorabilia for the exhibition that was held during December 2023 and January 2024 at Crawley Museum. The success of both these projects features in the articles written during those months later in this book.

23rd June 2023

Plenty happening down at the Broadfield Stadium over the last two weeks; pitch renovation has started and the hot weather, the irrigation sprinklers and the occasional thunderstorm, will hopefully give Ben and his team the opportunity to get the pitch back up to its usual impeccable standard, and most importantly Rafiq Khaleel has signed a new contract which keeps him at the club for at least another two seasons.

Patience, I am sure, will see the strengthening of our team in order that we can put behind us the anxious finale to last season. There is arguably, already, the basis of a good League 2 side at Crawley Town with eighteen players available for kit sponsorship, according to the Crawley Town website on 9th June 2023. However, when that eighteen includes Kwesi Appiah and Jake Hessenthaler, who for some reason last year were out of favour at the club, you could consider the number to be slightly smaller. I have always appreciated the effort put in by both but, without knowing the reasons why they went off the radar last year, their future with the Red Devils is up for debate.

That debate is something that needs to be cleared up soon as possible and these are the questions that need answering by the club and its owners so that we can move forward and start to rebuild links between the two parties that are the furthest apart now, the owners and a sizeable number of the fans.

The referendum issued by the CTSA last week, which I couldn't vote in because it did not offer an alternative option, has shown that a small, but significant, number of CTSA members want a change in the ownership, but not necessarily a change of the owners. In my opinion this vote would have had more validity if the alternative option, of allowing Wagmi to prove they have learnt from mistakes made last year, had been made available. I am not saying I would have voted for that option but having it on the ballot paper would have given any result more credibility.

Back to the subject that matters most, if the squad slims down by two or three players, see above the comments re Kwesi and Jake, and Aramide does not extend his contract, then we would be down to fifteen players, meaning, in my opinion, that we would need at least another seven players to make us viable to continue our Football League experience into a fourteenth season.

Once again in my opinion, those seven players must include another keeper, at least to challenge Corey, and two quality players in defence, midfield and up front.

Fixtures out this Thursday, season ticket bought last week, and six pre-season friendlies arranged between the 11th and 29th July will make the time fly between now and the beginning of the season on 5th August.

Exciting or Worrying times? We will see in time. But here are a few tips for both the owners and the CTSA. Talk to one another with a sense of cooperation, drop negative words like "demand" from your rhetoric and stop trying to see things which may not be there.

25 June 2023
   Summers Here
   The grass has ris,
   I wonder where the players is?

Not grammatically correct I know, but when I was at the club yesterday (Friday) I was amazed to see how much the grass had grown since last week. There were a few brown patches to be seen, but 99% of the pitch had grown well enough to allow Ben and his team to be able to cut pitch length stripes into it. With another twenty-five days to go until we play Crystal Palace there is still time for it to be in perfect condition, and still enough time for Scott Lindsey to add to the playing squad.

I note that James Tilley has gone off to play for the plastics from Kingston, or is it Merton now, and would like to wish him every success in 44 games next season, but not against us. Will he be missed? As a person of great character, certainly, as a player, only time will tell. We have added to the squad in the signing of Liam Kelly, and I know you shouldn't judge his quality by YouTube clips, albeit that they show he knows where the goal is, but likewise you shouldn't negatively judge him without ever having seen him play.

I anticipate more player announcements this week, as they return to the club for testing and the commencement of serious training, and two bits of news I would like to see announced are the re-signing of Aramide Oteh and the finalisation of the Kwesi Appiah and Jake Hessenthaler situations.

Off the pitch, a meeting was held last Wednesday between the CTSA and Preston Johnson and Eben Smith, hosted by Ashley Brown, the Head of Supporter Engagement of the Football Supporters Association (FSA) and, after some discussion, a set of minutes was agreed and can be read on the CTSA website. It may seem a bit neutral to some, but for me that is what is needed now.

Positivity needs to be the mantra as we seek to rise from last season's depths, from all who love Crawley Town FC and that includes players, management, owners and supporters, and I would like to start by saying I am glad to see that, after just a week of sales, season tickets are already up to 50% of last season's number, and we have end of month pay days around the corner, which I think will take it even higher. It's easy to imagine how that statement could have been made negatively, but every negative statement has an adverse effect on the club we support, by putting off new sets of supporters coming through the gates.

Hope that I am not appearing blinkered or righteous, but everyone should know by now that, after family and my faith, Crawley Town are number one in my list of interests. See you at a friendly soon, where, if you disagree with my half cup full approach, we can have a respectful chat and perhaps share a drink or two.

1st July 2023

If anyone wants something to do, whilst we are waiting ever so patiently for transfers into the club to occur, may I recommend the latest Indianna Jones film now at the place where we used to play before 1997. Seriously, it's well worth a look, but it still doesn't soothe my anxious mind as much as some decent players signing for the Red Devils would. True, we have signed Danilo Orsi from Grimsby, and he will hopefully score a fair number of goals for us in the coming season and hopefully provide the ammunition for our other forwards as well. However, we have also transferred Jack Powell to Crewe Alexandra, which understandably has met with mixed opinions on the various forums. I will miss him for his attitude, in that he makes an effort before each game to applaud the crowd, but on the other hand I will not miss his inconsistent corner taking which seldom seems to beat the near post defenders. He is a good league player who sometimes produces out-of-this world moments, whilst at other times he can fail to impress. What I don't understand is how some of our fans can say he's not good enough, whilst still criticising WAGMI for transferring him out. Still, no one is perfect, so if you know of any footballers with Noone as a surname perhaps you could give him a call.

Still waiting to hear about Aramide Oteh and Jake Hessenthaler and where they stand as regards re-signing, in Remi's case, and if Scott is allowed to play Jake after appearing to be frozen out last year. I believe, if WAGMI are prepared to "back Scott and his decisions" he should be at least able to assess him for himself in the upcoming friendlies. Of course, this also depends on whether the player himself is prepared to put the last season behind him and once again show his loyalty to the club.

I have addressed my concerns to Preston Johnson, and he insists that Wagmi are "still making moves, nothing is done yet". Of course, he could well be right, and, in the past, other regimes have made the same sort of statement and signed players on the eve of the season's first game and played them immediately. This is the second time I have written this article, and I am sorry to see Kwesi depart the club in the manner he has and am probably now coming round to the conclusion that perhaps Jake and Remi might be the next departees. Having said that, money for incoming players must certainly now be used and I hear rumours that a winger from Bromley might be coming soon.

The move to the University of Sussex, Falmer training facility, is good news I believe, and news that should be applauded by all our supporters. My point being that if you criticise every decision you don't like, you should also applaud every decision you do like, whilst also taking care as to who you attribute the blame or credit to.

Next week, we could all be licking our lips at the signing of some class players. Let's hope that's true

9th July 2023

I watched a Jason Manford stand up performance the other night, which he closed by getting the audience to sing along to some "Assembly bangers". The sort of songs we all know because school assemblies, so I offer no apologies for giving you my interpretation of "Sing Hosannah", inspired by the signing of our new centre back.

Give us Joy in our team, keep him playing.
Give us Joy in our team, we pray.
Give us Joy in our team, keep him playing.
Keep him playing till the end of play. (Refrain)
Joy Mukena, Joy Mukena,
Joy Mukena is our centre back!
Joy Mukena, Joy Mukena
Joy Mukena at the back!

Now all we need are appropriate tunes to welcome Liam Kelly, Danilo Orsi, Harry Forster and any others that may join us.

This is what I mean about being positive about incoming players, giving them a chance and not prejudging them. I know I will be accused of doing exactly that, but at least I'm giving them the benefit of the doubt and supporting them as they come to play for the mighty Reds.

Another thing to consider is, why criticise WAGMI for the use of data and statistics when that is exactly what some fans do to try and prove a point about the quality of incoming players?

As Jimmy Greaves used to say, "it's a funny old game Saint, a funny old game".

The latest on Aramedi Oteh is there is no news on him, and that is from our owners' "mouths". The saying "No news is good news" doesn't fill me with much confidence I'm afraid, but I still hope to be proven wrong and that he will be made an offer that is good for both him and the club overall. If that doesn't prove to be the outcome, then both parties should move on, and we should get another forward who really does want to play for us for whatever we are offering him. I don't want anyone to think I know about what is happening in this matter, as all I know is there no conclusion to it as I sit here typing this article buoyed by England U21s being crowned European champions and the England Cricket team prolonging the Ashes for at least one more game. Let's hope there is some much-needed communication from our owners this week.

And then there is Jake!!!!! But that's a whole other matter.

Friendlies start this week with away games against East Grinstead and Three Bridges, followed by a trip to the Crabble the week after and a home game against Crystal Palace on Wednesday 19th July. These games will give us all the opportunity to see what Scott's recruitment has given us for the coming season and will also enable our younger fans to know what they are singing about when they burst into song about teams we have played in the past.

The Crystal Palace game, against hopefully a strong Eagles side, will be watched by a big crowd at the Broadfield Stadium, according to messages from the Club, and whatever the score line should provide us with an indication of our abilities for the upcoming season.

You never know, the Aramide Oteh and Jake Hessenthaler conundrums may even have been solved by then.

16 July 2023

New Players in: Luca Ashby-Hammond, Liam Kelly, Harry Forster, Danilo Orsi, Klaidi Lollos and Joy Mukena.

Several players with contracts extended and still a couple of queries about Remi Oteh and Jake Hessenthaler as to what their status is.

I have watched both games, East Grinstead and Three Bridges away from home, and although we haven't repeated the thrashings of previous years, I think it is fair to say we should have beaten both sides by considerably more goals and were only stopped from doing so by man of the match performances by both the home goalkeepers.

In the first game, as in the second, Scott Lindsey played arguably his stronger eleven in the first half and, if we had converted half of our chances, should have been four up by the interval. As it was, a total change of participants at half time, with the score still unbelievably at nil – nil, saw Crawley Town win by two goals to one, with goals from Nick Tsaroulla and Florian Kastrati, the winner coming virtually on the final whistle. Several promising triallists, Sonny Fish (ex Orient) and Ade Adeyemo (Arsenal Youth), proved they are certainly worth looking at again, but I feel the person who got the most from the game was Scott Lindsey.

The shortest trip to an away game followed just four days later, courtesy of the number 5 bus, with the short journey to Jubilee Fields, when once again the "better" team, in my opinion, started the game. Nick Tsaroulla started this time, under the well-deserved captaincy of Harry Ransom, and played really well down the left, combining well with Danilo Orsi and new signing Klaidi Lollos. In goal was new loan signing Luca Ashby-Hammond, from Fulham, and it must be said he will offer real competition for the first team goal keeping slot. Town went in at half time two goals to the good, courtesy of Orsi's brace and then the second half "all change" took place. However, the improvement that occurred on Tuesday didn't seem to materialise this time despite the introduction of Khaleel, Gordon, Telford and Nadesan. In my opinion Harry Forster and Sonny Fish impressed the most in difficult, almost autumnal windy conditions, along with the Three Bridges keeper who kept the score down to two, with Bridges grabbing a consolation after a defensive mix up in the Town defense.

So, there we have it, a brace of two one wins on the road with the majority of discerning supporters appreciating that both games were played to assess the participants and not necessarily for the results.

Away from the pitch, I was saddened to hear of the loss of one of our supporters and my thoughts and prayers go out to his family and friends and all who knew him.

I am still in conversation with Preston Johnson about various projects around the club and the town and am pleased to see we have signed decent players, are extending the fan zone and joining together, as fans, players and management, in the organising of the Crawley Museum exhibition to celebrate the past, present and future of our fantastic club.

23rd July 2023

What have we learnt over the last week?

Well, we now know that we can grab a last-minute win after having let a team equalise and we can also hold on to a win after going two nil up. Arguably you might also say we have learnt how to tighten up at the back after being given a mauling in the first half, albeit against an almost full-strength Premier League side.

Whilst it was good to see a crowd of 5500 at the Crystal Palace game, I thought it was a bit of a stretch to say only 1300 were from South London. I would have put it at 50/50 myself, what about you? The atmosphere was good throughout, I thought, which was helped by the extended Fan Zone and the obvious lessons learnt from last year's games against well supported teams.

The second half of that game saw a much-improved effort from the Reds and Nick Tsaroulla was extremely unlucky not to score when his volley from the edge of the area came back off the post with the keeper beaten.

On to the weekend I thought I would be able to concentrate on the Ashes, only to find the Crawley Town media team reporting on a humiliating 9 – 1 away defeat to Portsmouth. They did point out that the game was played over four thirty-minute quarters but didn't supply any further details. A little later in the afternoon details of the match, or should it be matches, came out to clarify what had occurred. The exercise was then described as two 60-minute matches, and in the first one Crawley held a very strong Pompey side to one all, only to concede a penalty in the last minute to lose two one.

In the second game Scott Lindsey put on a completely different eleven who conceded three in the first half and four in the second. I am an eternal optimist where CTFC are concerned, so I will accept at very best a two-one defeat and a seven-nil defeat, or a five- one defeat followed by a kick about, be it that games should only last ninety minutes.

Being serious for a moment, I am encouraged by Scott's assessment of both sixty-minute games, but also slightly concerned that there were surely some contracted players in the second game, some of which he may have recently signed on contracts and some of which were already contracted to the club. I may of course be wrong, but it doesn't help when the team line-ups for both matches have not, as far as I am aware, been published. In hindsight I don't think our Media team should have tweeted it as a nine one defeat in the first instance, as according to our manager that isn't what it was. There is a lot to be said for communication between the club and the fans, but in my opinion, it is sometimes best thought over before passing it into the public arena.

Heybridge Swifts and Bromley to come, and hopefully some more encouraging results.

30th July 2023

Is it now time to start thinking positively about the team Scott Lindsey is building? Asking for a friend.

Before you accuse me of going over the top after two wins against non-league sides, I know there is a great deal of difference between friendly victories and playing the likes of Bradford City, who we face next Saturday, but we should be encouraged, I believe, in the way our new signings have found the net in pre-season.

Welcome to our new players, all ten of them. I hope you settle in quickly and you soon become fans' favourites like some of the players you have replaced. You can be assured that if you play for the shirt with 100% effort you will get the support from all Crawley Town fans. The results this week have shown that Danilo and Klaidi could well turn out to be regular scorers for the Reds, whoever we are playing against.

The last match, against Bromley who finished in the National League Playoffs last season, going out in the semi-finals against Chesterfield, shows that we are not far off a team that will bring the smiles back to the Broadfield faithful.

On the love hate relationship that some fans seem to have with our owners and vice versa, I would encourage both sides of the divide to seek ways of bridging the gap between each other. Owners need to understand that fans need to know the direction in which they are taking US, and fans need to realise that owners can communicate with the fans without putting a WAGMI label on it. The club update we received from Tom Allman on Friday shows how much work goes into running the club and for me was very encouraging. Whilst I appreciate that last season was a very big disappointment for us all, I would ask all our fans to look at the club and how it has improved off the field, which can only be attributed to the hard work of all that work at the club and the backing they get from our owners.

I know, through regular conversations with Preston Johnson, that he truly wants Crawley Town to prosper and that he is open to criticism as long as it is positive. This, I have to say, does not include going on to non-football related podcasts and then feeling aggrieved when they get an emotional response in return. We do have some "crazy" supporters, just like every other club does, but to add the word "loser" to what was supposedly said is tantamount to creating fake news.

Anyway, back to what should unite us, increasing the level of support in our club. Mick Fox, of Retro Reds fame, and I are organising an exhibition at Crawley Museum in December and January covering the history of our great club, which needs some financing. I have offered the royalties from "Tinpot and Proud", towards the funding of this venture and Preston Johnson has also pledged around £500 to the cause.

Remember, TOWN TEAM TOGETHER

5th August 2023
    Crawley Town 1 Bradford City 0
    CTFC Scorer Will Wright (14)
    Attendance 3883
    Rivals' results, Grimsby 0 AFC Wimbledon 0, Wrexham 3 MK Dons 5

I am writing this article on Sunday 6th August 2023 which, if he had still been alive, would have been my dad's 100th birthday. This weekend also marks the start of my 68th year watching the Red Devils and this weekend has proved to be more successful than my first match back in 1956 when we lost our first game in the Metropolitan league, going down one nil to the mighty Tonbridge Reserves.

That first match would have been in front of a few hundred people, whereas Saturday's attendance was a credible 3883, of which just over 1000 were from Yorkshire, whether in mind, body or spirit. This, to me, shows that the majority of our fans are willing to close the door on last season's mistakes and get behind the good work that Scott, Jamie and the rest of his staff are doing to rebuild our team into one that knows how to fight and battle to gain a result against anyone we are faced with.

From the moment the "fifth best centre back from Gillingham" put us ahead with his exquisite free kick in the 14th minute there was a feeling that this was going to be our day, certainly in Torres corner where I was stood with eight of my family and even more of my friends. Bradford City are a good side, who played well but were sent home regretting their journey to the Broadfield Stadium. Indeed, if they had played more football, rather than playing in the image of their manager most of the time, they may well have got a draw. As it was, all of Scott's signings showed promise in differing levels, but all displayed a character that will go down well with the Red Devils faithful. The signings that were sanctioned by the club's owners that Scott speaks to on a daily basis and appears to get on well with.

Of course, our next two games are away, at Exeter in the League Cup and Salford in the League, and it is possible that we could get nothing from these games, which is why it is important that we continue our 8-game unbeaten run at home against MK Dons a week on Tuesday.

In closing, my latest book "Tinpot and Proud" will not, at the moment, be available from the club shop because of the title.

An opinion which is not shared by our owners.

Go Figure!!

8th August 2023
EFL Cup
Exeter City 2 Crawley Town 1
CTFC Scorer Lolos (15), Exeter scorers Taylor (73) Scott (84)
Rivals' results
EFL Cup
8th August 2023   Mk Dons 0 Wycombe Wanderers 2
9th August 2023 AFC Wimbledon 2 Coventry City 1

12th August 2023
EFL League 2
Salford City 1 Crawley Town 1
Salford scorer McAleny (47) CTFC scorer Garbutt OG (40)
Rivals' results
AFC Wimbledon 1 Wrexham 1, MK Dons 1 Tranmere Rovers 0

Having just got back from Salford, I thought I had better write this article whilst listening to Brentford V Spurs on Radio 5 before I fall asleep.

What a weekend, two nights in Manchester and a great performance by the Mint Greens to make it all worthwhile.

I was lucky enough to be sitting behind Will Wright's mum and dad, who had nothing but good things to say about how Will has been impressed with the way Scott wants the Reds to play, and when we got the free kick out on the left, we joked whether Will would shoot or not. As it was, the delivery by Will ended up in the net courtesy of Garbutt putting through his own net. It certainly was a deserved lead as we had already hit the bar twice and the left-hand post once before we had scored. Unfortunately, we let in the equaliser virtually from the second half kickoff, but even then, could have and should have gone on to win.

Before the game I would have taken a point without hesitation, but I can understand Scott's disappointment with it, especially considering the way we played, full of energy, commitment and attacking intention throughout. When you can take off Telford and Orsi and replace them with Campbell and Lollos it shows that Scott was not prepared to settle with just the one point but wanted all three. Indeed, if Adam Campbell's curling effort had curved by another centimetre it would have given us the victory which we deserved.

Comparing this season's start with last year is like comparing apples with bananas, but I'm going to do it anyway. This year after two games we have four points and lie in sixth place, last year it took us seven games to get to five points, and we knew we were in for a struggle for the season. With two home games to come this week, if we perform as well as we have shown we can, there is no reason why we should be worried about how this season will proceed.

I know I'm an optimist, but I feel it's better than what I witnessed on Saturday at the game. Everyone is entitled to their own opinions, but if we continue to play like we are at the moment will there come a point when the banners of distrust are put away and the pointless chants, requesting people to stand up if they hate the people who are financing and backing Scott in the way he is building the team, are no longer heard?

I will now probably be accused of being in the pay of our owners, which I most certainly am not, but it did make me smile when people, already standing up, started the stand-up chant. I don't recall anyone who was seated getting up to join them either.

MK Dons next and Gillingham on Saturday could see us almost top or back in the pack, but whatever the results this next week I will continue to be positive about our current squad of players.

15th August 2023
Crawley Town 2 MK Dons 1
CTFC Scorers Tsaroulla (16) Orsi (62) MK Dons scorer Eisa (27)
Rivals' results Colchester United 0 AFC Wimbledon 2

19th August 2023
Crawley Town 0 Gillingham 1 Gillingham's scorer Ransom OG (40)
Rivals' results Colchester Utd 2 MK Dons 3, Sutton Utd 0 AFC 3

In last week's article, I said that after our two games against MK Dons and Gillingham we would either be top or back in the pack. We are eighth, having won one and lost one, but in my opinion, we should be at least one point better off, which would have put us on eight points, just two behind Gillingham, and in fourth place. Am I still positive? Yes, I am and now it just needs us to break our away duck in order for us to maintain our good start to the season. Swindon and Stockport on the road over the next two weeks and a chance for some away glory.

If you're disappointed with seven points from four games, then please do your Maths' homework and you will see that over forty-six games that is certainly play off form. Of course, we could face a dip in form, whereas it's just as likely we might get better. The crowd against Gillingham, with just under 3000 home supporters present, gave full-blooded support throughout and some fans have pointed out we were ahead on all the stats except for the one that ultimately counts, the final score.

The difference between the two games for me, was that in my opinion our shooting was less powerful in the game we lost, less clinical, but even with that observation we should have got at least a point against a team who hardly threatened us at all. But that's football.

What has pleased me in the last couple of weeks is the sense of togetherness around the club, whether that's in the team or in the upward trend in our home attendances. There also appears to be a change in attitude amongst our fan base to our ownership. I'm not saying that a "WAGMI forever!" banner has been ordered, but there seems to be a move towards reconciliation in some quarters.

I would like to mention some of our fans who have shown what it means to them to be a Reds supporter.

Take Paul "Four Nil" Tarran for instance. He has stopped betting on four nil home victories, but that is not why I am writing about him in this week's article. No, his mention is because he, and his family, interrupted their holiday in Weymouth to turn the Gillingham home game into an "away at home" game by travelling back to Crawley by train, only to get back on the train post-game to resume their holiday.

There are also those supporters who have bought a copy of "TINPOT AND PROUD" from me since the season began, enabling me to meet my pledge towards the cost of the upcoming Crawley Town Exhibition due to be held at Crawley Museum later this year. Sales are going well, and the book can now be ordered from Amazon and other book wholesalers such as Goodreads and will shortly be available from Waterstones, Crawley.

Lastly, a thank you to Preston Johnson, Simon King, Sarah Markham and Kevin Neylon, who have all generously contributed to the exhibition fund and, as a result, will all be invited to its opening in December.

26th August 2023
Swindon 6 Crawley Town 0 Swindon scorers Kemp (38) Young (47,51,60,71) Shade (90+9)
Rivals' results AFC Wimbledon 1 Forest Green Rovers 1, MK Dons 2 Doncaster Rovers 1.

Where do we start this week?

Well, let's start with some good news, first of all with the news that a founding member of the Junior Reds, Sam Jordan, has been appointed onto the board and will be taking the EFL's fit and proper person test. This, I believe, is on top of having Hugh McKinney as fan representative to the board. This is a move in the right direction and both WAGMI and the CTSA should be applauded for it.

Secondly, thanks to Preston Johnson, Paul Hayward, Tinpot and Proud, Kevin Neylon, Simon King, Steve Herbert and Sarah Markham for enabling us to reach our initial target of £1500 to fund the upcoming exhibition at Crawley Museum, scheduled for December and January. If you still wish to contribute, either with funding or memorabilia, photographs, memories etc. please feel free to do so, as it will only help improve the exhibition.

The last bit of good news, before I get on to "that" game, is we have a chance to snap back out of our two-match losing streak at Stockport next Saturday and then with a couple of home games on the trot.

I don't want to make light of losing six nil away, but we have done it before and gone on to reach the 5th round of the FA Cup and win promotion at the end of that season. I know we are looking fervently for a goal scoring forward and that, even if you are reading this on Wednesday, the window is still slightly ajar.

Back in 2011/2012, after the first five games, we had 10 points. This year we are just three points behind that after having played five highly rated teams. After six games in our first season in the EFL, we had 13 points, and hopefully if we get a result at Stockport on Saturday, we could be just three or five points behind that tally come 5pm on the 2nd of September. What am I getting at? Well in the words of Corporal Jones, "Don't panic". Back in our promotion season to League One, we lost our 7th and 8th games, six nil away to Morecambe and three nil at home to Swindon leaving us on 13 points before we went on a thirteen-match unbeaten run till Christmas. I believe that Scott Lindsey is capable of a similar turn of events, given the means to strengthen the squad with the funds released by Dom's departure. Keep the faith TTT.

29th August 2023
Rivals' results
EFL Trophy
MK Dons 4 Charlton Athletic 1

30th August 2023
Rivals' results
EFL Cup
Chelsea 2 AFC Wimbledon 1

2nd September 2023
EFL 2
Stockport County 3 Crawley Town 3
Stockport Scorers Barry (13), Sarcevic (36) Olaofe (89)
CTFC Scorers Campbell (42), Maguire (54), Orsi (66)
Rivals' results Crewe Alexandra 3 MK Dons 1, Newport County 2 AFC Wimbledon 2.

   I am writing this on a Sunday evening, not because the game was terrible but as a result of having a very busy weekend. Before the game started, that age old cliché about being happy with a point got used quite a lot during the day, although it changed several times during the actual one hundred and four minutes played.
   As we kicked off, against a team below us in EFL 2 but more fancied by the bookies than Crawley to achieve a second play off place in consecutive years, I did indeed share the opinion that a draw at Edgely Park would be a point gained, rather than two lost. Actually, after 36 minutes and with us two down, I would have been ecstatic if we managed to nick a comeback point. With memories of our six-nil drubbing at the hands of Swindon in my mind, I was rather pleasantly surprised as the dulcet tones of John Barnett, along with his rather hushed compatriot Ken Blackmore informed me that Adam Campbell had halved our deficit and that we were back in the game. Half time team talk and work on Ken's microphone certainly improved our fortunes and our listening pleasure, as first, in the 54th minute, new signing Laurence Maguire drew us level, followed by Danilo Orsi giving us the lead just twelve minutes later. "Feed the 'Ors" or "Orsi, Orsi, don't you stop, just let your goals take us to the top" could be heard throughout my flat and beyond, and I would hazard to guess that no longer would we be happy with a single point.
   However, Football can be a cruel game, and when Stockport equalised in the 89th minute and the fourth official showed that there would be at least another ten minutes of added time, the cliché turned full circle and we were content, if not a little disappointed, with our point gained away from home. The fact that Scott and our players were downbeat about the result is, for

me, a sign that better times are on the way. Last year we would have been ecstatic with a point from Stockport.

That brings me to another way of looking at our results so far. Last year we drew with Bradford at home, whereas our victory over them on the 5th of August gave us a two-point gain over last season. Similarly, our fixture at Salford gained us another point, which was cancelled out by the point loss against Gillingham. We lost at Swindon and Stockport last season, so we are another point to the good thanks to Saturday's draw. That just leaves us with our win against MK Dons to factor in, and as we can't really do that the only pieces of data we can use are the home results against the four relegated sides from League 1 at the end of the 2021/2022 season. Those clubs were Crewe, Doncaster, Gillingham and AFC Wimbledon. We drew against the first three and lost to the Wombles. This means that through my rose coloured specs, we are six points better off than last season already.

Now let's win against Newport and Tranmere at home, as we did last season, to maintain that gain.

5th September 2023
EFL Trophy
Crawley Town 4 Charlton Athletic 3
CTFC Scorers Forster (1), Lolos (45+4), Tsaroulla (70), Khaleel (81)
Charlton Scorers Leaburn (23), Campbell (26), Dobson (57)
Rivals' results AFC Wimbledon 1 Stevenage 1

9th September 2023
EFL 2
Crawley Town 4 Newport County 1
CTFC Scorers Tsaroulla (5), Campbell (54, 67) Gladwin (79)
Newport Scorer Bogle (10)
Rivals' results AFC Wimbledon 1 Stockport County 2, MK Dons 1 Notts County 1

What a wonderful week of pulsating, attacking football from the Red Devils. After the three all draw at Stockport, we followed it up with a great four three win over Charlton Athletic with a side that showed a plethora of changes from the Edgely Park encounter. Charlton fans will claim they also made changes, but when you look at both squads, it seems that both sides had eight players from their last match on the field at some point in the 90 plus minutes played. To score after just forty-one seconds, courtesy of Harry Forster, certainly helped create an atmosphere which never dissipated, even when the Addicks equalised and then took the lead. Klaudi Lolos ensured a symmetrical end to the half by rising above the Charlton defender to head home to make it two all at the break.

The second half saw Town bring on Kelly, Tsaroulla and Wright, but it was Charlton who took the lead again through their captain, Dobson, who hit a Bulmanesque type shot, which gave Luca Ashby Hammond no chance at all. In seasons past, that would probably have been the end of the contest, with people saying, "who wants to win this cup anyway?" However, this is a different set of players who seemingly want to prove their capability and determination in any game they play, and Tsaroulla and Rafiq Khaleel scored the goals that won the game and have given us a great chance to qualify from our group. If we do, we will only be four games from Wembley.

Calm down Steve, it's the league that matters most, and that was certainly evident on Saturday when we tore into Newport County from the start. The game started with another early goal for Crawley when Campbell fed Tsaroulla and he stroked the ball home in front of the Winfield Terrace, Ben Gladwin having seemingly lost the toss at kick off. Omar Bogle, after being almost seemingly unable to carry on after an early robust, but completely good challenge, then showed an almost Lazarene recovery to equalise and we had only been playing 10 minutes. Once again, the players showed after half time that they weren't prepared to settle for a point and what followed was a wonderful display of attacking football which saw the Reds run out four goals to one winners, with a brace from Adam Campbell and a fourth from captain Ben Gladwin.

Who should get the credit for the way we are playing? Well, obviously Scott, his coaching team and the players deserve a great deal of credit, but I couldn't help having a wry smile on my face, when Scott praised the efforts of the owners in getting

Adam Campbell into the club, which Adam himself confirmed in his interview. Players come and go in every club in the land, as do owners, but surely now is the time to believe what Scott is saying about our owners and drop the negativity for a stance more positive. You never know, you might enjoy it more.

16th September 2023
EFL2
Crawley Town 3 Tranmere Rovers 2
CTFC Scorers Darcy (61), Tsaroulla (68), Lolos (90+6)
Tranmere scorers Jolley (21) Taylor (66)
Rivals' results AFC Wimbledon 2 Crewe Alexandra 2, MK Dons 1 Stockport County 2

Let's get the moaning out of the way shall we? Why do some of our supporters seemingly want to drag the reputation of our club through the dirt? Why do they upset the momentum of our team when they are getting on top? Why do they want to run the risk of our club having to pay a hefty fine, a ground closure or, even worse, a points deduction because of their behaviour? Please tell me, as I am obviously missing something. The club have rightly condemned Saturday's flare and bottle throwing but perhaps it would be a good idea for our media guys to raise the issue in the post-match interviews with Scott Lindsey, so that he can praise the fans for their noise and passion but ask them not to stall our momentum through idiotic behaviour. If you doubt what I am saying, then look at the timings of the goals from Saturday. The delay after Ronan's equaliser, on 61 minutes, gave Tranmere a bit of respite and allowed them to regroup and go ahead for the second time in the match. Thankfully, our players responded with intensity and passion, with Nick Tsaroulla drawing us level and Klaidi "Fairclough" Lolos grabbing the winner in added time.

Rant over, and I, for one, am looking forward to seeing us grab our first away win on Saturday up at Cleethorpes when we take on Grimsby Town. We haven't been very successful up at Blundell Park in recent years, but I'm sure Scott and his team will have the players up for the battle to get the points to take us into the automatic promotion places.

After eight games we have won four, all at home, drawn two, both away and lost two, one at home and one away. We have fourteen points, in comparison to just seven at the same point last season when it took us until our fourteenth game to achieve our current points total. This means a 100% improvement from the team, and one that has been recognised by our home core support getting to around 2700.

The week after the Grimsby game we are at home again to our near neighbours Sutton United. They haven't picked up any points since the first day of the season, when they destroyed ten-man Notts County, and currently sit in 24th place at the bottom of the table. I am sure Scott will be impressing on our lads that we have yet to garner any points from our four league meetings with them so far and that now is the time to put that right.

At that game, Andy Taylor, a former Reds centre back who played 113 games for us between 1998 (away at Halesowen) and 2001 (away at Kings Lynn) scoring seven goals in total, will be presented with a shirt of his vintage by John Barnett, in response to a Facebook request by Andy himself. The club have given him complimentary tickets for the game, and if we can arrange for the presentation to be on the pitch, I hope you will show him the welcome I know you are capable of. Come on you Reds!!!!!!!!!!!!!!

19th September 2023
Rivals' results EFL TROPHY
Oxford United 0 MK Dons 1
23rd September 2023
EFL2
Grimsby Town 2 Crawley Town 3
Grimsby Scorers Holohan (24) Eisa (30)
CTFC Scorers L.Kelly (32), Darcy (35), Orsi (90+6)
Rivals' results
Sutton United 1 Mk Dons 1, Walsall 1 AFC Wimbledon 3

How to fit the events of Saturday 23rd September 2023 into just over 520 words? Well, we won three two after being two goals down thanks to Liam Kelly, Ronan Darcy and, of course, Danilo Orsi.

When we got to Kings Cross the Hull Trains 9.48 was packed and the seven strong group that I was travelling with had to split up to sit in our booked seats. I was in a carriage with some Crawley supporting youngsters, a couple of Gillingham supporters on their way to what was to be a two one defeat at Doncaster, and the general travelling public who must have wondered what they were in for. As it was, the journey turned out to be noisy but generally good natured, but it soon became apparent that we were going to miss our connection at Doncaster due to being stuck behind a privately chartered steam train excursion.

When we finally caught our Cleethorpes bound train, an hour behind schedule, I was able to rejoin my travelling group and it was on this leg of the journey that Ivan Noel and I realised that we were operating on a different wavelength to our younger travelling companions. More of this later.

Being an hour late, we walked along the prom eating fish and chips towards Blundell Park hoping that nothing else could possibly happen to blight our day. However, when we went two down in the first half hour several people were beginning to wonder if we were in for another Swindon type display. Liam Kelly and Ronan Darcy had other ideas however and, when we got to half time at two all the mood was electric, giving me a chance to look around me at who else was in attendance.

The first person I spoke to was Viv Jeffery, an ex-Red in the Liam Kelly mould, or perhaps that should be the other way round? Viv lives and teaches in Lincolnshire and tries to attend all our matches in the area with his son. I invited him to the upcoming exhibition in December for the family Sunday, the day after the Mansfield home game, and he seemed very keen to attend. 90% of the Maguire family were in attendance as well, and some exiled Reds supporters such as Mick O'Donnell from York, However, what amazed me most was two supporters from Newcastle, Connor and Angela Brown and scouser Dan who travels to most of our games from Leeds. I have told Daniel's story before, so I want to tell you this time about Connor. He picked Crawley Town as his team in FIFA when he was much younger and has now turned into a supporter of the human version of the team. Unbelievable!!

Different wavelength time now, both Ivan and I noticed that when Matt "drummer" Jenkins sang the Ronan Darcy song he sang Roman. We pointed out to him his error, and I quipped "Ronan, what has he ever done for us?" Ivan laughed; the rest looked perplexed, and we had to explain it to them all. Not you though, eh?

So much more to tell, sticker dares and counter strikes, befriending a north London Leeds supporter and a young girl with a red friendly name conducting the singing, but that will have to wait until the fourth book. Title, please Ivan. (yes, this is the fourth book, but when I wrote about the Grimsby game even the thought of it was a long way off. On the train home from Grimsby, we dared Matt Jenkins to get off the train at the first stop and stick a CTFC sticker on the station name plate. He duly accomplished his task only to see a Grimsby supporter stick his own club's sticker over ours. The Leeds supporter from north London appeared to have no recollection of their three-nil drubbing at the hands of the mighty Red Devils and the young girl leading the Crawley choir was, of course, Scarlett.)

30th September 2023
EFL 2
Crawley Town 3 Sutton United 0
CTFC Scorers Campbell (6), Maguire (53), Orsi (66)
Rivals' results
AFC Wimbledon 4 Tranmere Rovers 1, MK Dons 0 Harrogate 1

Another weekend full of incident as far as football is concerned in the Leake and Humphrey households. The best part of the weekend was Saturday afternoon, when the mighty Reds finally put an end to the Sutton United jinx, which to my fading memory goes back about 60 years when we beat them one nil, at Gander Green Lane, thanks to a David Heard wonder goal. Three superbly well taken goals from Cambell, Maguire and Orsi snuffed out the Sutton endeavour, which threatened at times to get them back into the game, and the victory took us to second place, behind Notts County on goal difference. In fact, if Liam Kelly's audacious free kick from the halfway line or Rafiq Khaleel's volley late on, had been just a few inches lower, we would now be top. Ten games played; twenty points won, two points per game gained, if repeated, would see us safe from relegation by Christmas and automatically promoted at the end of the season. Over optimistic? Maybe, but as Juanita Hall and Bloody Mary sang in South Pacific, back in 1958 "If you don't have a dream, how you gonna have a dream come true?"

What made the afternoon even better was seeing Preston Johnson at the game and him being able to walk through our supporters with no hassle, coupled with the visit by ex-Red Andy Taylor to collect a shirt from the time he played for us back in the late 90s and early noughties. He played 113 games for the Red Devils, scoring seven goals, including two against Atherstone United after having come on in the 83rd minute. Andy was accompanied by his teenage daughter Bella who, herself, is an 800 metre athlete back in their hometown of Bury St Edmunds. One to watch for in future international athletics competitions. Andy owns his own building firm but is also heavily involved in the training of athletes to a high standard.

Away from football, Europe took the Ryder cup, which Preston did not enjoy, and while we were watching a Womens FA Cup game we talked about the difference between the European and American attitudes to playing as a team. We put it down to the American golfers being more self centred in their approach to golf and not understanding the team concept in what is traditionally an individual's sport. Just as the game between Crawley AFC and Ashmount Leigh was coming to a conclusion, with Crawley winning one nil, one of the visitors' coaches collapsed to the ground in the dugout, causing players from the Crawley team to quickly offer first aid assistance. Within minutes, a defibrillator was being called for and the twenty-two players formed a virtual curtain around the intense activity taking place, reminiscent of that afforded to Christian Eriksen whilst playing for Denmark in the Euros. The latest information as to the coach's condition was that she was responsive to treatment. Perspective is far more important than winning or losing in instances like this, and I will never forget the day when I went to watch my granddaughter be the first person in my family to play in an FA Cup match.

Back to Crawley Town, Doncaster away beckons on Tuesday followed by a full house on Saturday against Wrexham. If we are six points better off by 5pm Saturday, the dream might just start to appear like a reality.

3rd October 2023
EFL 2
Doncaster Rover 2 Crawley Town 0
Doncaster scorers Faal (27), Ironside (62P)
Rivals' results
Harrogate 0 AFC Wimbledon 1, Walsall 0 MK Dons 0

7th October 2023
EFL 2
Crawley Town 0 Wrexham 1
Wrexham Scorer Palmer (13)
Rivals' results
Gillingham 2 MK Dons 1, Mansfield 0 AFC Wimbledon 0

Well, that didn't go to plan, did it? I wanted six points from the week but that got amended, after Doncaster away, to three and when Ollie Palmer put Wrexham ahead, I would have settled for the draw. I am disappointed with our weekly points total but not with the way we played. Indeed, it looked like we might equalise almost straight away, but it wasn't to be, and we now sit in 8th place after twelve games played, just four points behind the leaders Notts County, two behind an automatic promotion place and just a couple of goals from the play-off positions. We could find ourselves as low as 10th after next weekend because we have no game due to Morecambe having players away for the international break, but we will have a game in hand.

I think this could be a blessing as it will give some time for Liam Kelly and others to recover from their injuries. It will also give valuable game time to those who are just outside the first team, as we have the visit to Gander green lane in the Papa John's Cup, followed by our Sussex Transport Senior Cup match against Worthing just one week later. I want to win both these games, but they should also be used to give other players a chance to stake their claims for a first team place.

The most disappointing aspect of Saturday for me was the reaction from some stalwart fans to the extra 2500 fans we had in for the game. Whether they will come again remains to be seen, but fans have to start somewhere and, judging from comments I heard from some of them, they were impressed by our standard of play and thought we deserved at least a draw. Crewe is up next on the 21st of October and will give us an opportunity to beat a team above us before we go on the road to Walsall and Forest Green.

Away from the on-pitch stuff Mick Fox and I are working tirelessly to pull the upcoming Crawley Town Exhibition together and are fast getting to the point of what do we leave out, rather than worrying about will we have enough to display. Past players such as Viv Jeffery, Andy Taylor, Tony Vessey, Ian Payne etc will be invited to the opening on the 7th of December and the fun day on the 17th, whilst it is also hoped that Scott Lindsey and some of the current squad will also be able to attend. There will be craft activities and a kit design competition for people to take part in and I have heard that two people who like to dress up in red, one once a year and the other one at home games, will also be in attendance. Keep the faith Reds fans, for whilst it is good to learn from the past, it is best to live for the present and plan for the future.

10th October 2023
EFL Trophy
Sutton United 0 Crawley Town 0
(Sutton take extra point on penalties)

14th October 2023
EFL 2
Rivals' results
AFC Wimbledon 0 Bradford City 1, MK Dons 2 Barrow 2

First, let's look at our position in the JPPJ Freightrover Sherpavan trophy. Still unbeaten in normal time. We currently sit on four points in first place with a plus one goal difference with Charlton and Sutton in 2nd and 3rd on 2 points each with plus one and zero goal differences respectively. The Aston Villa u21 team are bottom on two points and with a minus 2 goal difference. From this position we have only ourselves to blame if we don't qualify for the knockout rounds. Even a loss on penalties would see us end on 5 points and see us qualify whatever Sutton and Charlton collude to achieve. Personally, I think we will win outright on the 7th of November leaving us only four matches away from Wembley.

Coming back down to earth, before our progress in the EFL Trophy is decided we will have played our first game in the FA Cup for this season and hopefully will have picked up Forty-One thousand pounds in Prize money by beating Notts County away. I was hoping for Ramsgate or Horsham at home. If we were to repeat our memorable runs in 2010/2011 and 2011/2012, we would have made £333000 in winnings and that is why the FA Cup is so important to us at our level and below. And that's me coming back down to earth. A difficult tie, but you must think they won't be that pleased either.

Before the magic of the FA CUP though, we face the holders of the Sussex Senior Cup on their own ground in Worthing and Crewe Alexandra, Walsall and Forest Green Rovers in the league. I see no reason why we shouldn't be in the next round of the Sussex Senior Cup and on at least twenty-seven points in the league table by the time we start our FA Cup exploits. We do have an unpredictable young side, but in my opinion, they are a joy to watch when they are on song.

The results on the 14th of October saw us drop to tenth place with new leaders, in Stockport County, just six points ahead of us but with Crawley having a game in hand. There were defeats for Notts County and Wimbledon whilst Wrexham came back from two down to win three two and Stockport won at Harrogate, whilst Mansfield, having thrashed Notts County, are still unbeaten, having won five and drawn eight games. Six points cover the top ten and next week's game at home to Crewe, currently in fourth on 23 points with a plus 9 goal difference, hopefully will bring out the killer instinct in Crawley. Our home form, five wins in seven against Crewe's away form of just one win in six, certainly seems to indicate that we should be favourites on paper. However, we don't play on paper, do we?

Two weeks ago, I mentioned a Women's FA Cup match that was abandoned with a minute to go because of a medical incident on the away team's bench. I'm happy to say that the lady concerned is now making good progress at home, but not so happy to report that the FA ordered the whole match to be replayed and murphy's law will tell you that the losing team in Sunday's game was the team who were one minute away from victory in the first game. Football, eh? Who'd credit it?

17th October 2023
Sussex Senior Cup
Worthing 6 (Six) Crawley Town 2
Worthing scorers
Starkey (16), Robinson (26,37), Luque (84), Pearce (87) Smith (90)
CTFC Scorer Adeyemo (6,21)

21st October 2023
EFL League 2
Crawley Town 2 Crewe Alexandra 4
CTFC Scorers Lolos (15), Darcy (28)
Crewe Scorers
Tracey (20), Conroy OG (56), Baker-Richardson 75, Nevitt (90+4)
Rivals' results
Accrington Stanley 1 MK Dons 0, Barrow 0 AFC Wimbledon 0

Oh, what a week, late October 2023, what a dreadful week for me, late October 23.

Well, it has been. Two English cricket defeats to South African opposition and one to the Afghans, plus ten goals let in by the Reds and only four scored in return. I went to both games this week, giving up watching England beat Italy on the tele to qualify for next year's Euros for a trip to Worthing, and also watching Crawley on Saturday losing to Jack Powell's Crewe. In both games Crawley took the lead twice, and in both games surrendered rather tamely in the second half, allowing Worthing to progress in the Sussex Senior Cup and letting Crewe take the full number of points back to the midlands.

The Tuesday game saw Adeyemo score twice in the first half to put us one nil and two one up respectively. Even when we went three two down just before the break, I was fully confident that we would turn it around, but then injuries to Ransom and Adeyemo and a lack of discipline from Johnson earning him a red card put paid to that optimism and we went down all too easily by six goals to two. Worthing fielded half of the team that played the previous Saturday to beat Bath City, whereas we made ten changes from the team that had lost to Wrexham the week before. I am not a football manager but, perhaps if we had used the same approach to the game as Worthing, we would still be in the Sussex Senior Cup.

Perhaps Scott had been distracted by all the rumours coming out of Kent, however it certainly didn't show on Saturday when Klaudi Lollos, starting the game, swept the Reds into an early lead. It didn't last long though as Crewe took full advantage of us giving the ball away in midfield to equalise just eight minutes later. With Jack Powell returning to Broadfield Stadium for the first time with Crewe, it soon became apparent that his habit of not being able to get a corner over the first defender has seemingly been coached out of him. Darcy sent us into the break two one up with a tremendous shot but unfortunately Crewe took the three points with two goals of their own and one own goal scored by Dion Conroy in the second half.

A disappointing result which seemed to come about after what looked like a bad injury to key man Liam Kelly and the substituting of Darcy, who for me seemed to be playing really well. I am prepared to take some of the blame for this defeat, by pointing out our good home record and their poor away record in last week's article.

And if all that wasn't bad enough, the news came through about Sir Bobby Charlton and then South Africa beat England in the Rugby, albeit by only one point. When I was 14, a long time ago, my dad took me to see England v Mexico in the World Cup, and we were lucky to be standing directly in line with Bobby when he unleashed the shot that started our journey to World Cup glory. Sir Bobby RIP.

Sadly, it is only right that I mention the passing of Neil Le Bihan, who played for Crawley Town in 2002/2003 making 43 appearances and scoring three goals in his one season with us. Neil Le Bihan RIP

24th October 2023
Walsall 1 Crawley Town 1
Walsall Scorer Johnson (88)
CTFC Scorer Orsi (90+4)
Rivals' results
AFC Wimbledon 2 Accrington Stanley 4, MK Dons 4 Bradford City 1

28th October 2023
Forest Green Rovers 2 Crawley Town 1
Forest Green Rovers scorers Morton (27,45+2)
CTFC Scorer Darcy (7)
Rivals' results
Morecambe 4 AFC Wimbledon 1, MK Dons 3 Swindon 2

    Where to start? Well, if Danilo hadn't scored his injury time equaliser last Tuesday against Walsall, we would have been on a run of five league defeats in a row. Then again, if Old Moore's horse hadn't stopped for a tinkle, he would have won the Derby. According to my Grandad. that is.
    Let's look at what has happened in October, shall we? First of all, we went to Doncaster on a Tuesday evening and lost two nil. This game ended a four-match winning streak in September, a month in which we also drew at Stockport and beat Charlton in the Papa John's Trophy.
    Then, on the 4th of October, our Kentish friends sacked Neil Harris, despite them being in a promising position in the League. Since then, we have lost another three league games, lost to Worthing in the Sussex Senior Cup and were beaten on penalties in the PJT by bottom club Sutton United. We have gone from almost taking top spot to fourteenth in the league, and one has to wonder whether this loss in form has anything to do with the rumoured interest from the Gills in Scott Lindsey.
    Some of the factors that should be considered when trying to get to the bottom of the dilemma we find ourselves in are; Do our triumvirate of Scott, Jamie and Carl all live closer to the Gills

than they do to Crawley? Has Scott been approached by the Gills, as has been stated in the press? Is Scott interested in the position in Kent? and so on and so on.

I can understand, if the answers to all those questions are in the affirmative, why he might be interested, especially if the rumours about what they want to offer him are true. However, if the atmosphere of indecision is affecting our results, I would rather the situation was resolved one way or the other, as quickly as possible. Players and Managers can touch the badge as much as they like, but we all know they could be doing the same thing with another club's badge in the future.

A speedy conclusion, either by us needing to look for a new management team or in Gillingham appointing someone different, is what is needed. Southend United have refused Gillingham permission for them to talk to their manager, which begs the question of our owners, could we have done the same thing. Scott's departure, if it happens, will probably mean the departure of Jamie and Carl as well, and would leave us having to search for our sixth management team in under a year, and in the worst scenario could also mean some players following them in the next window.

On the other hand, I might go and have a shower, a la Bobby Ewing, and realise October was just a bad dream.

On Saturday's game, I thought we were going to get our second away win of the season when Ronan Darcy opened the scoring after six minutes but as has become a familiar pattern in some of our games, our well created and executed goal was outweighed by some seemingly sloppy play, gifting them two presents before half time. Oh well, at least we're still in the FA Cup.

4th November 2023
FA Cup
Notts County 3 Crawley Town 2
Notts County scorers Crowley (13), McGoldrick (38), Langstaff (76)
CTFC scorers Orsi (3, 66)
Rivals' results
AFC Wimbledon 5 Cheltenham Town 1, Reading 3 MK Dons 2

Lots of ex Reds in the draw for the second round of the FA Cup and a few notable results, indeed at the moment, I'm just settling down to watch Jack Powell v Sonny Bradley only to find Crewe are not playing Jack. Other names of note featuring in the first round were Matt Saddler and Isaac Hutchison for Walsall, the former as their manager, whilst Shamir Fenelon scored for Horsham at Barnsley after Max Watters had given the Tykes the lead. It sticks in my craw a bit, but well done to Horsham, who, if they beat Barnsley in their replay, will face Sutton United away at Gander Green Lane.

Crawley Town, however, despite a good display away to high flying rivals Notts County, find themselves with a free weekend at the beginning of December after losing three - two. I listened to the game curtesy of Ifollow, and I should have guessed it wasn't going to be a good afternoon when first of all the Oxford United match was being broadcast, followed by a few minutes of home commentary from our game, before I had the pleasure of hearing Gary Smith and Travel Ken Blackmore. Unfortunately, by the time I heard their southern twangs, Crowley of County had equalised Danilo Orsi's 3rd minute opener.

The mix up over the broadcast did give me the chance to hear another ex-Red mentioned, Ashley Nathaniel-George playing for Maidenhead United at Oxford.

Our team showed three changes from our last game with Addai, Darcy and Williams making way for Ashley-Hammond, Khaleel and Gladwin, with Adam Campbell making the bench after the injury he sustained against Wrexham. Neither Darcy nor Williams were on the bench, which I assumed meant they were both injured. I can't believe Ronan was rested because it was his birthday, although if he is injured that, in my opinion, would justify him being allowed to stay at home with his family. I hope personally that both get fit for selection as soon as possible so that Scott has a full squad to pick from.

The second half featured the same guts and glory cup action as did the first, and even though McGoldrick put County ahead, Kellan Gordon fed the Ors just eight minutes later, and the prospect of a replay in ten days' time started to loom large. However, County manager Luke Williams brought on talisman leading scorer McAullay Langstaff who put Notts back in the lead and that was how it stayed despite an additional seven minutes on top of the ninety.

Positives from a defeat? I'm sure there will be quite a few, including the availability of skipper Ben Gladwin and Adam Cambell, the way we played from the start of the game, to take the lead and then to come back from two one down to equalise and the fact that Luke Williams was reported as saying we deserved not to lose. Hopefully, we will get the upper hand and revenge when we play them in the league on the 28th of November.

Just as I was getting over the disappointment of defeat, another ex-Red came up on Final Score, Ludo Francillete scoring a brace in a 5-1 win for Eastleigh, and I thought of the 271 reds fans who were on their way back home. Great effort by the team and fans alike, which we must now take onto Tuesday against Aston Villa U21s, and most importantly into next Saturday's home against Accrington Stanley.

7th November 2023
EFL Trophy
Crawley Town 3 Aston Villa U21 2
CTFC scorers Roles (7,35) Simon-Swyer (15)
Aston Villa scorers Moore (42), Richards (56)
Rivals' results AFC Wimbledon 2 Crystal Palace U21 0

11th November 2023
EFL League 2
Crawley Town 3 Accrington Stanley 1
CTFC scorers Orsi (8,76) Wright (48)
Accrington Stanley scorer Nolan (2)
Rivals' results AFC Wimbledon 2 Doncaster Rovers 0, Newport County 0 MK Dons 0

Picture a Merseyside kitchen back in 1989. Two young Liverpool fans are chatting over a glass of milk. One tells the other that Liverpool's star striker Ian Rush had told him that if he didn't drink milk, he would only be good enough to play for Accrington Stanley. The other fan asks, "Accrington Stanley, who are they?", to which the first replies, "Exactly." Apparently, the advertising agency that thought this advert up wanted it to be Tottenham Hotspur who were taken the micky out of, but they objected. Stanley made £10000 out of the advert and one of the boys starring in the ad is now spending time behind bars for murder. Perhaps he gave up the milk.

Anyway, the game on Saturday against Accrington Stanley had me thinking about them in the same frame of mind as the "Exactly" boys for about one minute, as they tore into us from the start and took the lead in the first minute. I don't think we had fallen asleep in defence, I just think we hadn't woken up.

Scott must have been thinking about his decision to play Ashby-Hammond, but we weren't behind for long as Klaudi Lolos set up the ball for "The 'Ors" to equalise, which should have been followed by Danilo putting us two one up after a mazy run and pass by Nick Tsaroulla, deserving the label of move of the season, somehow evaded Orsi at the far post.

Accrington showed in flashes why they started the game in the last playoff place, but in the end were soundly beaten by three goals to one thanks to a bullet of a shot from Will Wright, which put us into the lead, and a third from the spot by Orsi, after he had been brought down in the box. We should really have gone for more goals as Accrington were reduced to ten men because of that incident, but we now sit in 11th place just two points behind Accrington in 8th and only one point behind both Wimbledon and Gillingham, with a game in hand on all three.

Saturday coming sees us visit the longest Cul de sac in England, when we try and stop the Telford goal machine at Barrow, and then just one week later we entertain Harrogate at home before making the second trip to Nottingham this season, this time in the League. Scott will no doubt be saying we want to win all three, and I think it's possible, although the pragmatist in me thinks five points would be an acceptable haul of points. At the moment we have a week off after those three games because of our FA Cup exit, so in my view we should put everything into the next two weeks.

I haven't forgotten our success against Aston Villa U21s on a cold night at the Broadfield, where two Jack Roles goals and one from Kamarai Simon-Swyer saw us win three two, top the group, and most importantly sets us up for a home tie in the next round against a second placed southern team from another group. There is no prize money for winning through the group or any of the knockout rounds, that is unless you get to Wembley and win the whole competition. This is why we must now put aside any boycotts, due to Premier League club's U21s taking part, and get behind the lads as they seek to tick off one event from my bucket list. COYR

18th November 2023
EFL2
Barrow 1 Crawley Town 0
Barrow scorer Telford (46)
EFL Trophy
Wycombe Wanderers 1 AFC Wimbledon 0

Uncut diamonds are rough and raw in formation, and with the proper cutting and polishing process, they gain the actual value, which sometimes reaches the millions. But, without the cutting and polishing, the raw diamonds fail to surge a spark in price and remain cheaper than the brilliant-cut polished gems.

But diamonds are not polished in the rough; they are polished after cleaving and cutting. Trying to polish a rough diamond into anything looking like a gem would be an incredibly tedious and time-consuming process.

And that is what Scott, Jamie and Carl are attempting to do with our, I was going to say half cut, squad. But that might be misconstrued. Suffice it to say, I compare our team to a bag full of rough uncut diamonds, that are beginning to shine thanks to the hard work put in by our management and coaching team, but, as yet, are in need of some more work.

On Saturday, as I am typing this, I note that we face two ex-Red Devils in Dom Telford, who starts, and Jamie Proctor on the bench. I know both will have been treated with respect by the travelling Red Devil supporters for their efforts while with us, but now is the time to see what Gary Smith and Travel Ken think. I'll be back..........

Soon as "I follow" creaks into activity, we learn that the team on the pitch is unchanged but the team on the mic is down to

Gary Smith without his partner, Travel Ken, and that left me with a sense of foreboding, which unfortunately proved to be correct.

Predictably, Dom Telford hit the winner for Barrow whilst we were still waking up at the beginning of the second half, and try as we might, we couldn't equalise and probably wouldn't have if the game had gone on for longer than the seven added on minutes. There was some discussion that Will Wright was fouled in the buildup to the goal, but for me the incident appeared to be off camera, or I had glanced away for a moment

The diamonds are still showing their rough edges and in need of a bit more polishing and now I will have to revise my target as published in last week's Observer, but not down, as that would be pessimistic. We now need to win at home against Harrogate and follow that up with a win at Meadow Lane against Notts County, if we are to put in a realistic charge for a league position that would warrant further investment in the upcoming January transfer window.

If you, as a team have twice as much possession as your opposition and almost the same stats as far as shots and shots on target are concerned, then surely the result should tend to go your way in the end, but as several fans and Gary Smith observed "If you don't buy a ticket, you can't win the raffle"

In the end the game could have gone either way, and when Barrow attempted to clean up by bringing on Proctor and Campbell (sounds like Gamble) you just knew the 65 fantastic Red Devil supporters would have to travel home, 300 odd miles, disappointed

Next up, Harrogate at home. COYR

21st November 2023
EFL Trophy
Rivals' results MK Dons 3 Northampton 2

25th November 2023
EFL 2
Crawley Town 2 Harrogate 1
CTFC scorers Gladwin (23), Lolos (71)
Harrogate scorer Muldoon (45+6)

Rivals' results AFC Wimbledon 4 Notts County 2, Salford City 2 MK Dons 4

We have played worse and got results, and likewise, we have played better and not got our just rewards. Saturday's game against Harrogate, in my opinion, saw us play through some bad spells and get something from the game through sheer hard work and a fair amount of skill when it mattered most. I was particularly impressed with Luca Ashby-Hammond, and the midfield dynamism of the sponsors player of the match Liam Kelly and the cool leadership of Ben Gladwin. Nobody had a bad game, including the substitutes, but it has to be said we must try not to give the ball away so much as Harrogate could have punished us for those little errors on another day.

Having said that, Harrogate had won their last four away games, so to put an end to that has to be considered a major achievement. The game could have gone either way, with both keepers making a series of good saves, but for once it went our way thanks to a long-distance ground shot from Captain Ben and a header from Klaudi Lolos. I think we also had a couple of headers in the first half, which either hit the post or were saved at the foot of the post, and why the referee didn't give us a penalty for a blatant foul on Nick Tsaroulla is beyond me, and indeed the majority of the people watching. Anywhere else on the pitch it would have been given, as indeed he gave freekicks for less obvious fouls throughout the entire 102 minutes played.

Another pleasing aspect of the afternoon was the crowd of over 2800, with less than 100 from Yorkshire. Our support is growing because of the way the team are playing Scott Lindsey, and long may that continue. There will be times that we lose because of our taking risks but when it all comes together what a joy it is to watch. Roll on Tuesday, when hopefully we will achieve my revised target from last week by beating Notts County and thus inflict upon them their second defeat in a row

Away from the stadium we are very close to the opening evening of the CTFC Exhibition at Crawley Museum at Crawley Museum. The opening ceremony is by invitation only and will feature ex-players, ex owners, present owners, sponsors, exhibition backers, local councilors and hopefully some of the present players and management. The exhibition will be open to the public before the official opening, at 1030am on Thursday 7th of December until 4pm, and then every Thursday, Friday and Saturday throughout the remainder of December until the last week in January, apart from the period from closing on the 23rd of December to reopening on 4th January.

On Sunday 17th December (the day after we have beaten Mansfield at home) the museum will open especially for our family fun day which will be visited by Father Christmas, Reggie the Red and a dramatic representation of one of our founders, GFH Banks, as performed by the Half Time Orange Theatre Company. Admission to the Museum, which is situated at 103 High Street, Crawley, is free although donations are most welcome.

Throughout the exhibition children will be able to take part in the "Find a significant result" trail for confectionary rewards, and everyone will be eligible to take part in the "Design a CTFC kit" competition with Family tickets, signed shirts and a month's subscription to Brick Borrow as prizes.

Come on you rip roaring Reds Devils!

28th November 2023
Notts County 3 Crawley Town 1
Notts County scorers Mc Goldrick (20), O'Brien (61), Morias (70)
CTFC scorer Campbell (10)
Rivals' results
Gillingham 1 AFC Wimbledon 0, MK Dons 1 Grimsby 1

Another defeat on the road and I guess there are some fans feeling a bit glum, however we are still nearer the play offs than the bottom of the table, so at the moment I see no reason for any negativity. Our team is a young one, and when they are on song, they really do take the breath away. Alongside those performances there will be some where mistakes are made, and we don't get the results we all want. I watched a bit of a game today between Eastleigh and Reading where the non-league team had more Football League experience in their ranks than the League 1 side. On this occasion the more experienced side won the day, albeit with a last-minute winner, whereas on another day Reading might well have made the most of their territorial advantage and progressed through to the 3rd round. That, Ladies and Gentlemen, boys and girls, is what football is all about. Mind you, Eastleigh, did feature Ludwig and Enzio in their side, so well done to them.

As I write this, Nativity is on in the background and Crawley Town are due to play Bristol Rovers in the Bristol Street Motors Trophy the night before this article comes out on paper. Hopefully we will have progressed through to the next round, and we will only be three games from Wembley, and the dreams and bucket lists might just get ticked off. Now, though, is the time to field our strongest side, come on Scott, you know it makes sense.

Away from the playing side, Mick Fox and I have concluded that we never want to see another piece of Velcro again as we come towards the end of the preparation for the, soon to be opened, Crawley (Town) FC from 1890 to 2023 exhibition. The exhibition is open to the public from 1030am on Thursday 7th of December and will be opened officially at 7pm that night for invited guests only.

The exhibition will take you through all the different aspects of what it takes to make a football club, from the grassroots of the West Sussex Junior League through two World Wars, the Metropolitan and Southern Leagues and the Conference to finally reach the promised land of League Football. Yes, it has taken over 100 years to do it and that is why we cannot allow it to slip away, as we almost did last season. In the past we would have been pleased to beat the likes of Shephsed Charterhouse, Worcester City and others of a similar standard but now our list of conquests features such illustrious names as Bolton Wanderers, Norwich City, Wolves, Sheffield United, Leeds United and many more. Come along to the exhibition throughout December and January and relive the ups and downs associated with our wonderful club, and make a special note in your diary of the Family Fun Day on Sunday December 17th where there will be museum trails, competitions with prizes donated by the Club and Brick Borrow, a club commercial partner, craft activities, chats with players, past and present, and visits from "GFH Banks" Father Christmas and hopefully, Reggie the Red. See you soon, COYR.

2nd December 2023
FA CUP
Rivals' results AFC Wimbledon 5 Ramsgate 0

5th December 2023
EFL Trophy
Crawley Town 2 Bristol Rovers 1
CTFC scorers Roles (58), Forster (69)
Bristol Rovers' scorer Thomas (45)
Rivals' results MK Dons 0 Brighton 4

9th December 2023
EFL 2
Colchester United 1 Crawley Town 2
Colchester Utd scorer Taylor (90+7)
CTFC scorers L.Kelly (41), Orsi (64P)
Rivals' results AFC Wimbledon 4 Swindon Town 0

    Whilst listening to the agonising 13 minutes of added on time yesterday and thinking at the same time of the current "CTFC from its Victorian roots to the present day" exhibition on at Crawley Museum, I thought I would count the number of current Premier League and English Football League clubs, we, Crawley Town have played in competitive football. Not including reserves such as West Ham's World Cup winning team back before 1966 in the Metropolitan League days, or the under 21s/23s we face in the Johnson Painted Pizza Delivery Competition, so as not to upset some of our more principled fans, I reckon we have played 66 out of 92 clubs.
    The reason why I did this was spurred by the memories which have been brought into clear focus by the exhibition, currently on throughout December and January. I urge all of you, who have Red Devil blood flowing through your veins, to journey along to 103 High Street RH10 1DD, where you will have the chance to reminisce through the ups and downs of our existence. If you are

of my sort of age you might like to visit during the week, on Wednesday through Friday, when you will be able to take it all in in relative quiet, whereas, if you have a young family might I suggest you pay a visit this coming Saturday or Sunday. If going on Saturday, you and your family can take part in the Victorian family day, when local artist John Leech, who used to live at 103, will rise with a Lazarine style to tell you what it was like to illustrate for Charles Dickens. On Sunday, you can take part in the Crawley Town FC fun day where GFH Banks will rise in a similar fashion to tell you about the beginnings of our great club.

On both days Father Christmas will be present, along with, it is hoped, Reggie the Red and members of our current squad. A design a kit competition, with prizes donated by CTFC and associates Brick Borrow will be taking place, alongside a CTFC trail where people will hopefully discover a memorable CTFC result in return for a dip in the sweet tin. One person who will definitely be there is ex Red Devil Viv Jeffrey, who is travelling down from Lincolnshire for the weekend.

Advertisement over, Saturday saw us come back from Colchester with all three points thanks to our wonderful squad of players, a great team goal made by Will Wright and passed, superbly, into the net by Liam Kelly and an emphatic penalty from Danilo "Feed me and I will score" Orsi, won by Nick Tsaroulla.

We are now 11th in the League, one point from the playoff positions with a game in hand on most of the teams above us. However, our next two games are at home to Nigel "I'll never have to come to Crawley again" Clough's Mansfield and AFC Wombles featuring James Tilley. Victories against both would set up Christmas nicely and hopefully give us added impetus going into 2024.

Life is never boring with Crawley Town FC but now is the time to unite as a family, on and off the pitch, to make the most of what remains of this season.

(SEE BELOW FOR THERE BEING NO MANSFIELD REPORT)

16th December 2023
EFL 2
Crawley Town 1 Mansfield Town 3
CTFC scorer Orsi (36P)
Mansfield scorers Cargill (12), Kellor-Dunn (56), Maris (65)
Rivals' results MK Dons 2 Forest Green Rovers 0, Salford City 0 AFC Wimbledon 0

19th December 2023
EFL Trophy
Rivals Results Portsmouth 2 AFC Wimbledon 5

22nd December 2023
EFL 2
Crawley Town 1 AFC Wimbledon 2
CTFC scorer Wright (83)
AFC Wimbledon scorers Davison (13), Al-Hamadi (18)

Apologies first of all, for not being able to write in last week's Observer. It wasn't because of the defeat by Mansfield on the Saturday, but rather because of being at the Crawley Museum for 7 hours the day after. Coming home from that I was paid a visit by a chap called Parkinson, who gave me a bit of a fright, so much so that I spent most of the next day in a catatonic state.

I am happy to say I am now fully recovered and looking forward to a Christmas that will hopefully yield the gift of four victories over clubs that we need to beat if we are to threaten the playoff places. Writing this before we play AFC Wimbledon because of newspaper deadlines means that we might have started that possibility before you read this and hopefully continued it by beating our Kentish friends on Boxing Day.

I will be able to close this article with news of the defeat against the Wombles, but before we get to that I would like to update everyone on how the exhibition is going at Crawley Museum. The numbers attending the family fun day were a little disappointing, but those who did attend had nothing but good words to say of what Mick Fox and I had curated over the preceding 5 or 6 months and also of the dramatic performance entitled "Pastures New" acted out in the exhibition space, celebrating the first 54 years of our club from GFH Banks point of view, talking about his dear friend and Crawley legend, Bill "Wayfarer" Denman. Those who saw it were almost moved to tears, and it was also a great pleasure to have ex Red Devil, Viv Jeffrey, Tom Allman and the great grandson of Stan "Mr. Crawley Town" Markham, in the audience. Please visit the museum before the end of January 2024, although moves are already underway to find a permanent location at Broadfield Stadium for the exhibition, which we hope will help contribute to the already wonderful match day experience.

Having bought the Observer on Wednesday, I was encouraged by what I read about Scott's thinking on the upcoming transfer window, Laurence Maguire and his almost half season report, and I have to say I am looking forward to the second half of the season in a very positive frame of mind.

I still have a positive frame of mind, despite losing at home to Wimbledon by two sloppy goals to one in a game of the proverbial two halves. In the first half, after having almost taken the lead in the first minute, we gave another two goals away before responding in the second half with a much-improved performance which saw the Dons have a player sent off which almost allowed us to rescue a point. In the first half we failed to get a shot on target, but in the second, we outshot the opposition and turned the possession data in our favour, and if Will Wright had scored five minutes earlier than he did we might just have salvaged a valuable point. Wombles fans said on BBC Sports website that they were playing against twelve, and whilst I agree that the referee was of the usual EFL 2 standard, he certainly was not biased.

Anyway, here's hoping you have all had a great Christmas, improved, I hope, by a win on boxing Day against the Gills.

23rd December 2023
EFL 2
Rivals' result Morecambe 1 MK Dons 3

26th December 2023
EFL 2
Gillingham 0 Crawley Town 2

CTFC scorers Wright (24), Roles (71)
Rivals' results AFC Wimbledon 0 Sutton Utd 1, MK Dons 1 Colchester United 0

29th December 2023
MK Dons 2 Crawley Town 0
Rivals' result AFC Wimbledon 5 Colchester United 3

1st January 2024
Crawley Town 3 Swindon Town 1
CTFC scorers Orsi (9,53) Roles (26)
Swindon scorer Kemp (90+2)
Rivals' results
Doncaster 3 MK Dons 0, Forest Green Rovers 1 AFC Wimbledon 1

Well, that was an eventful festive season for Crawley Town, wasn't it? Let's hope the rest of this football season is at least as productive. Yes, I know we lost two games, but we also won two which leaves us just three points off the last playoff place and eighteen above the drop zone. I read on Facebook that one of our fans thought we were entering a relegation dogfight after the defeat against Wimbledon, which at the time I thought was a little pessimistic, and certainly the next three results/performances, I believe, should have hopefully put that thought out of his mind.

I, like Scott, thought we probably played our best football in the game we lost at Milton Keynes and thus am only too happy to take the six points in the other two games against Gillingham and Swindon. The other splendid result from the last ten days must be the size of our home support, which seems to indicate that more people consider us to be half full rather than half empty. Will Wright's free kick and two goals from Jack Roles, one on Boxing Day and one on New Years Day, plus the brace from Danilo Orsi against Swindon has put us in a great position as we enter Scott Lindsay's second year in charge.

January sees us play Bradford, Wimbledon and Wrexham away, although the fixture against the Welsh side might have to change if they beat Shrewsbury in the 3rd round of the FA Cup, and Salford City at home. On top of that we also visit League One side Peterborough United in the next round of the Bristol Street Motors Trophy, a game which would be great to win for various reasons. There is no reason why we should feel that we can't beat any of those teams, and yes, they will be saying the same, but I'm a Red Devil and believe if everything goes our way that we will be in a spectacular position by the beginning of February. We could be sitting on forty-eight points and also be closer to knocking off one item from my bucket list.

My bucket list item is to sing "Abide with me" at Wembley whilst waiting to watch Crawley Town play at the home of football. I have even gone as far as to ask in my prayers if I would be allowed to do this before I must go and sit in the upper rows of seats that are reserved for the likes of Bill Denman, GFH Banks, Stan Markham, Dave Haining and Bruce Winfield. The Sermon at my church on New Year's Eve was about Simeon, who had been told that he would not die until he had witnessed the arrival of the Messiah, and that came to pass. Now, that may seem to be a bit flippant, as you cannot compare us getting to Wembley with the arrival of Christ. Hopefully, I will be given the chance to sing "Abide with me" on more than one occasion.

I only hope our nickname is not held against me!!

6th January 2024
EFL 2
Bradford City 2 Crawley Town 4
CTFC scorers Orsi (12, 90+7P), Campbell (85), Lolos (90+10)
Bradford City scorers Ridehaigh (61), Addai OG (79)
Rivals' results
FA Cup
AFC Wimbledon 1 Ipswich 3
First Year Report
Scott Lindsey, Jan 11th, 2023, to Jan 6th, 2024

Scott started his first year at Broadfield in good form, but his good work ethic was not rewarded as it should have been in his first quarter in charge. Fortunately, a great improvement in the second quarter of 2023 secured his place at this level for another year. This effort must be considered as worthy of praise as any in the past by the fellows of this establishment, prolonging the status quo for the 13th year in a row.

Having learnt a lot about this wonderful cub in that first half of the year, his charges started the new season in an impressive manner, and if it hadn't been for a period of distraction in October, which led to some disappointing outcomes, his efforts would have seen us ensconced in the play-off positions. Now, with that distraction firmly behind him and us, and the form getting back to how we would want, we find ourselves three points away from the promotion places.

Grade: Low C, but with opportunity for vast improvement before the final assessment in May.

Seriously, apologies for the attempt at levity, but if you look at our results since Scott took over and you break them down into roughly four quarters you will see a steady improvement in his win percentage, from 30% up to 43 to 44% by the end of play on 6th January. Indeed, if we get back to our form in the first quarter of this season, we might conceivably end up with approximately 78 points, which would have put us into the playoffs last season.

I haven't included Cup matches, and it must be said, going out in the first round of three out of the four competitions we enter must be seen as slightly disappointing. However, up against those poor outcomes, we are in the round of 16 in the Bristol Street Motors Trophy, and hopefully by the time you read this will have progressed to the quarter finals, putting us just two matches from Wembley.

Listening to the Ifollow while I write this, I anticipate forty minutes of anxiety, as is usual when we play away, before the final whistle blows and we can celebrate another away win. What can I do to help the situation, sitting at home on my laptop? Absolutely nothing, except perhaps try the toilet trick and read "If" by Rudyard Kipling. Unfortunately, I should have read "If" earlier or gone to the loo, as Bradford are getting on top and have just equalised, leaving another twenty-five minutes for us to either hang on or pinch the win.

Come on Klaudi, as he comes on for Roles, with just twenty-two minutes to go. Twelve minutes to go and Conroy gives Bradford a penalty which Cook dispatches despite Addai saving it initially before he allows it to squirm under his body.

Forster now on and Orsi almost equalises for the Red Devils but IF it isn't to be our day, then all we can do is to treat it the same as any result and come back fighting on We....... Wait a minute Campbell equalises and the tension goes on. Eight minutes added on,,,,,, call 999. Penalty to Crawley Town as Nick is brought down in the box and Orsi puts us back in the lead. Feed the Ors and he will score.

IF, IF, IF and then Lollos wins the game for sure.

Let's hope the players make it to the Museum between three and four on Wednesday 11th where they can see where their exploits will appear in the future. YOU REDS!!!!!!!!!! C+ already

9th January 2024
EFL Trophy
Rivals' results AFC Wimbledon 2 Oxford United 0
10th January 2024
EFL Trophy
Peterborough United v Crawley Town, Postponed frozen pitch

13th January 2024
EFL 2
Crawley Town 0 Salford City 1
Salford scorer N'mai (80)
Rivals' results
Tranmere Rovers 1 MK Dons 2, Wrexham 1 AFC Wimbledon 0

I should have known what sort of week it was going to be when, after the euphoria of last Saturday, several things happened around football that got me thinking. The first, was at a game featuring Crawley Athletic against a team from London, in their League Cup. The game ended at ninety minutes with the score at one all. The referee then started the procedures for a penalty shootout, and up stepped my granddaughter, who calmly slotted home the first one in true Orsi style. Before the player from the other side had a chance to take their kick, a man in a blazer (I'm only surmising there) walked on to the pitch, rule book in hand, and pointed out to the referee that thirty minutes extra time had to be played first. Luckily, the Crawley side went on to win by two goals to one but left one of their players slightly miffed that her penalty will now not feature in the records.

The next talking point, on Monday afternoon, featured Desmond Andersen's girls' team, coached by my son and kit sponsored by Preston Johnson. You will remember that last Monday was a snow day, and after getting to K2 by bus the misnomer of all-weather pitches came to the fore and that afternoon's girls league matches were rightly called off and rescheduled for last Friday, and I was left to get on the same bus that I had arrived on for my journey back home and a nice cup of Bovril.

Anyway, onto Crawley Town, who last Wednesday travelled to Peterborough United in the EFL Trophy round of 16. The good news is we are in the draw for the Quarter Finals against AFC Wimbledon at home, but because of the pitch inspection fiasco we still have to beat the Posh, now scheduled for Tuesday 23rd January, before either club can even start to think about selling tickets for a game that should be played the next week beginning the 29th January. These things happen, but the weather was forecast to get colder before kickoff and in my opinion common sense should have prevailed. This would have saved all the Crawley supporters from spending at least five needless hours on a train and would not have disrupted the team's training routine for nothing.

That brings me to the Salford City game, where all the form and stats were pointing to a home victory. Before Saturday we had played Salford nine times, winning and drawing four games and losing only one away in March 2022. Added to those stats was Salford came into the game not having won for eleven league games. The one worrying bit of information prior to the game was that they had, only last week, sacked their manager, Neil Wood, and replaced him with Karl Robinson, which often leads to a bounce in fortune. In fairness, on the day, if it hadn't had been for a player of the match performance by Corey Addai, we could have lost by four or five. The only stat that we were "better" in was possession, but they outshot us by a factor of three, and by ten, in shots on target. I know Scott and the players will know it wasn't good enough and that hopefully we will see a much-improved performance on Saturday at Plough Lane,

20th January 2024
EFL 2
AFC Wimbledon v Crawley Town Postponed
Rivals' results MK Dons 1 Morecambe 2

    I dreamt last night (Friday) that an Orsi brace and a scorcher from Will Wright defeated AFC up at Plough Lane by three unanswered goals. Here's hoping that dream comes true when we finally get to play them, probably on a Tuesday night in the not-too-distant future.

    The news of the postponement came through to me whilst I was "assisting" my son at a Foundation tournament at K2, for Primary school boys' teams. Generally, the tournament was played in good spirits by all the teams there. Having qualified for the semifinals by finishing second in their group on goal difference, my son praised his team, Desmond Anderson, for their resilience, as they got through because of scoring a late consolation goal in the one group game they lost. A goal which not only assured their semifinal place but stopped their conquerors from going through instead.

    They went on to beat Our Lady Queen of Heaven, the team that is, in the semifinal by one goal to nil but unfortunately lost a bruising final against Pound Hill, by the same score. Their performances throughout the whole tournament earned them a special mention from Jamie of CTFC Community Foundation, for the way they approached all aspects of the competition with integrity and respect, which has earnt them a tour of the home of CTFC next month. They would, no doubt, rather have won the final, but that comment will be remembered by their watching parents forever.

    After two hours in the freezing cold, I went for a couple of pints with my son, and that is probably why I had my AFC dream.

    Anyway, back to the events of the week which concerned Crawley Town. There has been activity in the transfer window, but most of it has concerned loan players going back to their parent clubs and some of our fringe players going out on loan to National League clubs. The two bits of good news are the extension of Lawrence Maguire's loan from National league leaders, Chesterfield and the replacement of Luca Ashby-Hammond with the signing of Ryan Sandford from Dartford FC. Older supporters will remember Dartford as being one of our main rivals throughout the 60s and 70s. I know Preston and Scott are still looking for additions to the squad, and I also know they will only sign players who can make a difference in a positive manner to what has already been an eventful season, and a vast improvement on last year.

Last Wednesday, it was my real privilege to show Preston Johnson, Harry Maynard, and most importantly for this supporter of 67 years, Dion Conroy, Harry Forster, Ade Adeyemi and Jay Williams. They were joined by some CTFC supporters, who couldn't believe their luck, and all chatted together with a real sense that this season is by no means over, and that last week's game has been discussed and now firmly put in the past. All the squad are fit, apart from Ben Gladwin, and raring to go as soon as the weather allows. If we had played AFC, I honestly think we would have won and now I'm going to take that confident feeling into Tuesday's rescheduled Bristol Street Motors Trophy game against Peterborough.

The only question in my mind is do I buy my train ticket in advance or wait to see what affect Storm Isha has on their pitch.

23rd January 2024
EFL 2
Rivals' results MK Dons 3 AFC Wimbledon 1

27th January 2024
EFL 2
Rivals' results
AFC Wimbledon 2 Mansfield 1, MK Dons 2 Gillingham 1

28th January 2024
EFL Trophy
Peterborough United 2 Crawley Town 1
Peterborough scorers Burrows (28), Mason-Clark (37)
CTFC scorer Tsaroulla (22)

The first thing I must write about, on this Sunday afternoon, is how well Crawley Town played against Peterborough United last Tuesday evening. Indeed, if the referee had given the penalty, when Nick Tsaroulla was brought down in the box, we would have been two nil up and on our way to a quarter final tie against AFC Wimbledon. I know they scored two, so it could have been a draw, but I am a firm believer in moments in time affecting everything else that follows.

The journey up and back to Peterborough went off without incident and there was still a good following of Red Devil fans in attendance, albeit not as many as those who made the journey for the postponed game, a fortnight ago.

We are out now, and my dreams of singing "Abide with me" before Crawley play at Wembley, will have to be delayed a little while longer. I suppose I could sing it if we were to reach the playoff final, and I honestly believe that we, with a large bit of luck and a following wind, could just about make seventh place by the last day of the season. Of course, this could be made even more possible if we were able to strengthen our squad, with just a couple or three quality signings, before the window closes on Wednesday 31st January. Come on Wagmi, you know it makes sense!! Morecambe up next Saturday, and hopefully a return to winning ways at home, with or without any additions to our squad.

Yesterday, I, along with Mick Fox, dismantled the Crawley Town FC exhibition at Crawley Museum, and it must be said it was an emotional time for both of us. What took almost a day to install, took just over an hour to put back into its numerous boxes and files, but have no fear faithful Red Devils, hopefully some or all of it will be installed permanently in its new home at Broadfield Stadium. Tom Allman and I will be talking very soon about a room in the vicinity of Redz, which could be used, and I have already approached the CTSA, as to the possibility of receiving funding for this project from Rollover profits.

The exhibition at the Museum was attended by 1700 people in 22 days, doubling the attendance of any previous December/January exhibition held at The Tree. Mick and I talked to most of those who attended and had wonderful conversations with people who found real comfort in finding relatives amongst the many photographs on show. It was my privilege to be able to show Dion Conroy, Jay Williams, Ade Adeyemo and Harry Forster, along with Football Operations Manager, around the exhibition last week and they were all keen to make more memories to put on show, both in this season and the future.

We, the supporters and the Club, must ensure that these memories are able to be talked about in the days, weeks, months and years ahead and for that to happen we will have to purchase our own boards and cabinets, hence the appeal to the CTSA. Of course, if individuals would like to support this venture, then please watch this space.

As I come to the end of my article for this week, I must mention the exploits of Crawley Athletic Women, who last Friday defeated Guernsey FC by one goal to nil at Culver Road, Lancing. The winning goal being scored by Beth Humphrey, my granddaughter, who was voted Crawley's player of the match by Guernsey streaming service, who were seated behind us in the stand commentating on the game for the people back in the Channel Islands.

COYR

30th January 202EFL Trophy Quarter Final
Rivals' results
Peterborough 3 AFC Wimbledon 1
NB. Just two days after beating Crawley Town

3rd February 2024
EFL 2
Crawley Town 1 Morecambe 2
CTFC scorer Forster (17)
Morecambe scorers Garner (35, 84)
Rivals' results
Barrow 1 MK Dons 0, Bradford City 0 AFC Wimbledon 0,

Another extraordinary week in the life of being a football fan in general and a Crawley town fan in particular. The winter window for 2023/2024 finally closed, not on the 31st of January as I originally thought, but at 11pm GMT on Thursday the 1st of February. Apologies here to Preston Johnson, who I pestered a day early for any news as regards ins or, more worryingly, any possible outs. As it was, we did have some outs earlier in the window which have already been recorded, and in the last hour or so before the window closed, we added Jeremy Kelly and Mustapha Olagunju to our ranks alongside Goalkeeper Ryan Sandford who had signed earlier in January. Jeremy, coming to us from the USA, although he was born in the Czech Republic and Mustapha, coming in on loan from Huddersfield Town. Three departments of the team being strengthened, hopefully, but in my opinion missing an opportunity to add extra bite up front.

Don't get me wrong, I think our forward players are all valuable members of the squad and have all scored goals this season, albeit in varying amounts. However, I do think that we would have been improved by an old-fashioned type of centre forward, who would not only be able to score himself but also make it easier for our existing forwards to score more themselves.

The game against Morecambe, which I watched as frustratingly as the rest of the 2700 home supporters, recorded us as having 70% possession, five shots to their three but unfortunately only one on target as opposed to their two. All the shots on target, according to the BBC, resulted in goals, but I'm pretty sure Corey Addai saved at least four attempts from their forwards. Having just listened to Scott Lindsey's reaction to the result and the performance, it is obvious he holds much the same sort of opinions as most of the home crowd, which hopefully he will work on with the team before we face Crewe Alexandra next Saturday. Adding to the frustration of us not getting a result today was the fact that a lot of the teams around us also dropped points meaning that an opportunity to get closer to the playoff places was badly missed. Looking on the bright side though, we are still on the verge of the playoffs.

Being an eternal optimist, where the Red Devils are concerned, I am positive that, after another week on the training ground, we will see an improvement in our decision making and risk-taking next week. There is an old adage that if you don't shoot, you'll never score. We must make the opposing goalkeeper earn his money and to do that, our players must take on the responsibility of shooting on goal, rather than trying to find someone else to take the gamble of a shot.

Back to something more positive, the history of Crawley Town Football Club exhibition. In the 22 days the exhibition was open, 1700 people attended. The exhibition cost about £1580 to put on, which was financed by some very generous donations and helped raise about £2200 to go towards the Museums running costs. Such was the success of the exhibition that Mick Fox and I, along with Tom Allman from the Football Club have agreed to house it permanently at the stadium, hopefully in time for the beginning of the 2024/2025 season. Watch this space.

10th February 2024
EFL 2
Crewe Alexandra 1 Crawley Town 0
Crewe scorer Adebisi (61)
Rivals' results
AFC Wimbledon 2 Barrow 0, MK Dons 2 Accrington Stanley 1

Despite the loss last Saturday (3rd February), Scott showed full confidence in the players by fielding the same starting lineup but with both the new signings, Jeremy Kelly and Mustapha Olagunju, on the bench.

From all accounts, at least those from Crawley based media and fans, both at the game and watching on Ifollow, Crewe should have been reduced to ten men early on for an over the ball tackle. Even I thought it was a red card, and I was only listening. Unfortunately, VAR doesn't get used at our level and we all know that even if it had been available, it doesn't always guarantee the correct verdict.

Up until the Crewe goal, in the sixty first minute, we had uncharacteristically only had 35% possession but had outshot Crewe with shots on goal and on target. After the goal, we obviously started to play more passing football which saw the last thirty minutes turn the possession stats upside down, ending in 52-48% in the HomeSide's favour. They had one shot on target to our two, but unfortunately the main statistic, the one that counts, shows Crewe as winning one nil and cementing the last automatic promotion place.

Crawley started the afternoon in 14th, went down to 15th when Swindon went one up against Salford, went back up to 14th when Salford equalised, only to go back down to 15th when Bradford scored to beat Wrexham away. This is what this season is turning into, a season of ups and downs, and we must now regain our positive home form as we face Walsall and Forest Green Rovers at the Broadfield this week, before we travel to Plough Lane to face AFC Wimbledon.

No nine-point targets from me this week, except like Scott and the players I would like us to gain maximum points by taking each game as they come. Walsall lost three nil at home to Newport, whilst Forest Green lost by four at home with Tom Nichols on the score sheet, following his move from Gillingham. Will this see the wounded animal syndrome raise their levels of performance against us, or will it be us who put things right and start to claw back what has recently been lost?

By the time you read this, hopefully we will be halfway to gaining the home points, and if we do, who knows what the rest of the season will bring.

I, for one, will be attending the Forum this week and have submitted two questions, which I hope will be answered to all our satisfaction by either Preston Johnson or Tom Allman. My questions seek clarification of our actions in the recent transfer window and when we can expect to see the recent Exhibition rehoused at the Stadium. Hoping to have seen some of you there and at the victories over Walsall and FGR.

Finally, you should never despair, Tom Fellows, on loan from WBA last year, scored a goal in the Championship at the weekend. Pleased for him. Unfortunately, another ex-Red Devil, Jamie Proctor was sent off for Foul and Abusive Language playing for Barrow.

Noli Cedere

13th February 2024
EFL 2
Crawley Town 1 Walsall 1
CTFC scorer L.Kelly (64)
Walsall scorer Hutchinson (38P)
Rivals' results

Accrington Stanley 2 AFC Wimbledon 0, Bradford City 4 MK Dons 0

17th February 2024
EFL 2
Crawley Town 2 Forest Green Rovers 0
CTFC scorers Orsi (39) Lolos (87)
Rivals' results
AFC Wimbledon 1 Morecambe 1, Swindon 1 MK Dons 2

Where to start? Improved performances and results? Over the top ex player celebrations? Supporters' quotes? The Fans Forum?

Well, let's go in chronological order, shall we? I attended the forum last Monday and was impressed with the candidness exhibited by both Tom Allman and Preston Johnson. The whole forum is available on YouTube, so I will leave it up to you to judge for yourselves as to whether you choose to reelect Preston and Eben for another year, but I would say better the Red Devil you know than the one you don't. A lot of lessons will have been learnt over the past two seasons, and I see no point in starting on a new learning curve with people we don't know.

A day later we were given a chance to see an improved performance by the boys in red, when we played Walsall at home. Both teams came into the game after defeats, and both looked as if they wanted to make amends, but it was Walsall who gained the upper hand when an over officious referee adjudged that Jay Williams had fouled the Walsall attacker in the box. Whether or not it was a penalty is still something members of my family can't agree on, and we were all within 10 yards of the incident. Anyway, the referee gave it and up stepped ex Red Devil, Isaac Hutchinson to put the Saddlers one up from the spot. I have no objections to ex-players celebrating goals against their former clubs, but to do it the way Isaac did must surely be worth a yellow card. If taking your shirt off is a yellow card, then surely inciting the home support must be. He may have been jeered by the crowd, but Isaac is a professional and should rise above that. When you compare his actions to those from Declan Rice and Raheem Sterling in the last week you can see he has a lot to learn.

What we saw of both Jeremy Kelly and Mustapha Olagunju during the Walsall game needs to be backed up by more playing minutes before a solid judgement can be made as to their ability, but neither, in my opinion, looked out of place.

The second half on Tuesday shows that we can battle, and if Liam Kelly hadn't scored the equaliser it would have been an injustice. One-one and Forest Green, under Steve Cotterill up next, would surely show us whether our bad spell is coming to an end.

With again a core home support of around 2600 (as opposed to around 1800 two years ago) the players certainly showed they wanted to look up the table rather than down, and goals from Orsi and Lolos gave us our first win in five games and keeps us just on the verge of the play offs. Yes, we are 15^{th,} but, with at least one game in hand on most of the teams above us, there is still a lot to play for before we entertain Grimsby on the last day of the season. This brings me to some fan comments which make me smile. "I think we are safe now" "Our season is over" etc etc. In my opinion we have been safe for ages. We now have three less points than we had at the end of last season with another fifteen matches to play, and even with our current form that would see us finish on 64 points.

Will that happen? I don't think so, I think we will up our form and finish in the seventies, and hopefully in the playoffs. COYR

20th February 2024
EFL 2
AFC Wimbledon 0 Crawley Town 1
CTFC scorer Orsi (78)
Rivals' results MK Dons 1 Wrexham 1

24th February 2024
Accrington Stanley 0 Crawley Town 1
CTFC scorer Ransom (68)
Rivals' results
Doncaster 1 AFC Wimbledon 0, MK Dons 3 Newport County 0

Dear Lord, I don't know if you follow Crawley Town, especially with us being known as the Red Devils, but is it just a coincidence that since Shrove Tuesday we appear to have given up the habit of conceding silly goals and remain unbeaten since then? Indeed, we haven't conceded a goal in open play in the last four games and have scored five in return.

Of course, I don't believe He favours us more than any other team, but it does seem that Crawley may have given up losing for Lent. Indeed, if we remain unbeaten until Easter, seven games including four at home, three away and five of the seven against teams also in the playoff hunt we will find ourselves on a points total somewhere between 56 and 70 points.

Coming down from cloud nine for the rest of this article, but only for a little while, I really enjoyed the trip to Plough Lane last Tuesday, as did the rest of the 529 travelling support, especially being able to sing "We are your Champions" and "It's happened again", referring of course to the tremendous 2010/2011 season and last year's one nil victory when James Tilley laid on Ashley Nadesan's winner to help in our battle for survival. This year, Danilo Orsi's goal kept us in the playoff hunt, if you're like me, or took us three points clearer of the drop zone if you like looking over your shoulder.

And then we returned to the scene of the last game in the 2011/2012 season, Accrington Stanley, when a goal from Scott Neilson in the 67th minute saw us clinch the third automatic promotion place. Almost eerily, this year saw Harry Ransom score the winner in the 68th minute, prompting me to wake up everyone in my flats with a very loud solo rendition of "It's happened again".

The win would have seen us in 7th place, a rise of seven places, if it hadn't had been for a Glenn Morris save against Wrexham which saw the Gills hold on to their one nil win. Other ex-Red Devils featuring on the SKY teleprinter yesterday included Sonny Bradley, Karlan Grant and Nathan Ferguson scoring for Derby, Cardiff and Wealdstone respectively and Tony Craig getting sent off for Dorking. The next seven games for Crawley Town are against teams from 2nd to 20th, with five of them realistically still in with a chance of promotion, but interestingly with all of them in worse runs of recent form than Crawley Town.

Barrow, three defeats in a row, Morecambe and Harrogate, three games since last wins, Notts County, only one win in last six games and Stockport, 4 matches since last win. Am I tempting fate? Possibly, but why shouldn't it be our turn this year?

I do believe we need to win games by more than one goal and keep up our recently improved defensive form, but for me our strength is having a squad of players who can be moved in and out of the team without the standard of play deteriorating.

Back to God now, Dear Lord please can you ensure that Ben Gladwin, Liam Kelly and Laurence Maguire heal quickly, so they too can be used in the closing stages of this wonderful season. AMEN

2nd March 2024
EFL 2
Crawley Town v Barrow Postponed Waterlogged pitch
Rivals' results AFC Wimbledon 1 MK Dons 0

I found out on Friday evening that our game had been postponed due to a waterlogged pitch and, after an initial sense of disappointment at missing out on my Saturday afternoon at the Broadfield, accepted the decision as being the right one to make, especially considering the long journey for the away fans.

Flipping through the channels I came across a programme about Peter Schmeichel, in which Sir Alex Ferguson said, "he was worth ten points on his own in any season". This got me thinking about Corey Addai and his worth to Crawley Town. Up until this weekend we had featured in 12 games where we had either drawn or won by one goal. I am not sure if Corey played in all those, but you could justifiably say that whoever was in goal for those games we could be 20 points worse off if they had made just one less critical save per game.

The games this Saturday afternoon saw our friends from Kingston, sorry, Plough Lane beat the club who share their history, MK Dons, to send us down to tenth in the league before any other team had kicked off. Their winning goal came in the 94th minute of their early kick off. Other teams having a week off because of the weather, included Bradford City, Notts County,

Colchester and Stockport and at the end of the afternoon Crawley had slipped just one more place to eleventh because of Morecambe beating Crewe by three goals to two after being two down.

Hopefully, Morecambe have got that performance out of their system before we face them on Tuesday, as our next three games, against the Shrimps, Harrogate and Notts County, will I believe be vital if we are to have the end of season we all would like.

Scott will be, I am sure, aiming to win each of them as they come up. If we do win all of them it will be a significant point, or should I say nine, in what has already proved to be a very interesting season. However, we all know what football can do to people who start getting ahead of themselves, don't we?

For me, I would be pleased to take five points out of the next three games but would gladly accept all nine. If you look at the league table, we must play eight teams who would still consider themselves in with a chance of promotion or the playoffs. Included in those eight are Mansfield, Stockport and Wrexham in first, second and third respectively, with only Stockport coming to the Broadfield Stadium.

I know it sounds like a hard task, but if we get through those games without losing our way, we have three out of the bottom four to play in the last two weeks of the season.

I am now going for a sit down and an alcohol-free beer and hopefully by the time you read this we will be on 52 points and on our way to glory.

5th March 2024
EFL 2
Morecambe 1 Crawley Town 0
Morecambe scorer Slew (68)
Rivals' results AFC Wimbledon 0 Grimsby 0, Mansfield 1 MK Dons 2

9th March 2024
Harrogate 1 Crawley Town 2
CTFC scorers Forster (58), Lolos (66)
Harrogate scorer Thomson (26)
Rivals' results

MK Dons 3 Salford City 1, Notts County 0 AFC Wimbledon 2

This article comes in two parts, the first written after the Morecambe defeat, for which I take full responsibility, and the second being written just after listening to the ifollow coverage of the Harrogate away game.

Having just watched us play Morecambe on my television, connected to my laptop, I have to say that we played well enough to have won the game by at least two goals, but as the game slipped into its 68th minute, I wrote in my notes "I can see us losing this one nil, hope we don't regret our missed chances", when Morecambe scored against the run of play and that was how it stayed until the end, which also terminated our run of four games without defeat and our 390 minutes of not conceding a goal.

Those 390 minutes obviously contributed to Corey winning a very much deserved PFA League Two Fans' Player of the Month Award for February, and I am very sure that he can do that again as we seek to get back on a winning run.

The last comments on the first of two very difficult away games are that only two other teams above us managed a win, with AFC dropping two points and Gillingham and Mansfield dropping all three. Crawley sits 5 points below the playoffs with games in hand on most of those above us. The dream is still alive and a big shout out to the 65 Red Devils who managed the trip to Lancashire.

Team for Harrogate away. Unchanged from the starting line up on Tuesday.

What a great afternoon for all Red Devils everywhere. Tense, exciting and in the end so very joyous, and we are still in the race for the play offs. It may not have seemed like it after just twenty-seven minutes, with Dion Conroy being replaced by Joy Mukena and Harrogate taking the lead. Did we succumb? No, we did not. Whilst teams around us were changing their positions in the league, we sank to 14th place but were still only three points off the playoffs, and when Harry Forster equalised in the 58th minute, the fight back was most definitely on, and in the 66th minute Claudi Lolos scored what eventually turned out to be the winner. What a great afternoon that must have been for the estimated 200 plus Red Devils in the 2200 crowd but also for the thousands watching or listening around the world.

Two home games to come now against teams, I was going to say above us, but Notts County are on a bad run and, thanks to a club who we don't really get on with, now sit in 15th place on 47 points, five points adrift of Crawley in 11th with 52. Stockport, who are at the Broadfield on Monday 18th March, managed a 93rd minute winner against Newport County, which keeps them in second, with a game in hand over Mansfield, 3-2 winners over Swindon.

I am in danger of getting carried away, but (tongue firmly in cheek) we must remember we are not yet safe from relegation. Two wins at home and results going for us in matches concerning FGR and Sutton United, should guarantee our League status for at least another year.

Away from the current Red Devils, Bez Lubala scored from the spot for Wycombe, Mike Jones scored for Chesterfield and Kyle McFadzean was sent off for Blackburn Rovers.

Hope I've managed to celebrate another win before you can read this in a "real" newspaper. COYR

12th March 2024
EFL 2
Crawley Town 2 Notts County 1
CTFC scorers Lolos (79), Adeyemo (84)
Notts County scorer Austin (20)
Rivals' results
AFC Wimbledon 2 Gillingham 0, Grimsby 1 MK Dons 0

16th March 2024
EFL 2
Rivals' results
AFC Wimbledon 0 Newport County 2, MK Dons 3 Crewe 1

18th March 2024
EFL 2
Crawley Town 1 Stockport County 1
CTFC scorer Lolos (83)
Stockport County scorer Sarcevic (61)

Going into the game last Tuesday, it was imperative we came up with a win to keep us in the running for a playoff place. Not a bad position to be in, for the team that was the bookies favourites for a return to the National League; for a team consisting of non-league players with little or no experience and for a team that even some of our own supporters were worried about before the season had even started. Despite going a goal behind to Notts County, this Red Devils side showed they should not be written off, as two wonderful goals from Klaudi Lolos and Ade Adeyemo gained the rewards of three valuable points which took Crawley up to ninth place with games in hand on most of the teams above.

Stockport, in their televised game against Salford, fought back from two goals down to earn a point, which only served to condense the situation at the top of League 2 even more, prior to eleven games being played on Saturday and Sunday.

Unbelievably, after those games, Crawley found themselves in an even better position at the final whistle of the Salford v Morecambe game despite not playing themselves. Having slipped to 10th place, thanks to six teams above us (AFC Wimbledon, Barrow, Walsall, Gillingham, Crewe and Wrexham) and one just below us, Morecambe, dropping points, we now find ourselves in with a chance of .... and that is where I will stop for now as I don't want to jinx anything.

Part 2 Written at 11pm on Monday 18th March 2024.

At times, earlier tonight, it may have seemed that I had jinxed us as Stockport took the lead through a Sarcevic header just after the hour mark, but thankfully Crawley Town are proving to be the sort of team that just doesn't know how to give up, and when Klaudi Lolos scored in the 83rd minute, with what is rapidly becoming a trademark goal for the Greek Cypriot, it looked as if we might just sneak the win. The game ended in a one all draw, which stopped Stockport from rising to a points total that would have put them in touching distance of current leaders, Mansfield. They now sit four points off the top with only one game in hand on the Stags. A win for Crawley would have put us in the last playoff position ahead of Wimbledon, Walsall and Gillingham and still with games in hand. Because of the draw, which in my opinion was a good result for us, we did climb over the Gills into ninth place, level on points but still with games in hand.

Everyone who played against Stockport deserves credit for their hard work and resilience which has kept the momentum going.

We travel to Tranmere on Saturday knowing that on current form (0ver the last 6 games) we are currently second in the overall table and the away table, as opposed to Tranmere who are tenth in the overall table and seventh in the home table. I will be watching on Ifollow on Saturday and cheering the lads on as if I was there, knowing that four of the teams above us are facing each other. I really hope that our current away form enables us to secure at least a point and hopefully all three. TTT COYR NC

23rd March 2023
EFL 2
Tranmere Rovers 1 Crawley Town 3
CTFC scorers J.Kelly (2), Williams (10), Orsi (79)
Tranmere scorer Norris (21)
Rivals' results
Crewe Alexandra 1 AFC Wimbledon 1. Stockport 5 MK Dons 0

> Yesterday, football was such an easy game to play
> Kelly scored, and right away
> Oh, I believed in yesterday!!!!

Truly, what a remarkable performance by the Red Devils of Crawley Town. A sublime goal by our man from America, Jeremy Kelly, followed quickly by one from Jay Williams set us on our way to our eighth away win of the season.

But wait, I hear you say, wasn't Williams supposed to be representing St. Kitts and Nevis against San Marino? Yes, he was, but unfortunately for them he picked up a knock in training and was released to get medical treatment back in the UK. He was then declared fit to play, and with the permission of his national side was put back into our first team to don the arm band once again.

Watching the game on Ifollow I didn't see that the "contact" between Gordon and their keeper warranted Danilo Orsi's goal being disallowed, and felt that if it had stood, we would have gone on to win by four or five. As it was, the Wirralites came back into the game, with Lewis Young's brother-in-law, Luke Norris, reducing our lead on twenty-one minutes with a volley after having shrugged off the attentions of Will Wright. Two one in our favour, but with such a long time to go, some sides would have succumbed, but not this squad of players.

After some pressure from the hosts, Crawley, with the aid of substitutions, didn't just hold on, but in fact extended the lead when Ade Adeyemo fed the "Ors" and Danilo finished off the line of the song by putting the ball into the net to make the final score three one to the Red Devils.

This was the best squad performance I have seen in ages, and Scott was justifiably pleased with his charges in his interview after the game. Where this result leaves us, is in the final play off place, seventh in the league. With Mansfield drawing at home against relegation threatened Colchester in the early kick off, Stockport beating MK Dons in the evening game by five goals to nil and Wrexham winning away at Grimsby, it very much looks like the top three are almost confirmed as the claimants for automatic promotion. We have at least one game in hand on teams from 4th down 13th, except for Barrow and Walsall. All we can do now is attempt to take each game as it comes, seeking wins at every opportunity, knowing that sixteen points from four wins and four draws would give us 75 points, almost, but not absolutely, earning us a playoff place.

The run ins for the teams currently in 4th to 13th positions show us and MK facing four other teams in that group, or in the current top three. This would appear to be to our detriment but perhaps teams facing relegation threatened Colchester, Forest Green and Sutton United might think otherwise.

Our game on Friday, against Doncaster, is up first for us and we must not be complacent going into that one. They are ten points behind us on the same number of games played, seemingly safe from the drop, but are level with us at the top of the form table, with four wins, a draw and a loss in the last six games and with the same goal difference of plus four goals in that time. In those six games they have beaten Crewe and Wimbledon, so must not be underestimated.

On a positive note, we are now safe from relegation!!!!!

29th March 2024
EFL 2
Crawley Town 0 Doncaster Rovers 2
Doncaster Rovers' scorers Adelakun (57), Biamou (90+8)
Rivals' results AFC Wimbledon 1 Harrogate 1, MK Dons 5 Walsall 0

1st April 2024
EFL 2
Newport County 0 Crawley Town 4
CTFC scorers Conroy (1), Darcy (26), Maguire (69), Campbell (90+1)
Rivals' results
Notts County 3 MK Dons 3, Stockport County 1 AFC Wimbledon 0

Two games in four days, three points gained, and two records secured. The first record was set on Good Friday when a record number of home supporters attended a game at the Broadfield stadium. The only disappointing factors being that Paul Tarran wasted more money on betting on a four nil home win and Crawley Town produced a slightly under par performance in front of a bumper crowd.

Another disappointing feature of the result, for me, is how quickly some of our supporters go from the heights to the depths in the course of ninety odd minutes. We lost a game to a team that were level with us at the top of the last six matches form table, but I was still confident that we would bounce back away to Newport, and that is exactly what we did.

With Dion Conroy, Nick Tsaroulla and Kellan Gordon coming in to the team for Ade Adeyemo, Joy Mukena and Harry Forster, it always helps when one of the returning players scores in 50 seconds of the start. Against a team with an outside chance of making the playoffs themselves, Crawley fought hard to maintain their lead and increased it through Ronan Darcy on twenty-one minutes, following good work from Tsaroulla and Lolos in the buildup.

Although we could have increased our lead, when Darcy hit the post in the 31st minute, we could have also conceded as Newport inevitably came back at the "galacticos" and could have scored if Jay Williams hadn't got his "lower body" in the way of a goal bound shot just before half time.

The expected Welsh onslaught never really materialised in the second half, and I couldn't really agree with some of the comments sent to Gary Smith at half time suggesting early substitutions, especially when somebody thought Darcy should be the first one to come off.

As it was, Newport brought on Bogle for Zanzala in the 67th minute to attempt to get the Welsh side back into the game, but before he could do that Laurence Maguire put the game beyond them, volleying an exquisite Will Wright free kick past the Newport Keeper. (Note to the management and owners, please sign LM for next season).

Scott Lindsey then made the substitutions when he wanted, replacing Orsi with Adam Campbell (71st minute) and Jay Williams with Liam Kelly (76th minute). The latter probably being to avoid the player facing the possibility of a second yellow card.

Newport briefly threatened in the 83rd minute, but when Cory Addai caught the second of their corners in quick succession it clearly set off the fire alarm in the stadium as the home supporters started to leave on mass.

Mukena, Roles and Khaleel then replaced Conroy, Lolos and Darcy with three of the normal ninety minutes to go and the game was put well beyond the exiles when Liam Kelly and Rafiq Khaleel produced the ammunition for Adam Campbell to score the Red Devils fourth and final goal.

That goal, as far as I am aware, made the result our best away win in the Football League. We have scored five, in beating the Wombles five two, and we have also recorded four three nil victories against Cambridge United, Swindon twice and today's opponents. However, I don't think we have scored four without reply away from home, before this win.

What made it an even better day was seeing only Stockport above us picking up a victory.

Mansfield and Wrexham away come next, weather permitting, and I will be there for both. COYR

6th April 2024
EFL 2
Mansfield 1 Crawley Town 4
Mansfield scorer Boateng (80)
CTFC scorers Gordon (4), Tsaroulla (24), Orsi (55), Lolos (56)
Rivals' results
AFC Wimbledon 1 Salford City 0, Forest Green Rovers 0 MK Dons 2

The truth is, I am absolutely shattered, but in a happy and contented way. Having travelled to Mansfield on Saturday with stalwart Red Devils and having met exiled Red Devils, Lloyd and party from Leeds who moved north with his Mum and Dad when he was just three, I came home on the EMR Train and the Thames Link not knowing quite what had happened.

Basically, Mr. "no longer will I have to come to places like Crawley again" Clough was taught a valuable lesson. Don't underestimate Crawley Town. From the start of the game, it was apparent that we were in the right frame of mind and even I, someone who doesn't count chickens, joined in the promotionesque type chants.

Returning ex Stag, Kellan Gordon, suffered some rough house treatment from the Stags defenders, although the man in charge seemed to think he was simply falling over, but it was fitting that he should break the deadlock with yet another early Crawley goal, which was added to by "another three more years" Tsaroulla goal which had Crawley fans in ecstatic celebration, or in a dazed and poignant state.

Calming down at half time, I am sure we were all expecting an onslaught from the yellow shirted Stags, but it was Crawley who essentially finished off the game within the space of a minute, after just 10 minutes of the second half. The first coming from Danilo "feed the 'ors and he will score" Orsi and the second from Klaudi Lolos. Some home fans started to exit the Stadium when Klaudi streaked through the middle to score Crawley's fourth and Clough substituted five players before they kicked off for the last 28 minutes, two of them being Super Tommy Nichols and Hiram Boateng, both ex Red Devils. Indeed, Tom almost scored with a header and Hiram did snatch Mansfield's consolation on 80 minutes, but even five added minutes couldn't turn the tide and the celebrations on the final whistle, when people of all ages, from cheerleader Scarlett through to people older than me, saluted their players as if they were all family, were something to behold. One of the notable features of the away support is the presence of players' families who support their kin and the rest of the team as if they were born and bred in Crawley.

Having to write this report before facing Wrexham, I hope we go at them like we did against Mansfield and know that whatever the result, we will still be in the running for a glorious end to the season.

If you are one of the lucky rabbit foot types, then consider this. On the 16th of October 2010 we went to Nottinghamshire and beat Mansfield by four goals to one. The goals came from legends Bulman, Tubbs and McAllister (2) and our next game, which was away from home, we drew one-one thanks to Scott Neilson. A few weeks ago, I would have settled for that against Wrexham, but now I want us to have a go at them and, if we lose, go again against Colchester next Saturday. The main point of this jaunt down memory lane is that back in 2010/2011, after winning against Mansfield, we went on to win the League title and win promotion to League 2.

I believe, do you?

9th April 2024
EFL 2
Wrexham 4 Crawley Town 1
Wrexham scorers Barnett (21), Mullin (23, 87), Cannon (76)
CTFC scorer Lolos (90+4)

13th April 2024
EFL 2
Crawley Town 2 Colchester United 3
CTFC scorers Lolos (42), Forster (90+7)

Rivals' results MK Dons 1 Mansfield 4, Swindon 3 AFC Wimbledon 2

Still shattered, not quite so happy or content as last week, but still hanging on to the fact that our outcome to this wonderful season is still very much in our own hands, or should it be feet?

Before I write about what is to come, I would like to share with you the good aspects of our last two matches, and yes, despite two defeats, there were some. At Wrexham, 316 Crawley supporters travelled to the Racecourse ground by car, coach or train, and whilst we got the performance we had travelled for, the result was not forthcoming as the Welsh side showed why they are where they are in the league. We had supporters from Liverpool and the Wirral in Alf and Malc, Yorkshire in Mick, Lloyd, Lauren and Dan, Scotland in Pete Sayers and friends and even from the good old USA in Hunter Orrell. They all contributed to the atmosphere in the ground as the Red Devils bossed all the statistics, apart from the one that counts.

What, though, would be the reaction at the end of the game to a four one defeat? Well, it was a reaction which outdid the response to Wes Brown's goal at Old Trafford back in 2011, when 9000 Crawley supporters just got louder and louder. We stood and applauded them and sang our tribute to them as if they had just won the league and I am sure this was much appreciated by our mint green heroes. Unfortunately, it was at that point when I stumbled down the stone steps only to be rescued and assisted by my fellow fans. Thank you to all who helped me at that time, especially to Christina who magicked a chair from nowhere for me to regain my composure on.

Still in 7th place, still down to us, and surely we could beat relegation threatened Colchester on Saturday in front of a bumper home crowd, couldn't we?

Well, we lost 3-2 against a side who showed they didn't want to go down, but amazingly, as I write this article on Sunday morning, we are still in 7th place, still with it all in our own hands, thanks to all the other results going our way. The real threat to our place in the playoff positions must be Doncaster Rovers who stretched their incredible winning run to eight with a four-nil win over Accrington Stanley but, having said that, they face Barrow next Saturday who currently sit one place above us in 6th. Or do they?

Whether we won last night or not, there are still many twists and turns to come in this play-off race. What we must also remember is where we were, in terms of league position, this time last year. We have had a tremendous season, whether it ends a week on Saturday, or, as I think it will do, on a mid-May Day out at Wembley.

Noli Cedere

16th April 2024
EFL 2
Crawley Town 1 Barrow 1
CTFC scorer Orsi (64P)
Barrow scorer Acquah (36)

20th April 2024
EFL 2
Sutton United 2 Crawley Town 2
Sutton scorers Lakin (48), Sanderson (79)
CTFC scorers L.Kelly (42), Lolos (90+1)
Rivals' results
Harrogate 3 MK Dons 5, Tranmere Rovers 3 AFC Wimbledon 2

If a picture paints a thousand words – Telly Savalas or Bread, "If" by Rudyard Kipling or "If the following happens, Crawley Town will make the League 2 playoffs" by Steve Leake?

Guess which one you're going to get here?

Unbelievably, after having drawn our last two games against Barrow and Sutton, and lost the previous two to Wrexham and Colchester, we are still in the last playoff place.

Yesterday's game was like watching the whole season in one game, some moments of pure magic sandwiched between unfortunate decisions and some poor defending, capped by the celebration as Orsi scores "the winner", only for it to be chalked off for offside is what supporting any team should be like. Impatience, Frustration, Celebration and Realisation all rolled into just under 100 minutes of football. Do I still believe we can make the playoffs? Funnily enough, I do, albeit that we need some help from our friends, if that's what you call them. Firstly, we need a consistent referee who penalises dangerous play no matter what colour shirt the player is wearing (re the high boot which nearly took Nick Tsaroulla's head off in the run up to Sutton's first goal) and we also need Colchester to take points off Doncaster on Tuesday and Crewe next Saturday, Bradford to beat Barrow during the week coupled with a victory for Mansfield (I've always liked Nigel Clough) over the "Cul de Sac" boys on the last day as Joe Comper and the Gills end their season by beating Donny. Not much to ask for, is it? Of course I am assuming we will beat Grimsby, who now have nothing but pride to play for, having beaten Swindon on Saturday. We could even finish fifth!!

Going back to the Barrow and Sutton games, it was so good to see Crawley Town fans out in force to support the boys in Red and White. I know it was frustrating, just as we get so close to achieving our dream, that we should drop four points, but I like to look it in a slightly different way by looking at the season as a whole and comparing to where we were predicted to finish by all the pundits and betting shops back in August. We are not heading into the National League, as was foretold, but are still on the verge of making the playoffs. The disallowed goal by the Ors on Saturday reminded me so much of Sol Campbell's for England against Argentina in the 1998 World Cup, when I appeared to be the only person in the Town Mead Tavern (Redz as it is known now) who noticed that it had been disallowed. Similarly, it was my granddaughter, "Coach" Beth, who noticed the linesman's flag while all around us were jumping up and down celebrating a winner deep into added on time.

I don't want Grimsby to do us any favours on the last day of the season, because I believe we can get the three points on our own merits, and then it will depend on results from elsewhere to decide our fate. Don't write off the playoffs just yet. Noli Semper Cedere.

PS Just where did Sutton hide their 3000 odd fans on Saturday?

27th April 2024
EFL 2
Crawley Town 2 Grimsby Town 0
CTFC scorers Orsi (24), Lolos (34)
Rivals' results
AFC Wimbledon 5 Walsall 1, Mk Dons 4 Sutton United 4

Without being a party pooper, I just want to reinforce Scott Lindsey's thoughts about getting into the play offs, that we are only halfway through the job at hand. Now we are in the playoffs, against MK Dons, we must make the most of the opportunity on offer and do our utmost to get to Wembley.

At one point on Saturday, we thought we would be playing Doncaster in the semifinals, but thanks to a Crewe equaliser against Gillingham we now find ourselves playing MK Dons at home on Bank holiday Monday and away on Thursday the 9th of May.

Let us, as Crawley Town fans, do our utmost to be at both games so that we can contribute to the club's effort to get to Wembley. Whether you go to the away game by coach, car or train let's get together to support the Red Devils and truly be the twelfth man.

Back to last Saturday, I personally think it must have been hard to pick the player of the match, as everyone who made the field, whether it be for 90 minutes or coming on as a substitute, played with courage and commitment throughout. Yes, we could have been a couple of goals down before Danilo Orsi opened the scoring against his former side, but thankfully we weren't and, in the end, completed the double over the Lincolnshire side.

The support, from the start until the end, was immense in both quality and quantity, although I have to say that that opinion would not be shared by a certain YouTube pundit, from Wimbledon, who recently judged the supporters of all 92 clubs as to how good their fan bases are. His gradings bore the scientific descriptions of Massive, Elite, Decent, Bang Average, Poor and Tinpot. No prizes for what level he put us in, but I would of course add "and Proud" to that. His reason was because we only took just over 300 to their place in February. He failed to say it was a midweek fixture, but most importantly that our

300 out sung their 7000 throughout the whole game. He obviously uses the "Never mind the quality, feel the width" maxim for his judgement criteria. AFC, were of course, placed in the Decent category.

In a similar YouTube survey, judging the clubs on their history, we apparently don't have any, whilst AFC have loads including winning the FA Cup. Oh no they didn't.

Anyway, back to the season that has just ended for Barrow with Dom Telford, for AFC and James Tilley, for Gillingham and Ashley Nadesan and Glen Morris etc. etc., and all the other teams that have reached their final destination for 2023/24, but is continuing for MK Dons, Doncaster, Crewe and, of course, us.

I stood amongst my family on April 27th in a state of quiet euphoria at the end of the game, and as our fans invaded the pitch, I got very emotional thinking of all the Red Devils who weren't there to witness this team truly making history for our club and for our town.

Now let's complete the job. TOWN, TEAM, TOGETHER

29th April 2024

Didn't sleep much last night, a mixture of old age, Parkinson's, kidney stones and still buzzing about what happened on Saturday and what the next three weeks have in prospect for all who support the Red Devils.

Getting out of bed this morning, that is when I decided to change the title of this book from "The Rivals", mainly about our rivalry with AFC Wimbledon, to something that would encapsulate all the meanings of the word "Rival".

Looking at the word, not just as a noun but also as a verb. This season will now be thought of by many as a season that will go down in history as one that rivals the likes of 1968/69, 1983/84, 2003/04, 2010/11 and 2011/24 and hopefully will have years to rival it in the future.

Hopefully, I will have thought of a more encompassing title by the time I finish writing.

30th April 2024

Slept well last night and prepared myself for the ticket buying expedition at the world-famous Broadfield Stadium. I arrived there just at the ticket office opening time of 11am, only to find myself at the back of a rather long queue stretching back to past the away turnstiles. The whole process took just under two hours, which was no fault of the ticket sellers, and I came away with nearly all the tickets I needed thanks to Peter O'Brien buying one for me with his season ticket. I am now left with getting up early, when the general sale starts in two days' time for the one remaining ticket we need, to get all the Crawley Town loving members of the Leake/Humphrey family into the game that could just get us halfway to Wembley.

1st May 2024

After another hour and a half standing talking to fellow Red Devils in the general sale ticket queue, I finally got the remaining ticket I needed to ensure that all my family, who wanted to, could go to the game. Interesting talking to people I have never spoken to before and encouraging to hear about their love for the club we all support. One thing that did concern me was that whereas Season ticket holders and CTSA members were restricted to the number of tickets they could buy, there appeared to be no limit in the general sale. I hope the people who bought up to twenty tickets were real supporters, as if they weren't, and were selling them on for profit, this could potentially mean that some real supporters might be disappointed and have to pay over the odds to see this vital game.

3rd May 2024

And once again I found myself at the Stadium this morning, arriving there just before 1130 am to find there was absolutely no queue for the first day of the sale of tickets for the away semi-final in Milton Keynes. My dilemma was that because of my Parkinsons, I needed to ensure that David, my son, would also be able to get a ticket for the game when the tickets went on general sale on the 7th of May. I have to admit that I felt a bit guilty asking for preferential treatment, but luckily the club allowed me to buy two tickets because of my "disability". Talk in the Foundations Extra Time Hub was almost 100% about the two games ahead, and it was good to share optimistic feelings with all that were there.

6th May 2024

On this day back in 1547, Spanish and German soldiers sacked Rome, marking the end of the Renaissance, whilst in 1840 the Penny black became the first adhesive postage stamp. Scoot forward to 1910 and the day marked the succession to our throne by George V, upon the death of his father, Edward VII and some 30 years ago the excavators of the Channel Tunnel met under the English Channel (La Manche if you are a Francophile) after having dug from Dover and Calais.

This year it was going to mark the start of the beginning of our push for League 1 status with the Broadfield stadium playing host to the first leg of our play off semi-final with MK Dons. Someone else had other ideas. Receiving the news, just as I waited for my bus, I sadly returned home, soaking wet and decided to write my article anyway.

When I was at church yesterday morning, I discussed the game with Tim, our vicar, and we both agreed that we could pray for our lads to play to the best of their abilities and for the officials to have good games with no wrong decisions made. However, we didn't even think about the weather and forgot to add this to the list. I apologise sincerely for this and have already put in my request for good drying weather tomorrow, which according to the BBC is on the cards.

Of course, if you're reading this on Wednesday 8th you will already know whether the game was played or not, and if it was, what sort of result we will be taking on to Milton Keynes on Saturday. Watching the referee on Sky Sports News, he had no choice but to postpone the game, but with my anti blue and white mind in gear, I wonder if the Brighton Ladies playing on the pitch on Saturday may have contributed to the postponement decision. I am, of course, only joking.

Does this make any difference to our chances of progressing? Well, it shouldn't, but there may be some fans who won't have been able to make the rearranged fixture and what effect this has on either team will, by the time you read this, be known to all.

I, like many fans, have gone through all the permutations in my thoughts and dreams with varying results, but always have come out with the right ending as far as Crawley Town are concerned. Whatever the result in the first leg, it is only half time in the play offs and with our much-improved away form in 2023/2024 their stadium should hold no fear for us as a club, whether we are players, management or fans, indeed we might even take more fans to Wimbledon, ooops, I mean Milton Keynes, on Saturday afternoon. Keep the faith.

7th May 2024
EFL 2 Play off semifinal, first leg
Crawley Town 3 MK Dons 0
Scorers L.Kelly (5), Williams (45+1), Darcy (65)

    A Tale of Two Matches, the first at a thankfully dry Broadfield Stadium, and the second at the home of Milton Keynes Dons. Before even a ball had been kicked, I was somewhat surprised at the amount of support we appeared to be getting from around League 2 in particular and the whole of the EFL in general. Most of it posted by AFC Wimbledon fans for their own reasons, but surely there must come a time when the past has to be just that, the past.
    Anyway, the first game of our semifinal saw another bumper gate at the Broadfield, with near on 5000 Crawley Town fans in attendance, watch an almost impeccable performance from the Red Devils, with Liam Kelly, Jay Williams and Ronan Darcy scoring the goals in an emphatic three nil victory. Almost, because of two moments where we could have conceded in the first half, but even then, the brilliance of Will Wright's clearance off the line from Dean's shot in the first two minutes and the outstanding ball control from Corey Addai from a misplaced back pass, only added to the absolute euphoric atmosphere in the stadium.
    Jobi McAnuff (Sky Football) thought there would only be one winner in this semifinal before even a ball was kicked, and that it wouldn't be Crawley, but watching the game over as soon as I got home that night, it was good to hear the enthusiastic appreciation of our style of play by both the commentator and Lee Hendrie, his "Travel Ken". The highlight, for me, being Gary Taphouse's comment about Liam's mishit back pass and Corey's handling of it. He said it reminded him of an incident

involving Lee Dixon and David Seaman, to which Lee Hendry retorted "I couldn't see Seaman bringing the ball down like that, to be honest".

The most telling moment for me, being Scott Lindsey indicating to the supporters at the end of the game, that it was just half time.

Saturday 11th May 2024
EFL 2 Playoff semifinal 2nd leg
MK Dons 1 Crawley Town 5
MK Dons scorer Dean (45+1)
CTFC scorers Williams (3), Orsi (30, 48, 90+2), Roles (80)

> Then I awake and look around me
> At four magnolia walls that surround me
> And I realize, yes, I wasn't only dreaming
> For there's a score and it is in our favour
> On and on, we'll go to MK
> Again, we'll win another game away

Sorry, Sir Tom. I just couldn't resist. The best result last night, as far as focusing the minds of our players is concerned, saw Crewe come back from their first leg deficit to win on penalties against the in-form Doncaster Rovers. Would we suffer a similar fate and lose out on a Wembley place? Well, you, as well as I, know the answer to that one.

Backed by over 1600 vociferous fans, split in two by MK Dons ticketing chicanery, but united in the single goal ahead, Crawley Town out fought, out thought and out played Milton Keynes from the moment Jay Williams put us ahead in the second minute. Further goals, in chronological order, by Orsi, Orsi, Roles and Orsi completed an emphatic victory over the "favourites" by five goals to one. Having said that, it really should have been five nil, as their goal scorer should really have been sent off after a blatant stamp on Jay Willams stomach, which went unpunished by the officials. Even when MK were awarded a penalty for armpit ball, Corey Addai saved well at the left-hand post and now it is time to think about Wembley, where to sit, how to get there and enjoy the day and the victory over Crewe Alexandra.

TOWN TEAM TOGETHER

This one is for you Dad.

When I was five my Dad took me to Town Mead to see my first Crawley Town match and I was hooked even though we lost. He died in 2010, just before our promotion season which saw us gain league status for the first time. Whilst he was in Crawley Hospital, I would visit him on Saturday evenings and talk over the latest game, whether it was Crawley, Stoke City or England and just before he passed, I was able to tell him that both the Devils' and the Potters had won. We also talked about the future and whether we would ever see Crawley play at Wembley Stadium. He was positive we would, but for me, I was just happy to see Crawley Town receive their Ronny Radford Giantkillers award one year after his death, ironically as his other club, Stoke City, lost to Manchester City in the 2011 FA Cup final.

I'm older now and have shared so much joy with my family and friends watching the team we all love, and as I have grown older, I have ticked off a lot on my bucket list and will hopefully tick off three more this coming Sunday.

1. Watch Crawley Town play on Wembley's hallowed turf........ TICK

2. Sing (even if I am on my own) "Abide with me" whilst waiting to see Crawley Town as per number 1.

3. The most important, see Crawley Town win at Wembley

That will be enough for me, and I am sure my Dad will be watching too and singing along.

I always wished our dreams would be fulfilled through either an FA Trophy or FA Cup final appearance, and I guess the second option is always a possibility, but realistically the best chance we have of making Wembley is either through the EFL Trophy, or by playing in a play-off final, as we will be doing on Sunday 19th May 2024.

I know that getting there is a prize in itself, but now we are there, I am of the same opinion as Super Scotty Lindsey. No point in getting there and finishing second, let's win it, with the best footballing side we have had for many a year.

For my grandchildren, and for other youngsters in the Crawley area, this will be their biggest memory of watching the Red Devils, and it will be something to tell their children in years to come. This team is a history making team and I do not see any reason why they shouldn't go on to make even more in the years to come.

That leaves me with a dilemma. I need something else to add to my bucket list. Championship, Premier League or Europe?

15th May 2024

Being retired and with nothing much to do today, tickets bought, and plans made for Sunday, I decided to look at some YouTube entries based around the results of the last week. I looked first at two made by MK fans as the second leg approached and played out. They were confident before the game that they could overcome the three-goal deficit from the first leg, but as the goals went in and their hopes were shattered, they very quickly abandoned supporting their team, cheered our fourth and fifth goals and led the "We're F***ing sh*t" chants from the very area where Pete Winkleman had placed the red and white flags before the game. One comment I did agree with, apart from the excrement chant, was why did they think putting red and white flags on seats would help their cause? Yes, they do play in red, when they must away from home, but everyone knows they are our colours. I suppose they could have just put out white flags, but then again that might have looked like they were surrendering like their team did.

The other three clips were the official EFL podcast and two from a couple of fans, not sure which club, who I think were man and wife. The presenters of the EFL podcast were quick to say they didn't expect either Crewe or Crawley to win their semifinals but were also quick to show how much they were impressed by how both sides came through against the more fancied sides. They were particularly impressed by us and fancied us to take the final after a tight contest.

The other two clips were made before the first semifinals and after the second games had been completed. They, without going into too much detail, predicted an MK v Doncaster final, which they readily apologised for in their second clip, forecasting a close match but seeing us triumphant. Now, this has made me nervous for the first time this week. I think I would have preferred them to tip Crewe, which with their track record would have almost certainly guaranteed a win for the Mighty Red Devils.

17th May 2024

The sun shone this morning as I went to the Extra Time Hub at the Broadfield Stadium. It was very encouraging to see so many people there picking up their pre-ordered memorabilia and also to wave off the team as they boarded the coach, ironically based in Gillingham, to travel up to London for the weekend of a lifetime, not just for them but also for the 15000 plus Red Devil fans who will be there on Sunday to hopefully cheer them on to victory and promotion to League 1. All the players were in good spirits, even Harry Forster, who will not be available for selection due to an injury sustained in the second leg of the semi-final against Mk Dons. Kellan Gordon, Nick Tsaroulla and Ronan Darcy, or even Ade Adeyemo, in my opinion, will make good replacements for Harry, but you have to feel for him at this moment in time.

More YouTube watching saw me switching one off, halfway through this morning, as the betting "experts" are already writing us off for next season, even if we win on Sunday, but then I thought to myself that perhaps that means we are bound for the League 1 play offs this time next year.

19th May 2024
EFL 2 Playoff final, Wembley Stadium
Crewe Alexandra 0 CRAWLEY TOWN 2
CTFC SCORERS ORSI (42) L.KELLY (85)

The Reds are going up ole ole,
The Reds are going up ole ole,
The Reds are going up, the Reds are going up, the Reds are going up ole ole.

Yes, it is true, Crawley Town will be playing in EFL League One next season, and will initiate battles against Birmingham City, Huddersfield Town, Charlton Athletic, Reading and Wigan in terms of league games, although the only team we have never played in any competition is Huddersfield Town. All the other teams in League One we have played in either League 1 or League 2, and it will be especially good to renew our acquaintance with Mr. Clough as I bet, he thought he had finally left us behind.

Going back to yesterday (Sunday 19th May 2024), my family's day started at 7am as we set off for Three Bridges Station. Catching the 0759 am Thameslink to London Bridge it soon became apparent that we were actually the second wave of supporters making their way to the home of football, and that there would be many more waves during the morning taking the bulk of the travelling support to the game that would define our season. Meanwhile, in excess of 500 fans gathered at the Broadfield Stadium, to board the ten coaches organised by Alain Harper (G&H Coaches).

By ten o'clock we were at Wembley Park, snapping shots down Wembley Way of the iconic stadium and its arch, as we made our way to the Box Park, which was solely for the use of Crawley Town supporters on this great day. Now, I am not the sort of dyed in the wool supporter who doesn't welcome new supporters and it was very encouraging to talk to people who I had never met before alongside people who have followed the Red Devils since 2011 and those, who like me, can remember back to the Metropolitan League and even before that.

Entering the stadium, the emotions set in for me as I remembered those who couldn't be there because their dream had become reality too late for them. You will all know people in this category, and it was good to speak to some of you at the game. Rest assured; I certainly believe my Dad was there in spirit and I know by talking to others that they had the same feelings about their loved ones too.

As far as the match was concerned, the only time I had any anxiety at all was when the penalty was awarded and just before Liam (I wanna knowowowow how you scored that goal) scored our second and match winning goal. This, for the fans, long term, mid term or their first game, is the best way to win promotion and the day was made absolutely complete when the players, still in their kit, joined us in the Box Park after the game to celebrate with us all.

A truly remarkable day, and at the end, when most of our 17 to 18000 supporters had exited the stadium, I was lucky enough, along with my son and granddaughter, to be able to speak with Preston Johnson and thank him for all he has done in enabling us to gain promotion within the time period set by Wagmi when they took over. Don't get me wrong, I know Scott and the players are the people who won it on the pitches up and down the country, including Milton Keynes and Wembley, but without the data driven model used for player recruitment who knows where we would be.

Lastly, over 17000 at Wembley is great but the measure of our long-term success will be if we can convert a fraction of them into long-term supporters and even season ticket holders. I must sign off now, as I am partying tonight and may see some of you there!!!

21st May 2024

The entry dated 20th May 2024 was limited to between 600 and 700 words, so that it could appear in the 22nd of May 2024 issue of the Crawley Observer. Having now been to the presentation evening last night, here are some more of my thoughts about a truly magnificent accomplishment by a team that were the bookies favourites to leave League 2, but in the opposite direction.

Firstly, the expedition by well over 17000 Crawley Town fans, whether they were lifelong, or it was their first game, was a truly significant movement of people by road or rail, or indeed by air or boat. Wagmi were well represented in the posh seats, although I have to say Preston Johnson did not look at ease in a shirt and tie. I also met Tony Kerkove in the stadium, who had travelled over from Belgium with the Belgian branch of the CTFC fan club. As long as we are a welcoming club we will always attract people who may come upon us by chance and long may that continue.

The game itself, against Crewe Alexandra, has been judged by some as being a bit boring, however I am not sure what game they were watching if they were of this opinion, as for me it had me on the edge of my seat and struggling to keep my balance as I stood to catch the latest attack. I was sat next to a young six-year-old boy, called Rory, and his mum, For Rory, it was his first visit to a big football stadium, and I told him he was an extremely lucky boy to have been able to witness our achievement so early in his fledgling football watching life, as I have had to wait 68 years to accomplish the same goal.

What amazed me, when I got home at 8 pm-ish and switched on the tele to relive the day's amazing atmosphere and action, was how good Danilo Orsi's goal was, as whilst watching in real time I had not realised he had used the outside of his right foot to slot the ball home. What a player!

Much later, the next day in fact, I watched several YouTube clips created by people who had been at the game. I did not see one from any Crewe supporters but did catch two from Yorkshire based ground hopping types, who were very complimentary about how we had played and were adamant the right team had won. What was good to see and hear was the initial Crewe supporters' response to the "penalty". Utter silence followed by a guilty realisation that their player had conned the ref. Luckily, or should I say rightly, we all saw the ref's finger go to his ear, then his walk to the tv screen, where he saw for himself how good Mr. Addai's challenge had been. Yellow card rescinded, an uncontested drop ball for Crawley Town, but surprisingly no yellow card for the Crewe player who had clearly dived.

Unsurprisingly, in the clips, if that is the correct terminology nowadays, most fans predicted wins for their own team, ranging from five – two to Crewe (never going to happen) to three – one to the Red Devils. Only one person predicted penalties, and he was from Crewe. My cousin's son, who was visiting us from Stoke via Banbury, where he now lives with his wife Emma and his son Edgar, when asked about our style of play, was quoted as saying "definitely heart in mouth at times! Especially when you are used to watching a Tony Pulis coached side. Very entertaining though".

I think he may have been referring to the penalty moment, and the fact that it was of our own making that it happened at all.

One other thing I noticed in the one video that was produced by someone from Crawley, was that he tried to start chants where he was seated with no success and then referred to the people around him as being plastics. I have said before, you have to start somewhere in supporting your own town's team and not be derided in this manner, especially when it comes from someone who starts his broadcasts in front of Chelsea memorabilia.

After the game, my family returned to the Box Park where we joined in the celebrations with fans, both old and new, who made me proud of the town I live in. True, there were a few who let themselves down in their uncalled-for reaction to an unintended spilling of a drink, but it was good to see the almost instantaneous response, by real supporters and bar staff, to snuff out the incident and remove the guilty parties. I have to say that they were not, to my knowledge, regular supporters, and could best be summed up as being the sort of people for whom football interrupts their drinking.

I, for one, wasn't going to let it spoil my enjoyment, and shortly after we draped Steve Herbert's flag over the upper bar's balcony just in time to see the players enter the building, still in their kit, and after initially being mobbed, make their way upstairs to VIP area where Manchester United and England centre back, Harry Maguire, was waiting, along with what seemed like the entire Maguire and Orsi families, to congratulate the team. Never before has the motto "Town, Team, Together" resonated stronger with me than at that moment.

Leaving younger members of my family to enjoy the celebrations long into the night, I returned home with my son Matthew, his wife Claire and my grandson Oliver and plenty of other smiling Crawleyites and immediately switched on the tele to relive the whole of the match again. Now, I know that 90 minutes in real life is the same as 90 minutes action on the television, but for me, watching the game in the comfort of my own home the match seemed to whizz by before my eyes. The brilliance of Crawley's first goal, scored by the outside of Danilo's right foot, the penalty incident and Liam's clinching 85th minute goal seemed to take only a few minutes and did nothing to remove the stupid grin from my face, which is still there three days later, as I write this down for posterity.

    Waking up on the Monday, after the big day out and with that supercilious grin still on my face, news of a celebration event comes to light. The team will be presented to the fans later that night, with admission to the stadium by ticket only at £5 a go. This, rather predictably, got some people complaining about the club charging and also for there not being a window for season ticket holders to get their tickets first, although I have to say that these comments were probably made by long term fans taking the Michael. After about half an hour of fighting with the club's website, I managed to purchase 6 tickets at £5 each, which seemed good value to me, as it turned out to be. The whole evening was a joyous occasion of fans both long term and new, old and young enjoying the presentation of the staff, both off and on pitch, and the players, being presented with the EFL League 2 Trophy. Something that would not have happened if we had managed to sneak into the automatic promotion places. The players seemed a little bit the worst for wear, I can't think why, and after the presentation they spent well over an hour signing memorabilia for the fans, with Corey Addai seeming to be the most wanted signature amongst the fans.

23rd May 2024
    I must really stop watching YouTube clips about the playoff final, especially when they are made by people from Milton Keynes. He was supporting us I suppose, and he did think we deserved our win, but for me I would rather hear from a true Red Devil about our success. The couple, who said we wouldn't get to the final, graciously accepted they were wrong and accepted that we thoroughly deserved our triumph. Thankfully, they predicted we will struggle next season, so Championship here we come.
    As a bit of fun last night, I led the Inspire choir in that most beautiful of songs. You know the one.
The reds are going up, ole ,ole
The reds are going up, ole ,ole
The reds are going up, the reds are going up, the reds are going up, ole, ole

25th May 2024

I have just watched the other Red Devils win the FA cup, second week running for Devils to come out on top at Wembley, and below you can find a brief rundown of half of next year's opposition for CrawleyTown, which surprisingly only features one club we have never played before.

Crawley Observer article. 29th May 2024

I am going to leave commenting on our released and retained list for now until we are sure who are staying with us.

The full complement of clubs playing in League 1 next season has been completed by our magnificent Wembley victory last Sunday and I am going to review half of them this week, in alphabetical order, purely as it puts us, Crawley Town, just outside the playoff positions in ninth.

In 1, we have Barnsley, who play at Oakwell in a 23,287-capacity stadium, where we won one nil back on the 9th of August 2014, completing the double over them on the following St Valentine's Day by five goals to one. Despite those results we were relegated and Barnsley, relegated from the Championship the previous season, finished 11th.

Next up is Birmingham City, who we played in the League Cup back in August 2017, losing by five goals to one with Panutche Camara scoring our consolation in the 86th minute. Their stadium, St Andrews, is the largest in League 1 at 29,409 and they were relegated this season just gone.

Blackpool, sitting at number three with no balls being kicked, play at Bloomfield Road and will be our northernmost competitors this year and our longest away trip in the league. Past results include a one nil home win and a nil-nil away draw. Capacity 16,616.

Bolton Wanderers' Toughsheet Stadium, with a capacity of 28,723, is a stadium I have visited, but not for a Crawley game, and offers the opportunity to stay in the integral hotel. The season after their relegation from the Premier League and our promotion from League 2 we knocked them out of the League Cup and in the year of Covid we beat them away but lost 4-1 at home on the last day of the season.

Bristol Rovers' Memorial Stadium 9,832 is more well known to Red Devils, Crawley Town having played them a total of thirteen times in four different competitions since we became a League club. We have beaten them four times and lost six, drawing three. We have never beaten them at their place in the League.

Burton Albion are next in the alphabetical league table, and they play at the Pirelli Stadium which is the one just above ours in terms of capacity. We first came across Nigel Clough at Burton and it close to the much-vaunted Overseal Fish and Chip shop, where you can get deep fried black pudding.

Abbey Lane is the home of Cambridge United, capacity 8,127 and they hold a slight advantage over Crawley, having won seven against our five, all in League 2.

Next comes a team who we have only played in the EFL Trophy or friendlies. They are Alain Harper's second team, Charlton Athletic. They play at the Valley which has a capacity of 27,111, and in matches played against them we have both won two games.

Exeter City, who play at the real St James Park which has a capacity of 8,720. In fourteen league two games against them we have beaten them four times and drawn four times. They have also progressed twice in the FA Cup against us when we were non-league, and once in the League cup at the beginning of last season.

Huddersfield Town who play at the Kirklees Stadium, capacity 24,121, are the only team we have never played in a competitive match, so must be number one on the "Stadiums to Visit" list for me.

The last team in the write up for this week are one of our shortest trips. They play at Brisbane Road and are of course, our old friends Leyton Orient. We have won ten times against their seven victories and one draw. However, in April 2022, the referee and linesman, both being sponsored by Specsavers at the time, failed to notice the ball going into the Orient net, the play rumbled on, we were denied a justified equaliser and they go down the other end and score to seal a two-nil victory. Bitter??? Me???

28th May 2024

Having sat through just under five hours of watching the semi-finals and the final again yesterday, with tears streaming down my cheeks, happy tears that is, I am now just waiting to hear some news about contract extensions for the seven who I would like to keep, plus a permanent contract for Laurence Maguire. Hopefully by the end of the week, so I can finish this tome and start the next one.

30th May 2024

Carrying on from my review of next season's opposition the next team up are Lincoln City. They play at Sincil Bank, which has a capacity of 10,669, and just missed out on the League 1 Playoffs this year. A beautiful City where we are yet to concede a goal, having drawn and won there by one goal to nil. At home it's one all in victories.

Mansfield, who boast, rather amazingly, the EFL League 2 Manager of the season for 2023/2024, play at Field Mill with a capacity of 9,186 (be nice when it's finished) and are predicting, despite the footballing lesson we taught them at their place, that we will struggle and go down. Whatever!

With a capacity of 7,798, Sixfields, the home of Northampton FC, is a decent stadium surrounded by fast food outlets. We have won four, drawn three and lost five against them, all in League 2, but beat them back in 1991, in the FA Cup, by four goals to two.

The club who Posh Spice tried to sue, Peterborough United, play at London Road and the matches between us include two wins and two losses, all in League One and one defeat in the League Cup and the EFL Trophy. The stadium holds 13,511 spectators and is easy to get to by Thameslink.

The next team is Reading FC, who we have only played once in a competitive match, when they became the third Premier League team to knock us out of the FA Cup in 2013. For the first fifteen seconds we were well on top thanks to Nicky Adams but ended up losing three-one. We have beaten them in a Friendly since however, and their 24,111 capacity Madejski stadium is surely a stadium all Red Devils will want to visit.

Rotherham United, who we completed the double over in our first season of League football, play at the New York Stadium where we are undefeated in our two encounters up in Yorkshire. Having lost just once to them in four matches played this is definitely a trip I will be making. Their 12,021 all-seater stadium needs a large contingent from Sussex and our exiles, as they are managed by a certain Steve Evans. Remember him?

Nearing the bottom of the league now, the next club is Shrewsbury Town who play at New Meadow, which houses 9,875 spectators. We have played them six times, only won once, but only lost twice.

The New Town derby will reconvene next season between us and Stevenage. Their ground, Broadhall Way holds 7,800 spectators and we have played them twenty times in their latest reincarnation, winning five times and losing six. Another ground easily reached by Thameslink.

Last year's League 2 champions, Stockport County, who couldn't beat us last season, play at Edgeley Park, capacity 10,852. Out of the four games played between us over the years it's one won, one lost and two drawn.

The last three clubs in the division all begin with W. They are Wigan Athletic (25,138), Wrexham (12,600) and Wycombe Wanderers (10.137) and they play at the Brick Community Stadium, the Racecourse Ground and Adams Park respectively. Wigan Athletic have played us only once, knocking us out of the FA Cup in 2017, after Jordan Roberts had given us the lead, whilst Wrexham have been beaten three times by the Red Devils in our non-league days, winning twice and drawing once whilst they did the double over us in the season just gone.

Wycombe Wanderers have played us six times in League two, winning three, drawing once and losing twice They did beat us in the FA Trophy back in 1986 by two goals to nil in front of 1,200 fans at Town Mead.

All in all, there are no teams in League One that have outstanding records against us, so bring it on.

I've bought my season ticket, had my photograph taken with the Playoff trophy, purchased a pink polo shirt, a scarf, chatted to a lot of very happy Red Devils and now I'm just counting the days until Fixture release day on June 26th.

Before then though, we need to look at our players, the ones we know are with us for next season plus those who we hope will sign new contracts and those who have been reluctantly let go. Those that are on contract or have just extended their contracts are; Addai, Orsi, Forster, Mukena, Kelly L, Williams, Adeyemo, Darcy, Conroy, Sandford, Khaleel, Fish, Lolos. That is thirteen in total, and all, as far as I am concerned, should have no one asking, "Why have you kept him?" Even Sonny Fish, who has been out on loan for most of the season, deserves the chance to show us what he can do.

Those under negotiation or who are free agents included Campbell, Wright, Kelly J, Gordon, Roles, Gladwin and Maguire, and that is why I wrote "included" instead of "include". Sadly, Laurence Maguire has decided to stay in League 2 by joining MK Dons, and at this point I would like to thank him for all he did for us in helping gain promotion and hope, perhaps, that he can show Alex Dean how not to behave like a spoilt child.

I would like to see the rest of them offered new contracts, albeit Ben Gladwin's might have to be in a coaching role. The only player that has been let go and that I would have kept is Harry Ransom. Good luck with wherever you end up at Harry and thanks for your service.

Five more players, all of quality, whether it be because of their experience, character or potential, could make us a force to be reckoned with and I think we need a forward, two midfielders and two defenders please, Scott and Wagmi. Looking back, Dom Telford was signed a year before, almost to the day that Liam Kelly signed in 2023. The date, at least the date I wrote about it, was the 24th of June.

Patience is required but I would like to see better communication about the ins and outs, as I have not seen anything on our website about Maguire leaving, yet there is a clip on the MK website where he is in their training kit saying how big a club they are. Having just written that, I notice there is a tweet, if that's what it is still called, on our X link, if that's what Twitter is now called. Help, I'm getting old.

The other person who is stepping down from his vice chairman role is the much wrongly maligned, Preston Johnson. Personally, I would like to thank him for all his hard work over the last two- and a-bit seasons. He, along with Eben, met their target, and I for one would like to know what the next one is. He has become a friend to my family over the two seasons and helped sponsor two exhibitions at Crawley Museum. I wish him well, good health and hope he comes back to see us storm League 1.

Season ticket prices show an increase of around ten per cent, after two years of staying level. Considering the rates of inflation over the last two years, I for one was expecting more. Fact, we are cheaper than newly promoted Bromley, and as I write this the encouraging news is, that after five days of sales, over 1100 hundred plus tickets have been purchased, with just under half of them going to new buyers. I reckon that this will mean us selling at least 1600 by the time the early bird offer ends, and hopefully beat 2000 by the August 10th, season start date.

The one bit of really good news is that BET 365, according to two Birmingham City Youtuber types, have us down as favourites to finish 24th. Play offs, anyone?

Our rivalries with both AFC Wimbledon and MK Dons in the league, saw us beat both once, one at home and one away but also lose to both, one at home and one away. We scored four goals, two against each club and conceded five, two to AFC and three to MK.

However, both Crawley and MK finished in the playoffs, us in 7th on 70 points and MK in 4th on 79, whilst AFC finished 10th on 65.

In the playoffs, as we all know, we demolished MK by eight goals to one over the two legs, meaning, that for the first time ever, we will start a season in a higher division than both AFC and MK. I will leave it up to them to argue about who starts higher up in League 2 on alphabetical order, but I know what the BBC will probably do.

Now, do we keep them as rivals, or do we look now to Charlton or Orient? This is where I intended to finish the story of this wonderful season, but because of the departure of several of our players, and our best players at that, I have decided to carry on adding to this tome, at least until the end of September, so we can see what effect these departures have had on our start to our second stint in League 1.

PART TWO
YEARS v YEARS
THE BEST YEAR EVER (OR WAS IT?)

Chapter 6
2024/2025
Relegation to Tier 4

25th June 2024

Those players under negotiation or who are free agents include Campbell, Wright, Gordon and Gladwin.

Jack Roles and Jeremy Kelly have signed two-year contracts, keeping them at Crawley Town until the end of the 2025/2026 season. In my opinion they both deserve this, and I am keen to see them progress in their own careers and in their performances with Crawley Town.

We have made our first signing, ahead of the schedule of last year and the year before in midfielder Antony Papadopoulos, signed from National League South side, Welling United. At 21 he is another young player but comes with the experience of playing for Leyton Orient and will no doubt have been assessed using Eben Smith's mathematical model. A model which did pretty well last year, didn't it? I do know he played against us in the EFL Trophy for Orient, when they tore us apart at the Broadfield Stadium winning by four goals to nil, because I was there! Good luck Antony and welcome to Crawley.

Sadly, as one player with Greek ancestry joins the club another leaves. Nick Tsaroulla, who appeared to be saying goodbye to the fans from the Grimsby game on through the play offs, has sadly signed for Notts County for two years. I know the County fans will take him to their hearts, as we have done here at Crawley, and I for one will never forget his input into the club and into the town. I wish you well Nick, but hope we keep a promotion ahead of you in the next few years.

Looking at the players still under negotiation, I feel it is imperative we try to keep them all or get players in to replace them who are better. As it is we have lost two centre backs and one wing back so need to replace them as well as improve the squad, just a little, in order to properly compete in League 1. Fixtures out tomorrow (Thursday 26th June) and very soon the players will be back raring to go, as I'm sure we all are.

3rd July 2024

I am going to attempt to write this article with my very thoughtful, all things being considered, head on my shoulders.

Last season was a truly momentous one in the history of Crawley Town Football Club, and one where our owners could justifiably claim that their mathematical model contributed greatly to our success. The year before, their first year as owners, was, they will claim, a season where they did not fully utilise that model and thus, to achieve promotion as we did, just six weeks ago, must be considered even more remarkable.

The players they brought in at the beginning of the 2023/2024 season were actually written off by some of our fans before even a competitive ball was kicked. During the season, most of our fans warmed to the players that some had written off, and quite right too, considering what they achieved.

This close season has seen heroes leave the club, including Klaidi Lolos, Corey Addai, Will Wright, Danilo Orsi and Nick Tsaroulla for undisclosed fees, whilst Laurence Maguire chose not to sign on for Crawley because of what seems a better financial offer from MK Dons. The one departee who I can totally understand, but regret as much as any of them, is Adam Campbell, who has obviously decided to go home.

I am sure that there will be some supporters wishing we could have offered all these players more money to stay at Crawley, but there lies the crux of the matter. Despite the increase in home attendances over the last two seasons the income still will remain far below most of our competitors, last year in League Two, and even more so in League One when we start again in August. Perhaps our ticket prices should have been raised more this year, but can you imagine what the reaction would have been from some of our fans if that had happened?

I do understand, but don't agree with, the attitude of some people who want their money back on their season tickets, presumably thinking our team deserved the wage rises they have probably received from their new clubs. Without a doubt in my mind, I would have liked to have given them the chance to do it all again with us, but I'm afraid that, barring a Euro Lottery win, wasn't possible.

The signings of Jeremy Kelly and Jack Roles on new contracts are a plus in my opinion, and the new signings, so far, of Scott Malone, Rushian Hepburn-Murphy, Josh Flint, Antony Papadopolos and Charlie Barker also show a raised level of experience from those players that we signed this time last year. On top of that, players like Ade Adeyemo and Sonny Fish must also seize the opportunity and become the same level of heroes that have unfortunately just left us, and we must also sign at least another four players, one being a goalkeeper.

One question that does need answering is why our owners haven't communicated some sort of context behind the departures. Perhaps it's because Eben Smith has absolute confidence that his mathematical model will prove successful again for the new season, if so, then please communicate this to the fanbase. If he is proved right, I will be ecstatic this time next year, but the lack of communication does, I believe, still show a lack of understanding of football fans in this country and how they grow attached to the players wearing the shirt of the club they support. THIS IS ENGLAND, not the USA. Talking of England, Swiss roll anyone?

Up to this point in the never-ending story of Crawley Town Football Club, you, the reader, should have become accustomed to the fact that passages about last season were written as they happened or just after, and were written originally for "Thoughts of a lifelong fan" for the Crawley Observer. From this point on I am going to write the book first and take the articles from it. Hope you understand, I think I do.

6th July 2024

Since last week's article matters have moved on in different and slightly bewildering ways. First the news that no one wanted to hear. Liam Kelly, despite apparently telling someone whilst out shopping that there was no way he was going to leave, has left. He is joining Laurence Maguire at MK Dons, presumably for more money, and as yet there have been no more players coming in, other than the five we already know about. Whilst wishing Liam well, and I do understand that at our level players have to consider better offers when they come along, I would have thought that the challenge of playing in League 1 would have been enough to keep him here for at least one more season. We will miss him, but having said that, we haven't seen our five incoming players play yet and who knows, they might be even better than the ones who have departed.

In the last few weeks, I have also written about Preston Johnson leaving his role as Vice Chair, but now we learn, after a couple of weeks of consideration and talking with his family, he is coming to live in this country for the foreseeable future with his immediate family, and will not only continue as Vice Chair, but will also take on the role of CEO and oversee all day-to-day business and football operations at the Broadfield Stadium. On top of that, Ben Levin, another member of Wagmi, is replacing Eben Smith as our other Vice Chair and will largely be involved in building our commercial revenue, which hopefully will mean we can, in the future, put a lock on the revolving door.

As far as I am aware, we have seventeen players on our books at the moment, although there are still rumours about other players leaving, so I hope the promise of a fans' forum comes to pass sooner rather than later. Two questions I would like to have answered are, how many more players are we looking to sign and has Eben left his mathematical model to enable those signings to be as successful as the class of 23/24?

To close this day's output from my obsessive CTFC psyche, SCOTT LINDSEY MUST STAY.

I lied. To close this week's input, England 5 Switzerland 4, albeit on penalties but they were so good (the penalties that is) that it took me back to the days of Roy Jennings. Palmer, Bellingham, Toney and Alexander-Arnold, we salute you, but none more so than Bukayo Saka, who not only scored his penalty but also laid a few ghosts as well. Holland awaits us!!

14th July 2024

Last Wednesday, the day of the Euro semi-final against the Netherlands, I invited Preston Johnson to my son's house to watch the game with my family and he arrived just in time to see Harry Kane score the equaliser from the spot, just after he had been "viciously" fouled in the process of shooting. Whilst we watched the game and celebrated when Ollie Watkins scored the winner, we talked about Crawley Town, departures, signings, goalkeepers and ground improvements, and most importantly as to whether Redz would be open for the Euro final. There is not a lot that I can share with you at the moment, but suffice it to say, Preston is well aware of the concerns of ordinary fans and is confident that come the beginning of the season on the 10th August we will be ready to compete in League 1.

Then on Saturday the latest Agatha Christie thriller entitled "THEN THERE WAS THREE" came out. You know the plot; a group of eleven people have a wonderful weekend enjoying themselves in an iconic building, and then one by one they start to disappear. Seriously, Kellan Gordon has decided to join Nick Tsaroulla at Notts County as they seek not to be relegated to the National League, which now leaves us with just Jay Williams, Dion Conroy and Jeremy Kelly from the Play Off Final starting lineup. Now, I am prepared to wait and see what our new signings are like before I get too crestfallen, but what really hurts is that I can't look at my Father's Day present any more (a graphic representation of Liam Kelly's Wembley goal) or, indeed, the latest edition of Crawley Live, as the front cover is a picture of three of our departed heroes. I will get over it, just like I will get over the increase, yet again, of the number of years of hurt we have experienced since 1966. Friendlies started last night (Tuesday 16th July) against Lewes, and I wonder how many of the Riallist family will have taken part. Tim, Tom or Toby perhaps.

Preston was there in Redz to watch the England game, and although we lost, he got to experience what a reaction to an England goal is like, when Cole Palmer scored to equalise against Spain. I have to say that Spain, as they have been throughout the tournament, were the better side, but only just. The French referee gave us an excuse to feel hard done by when, after four minutes added on time was shown, he blew the final whistle exactly on four minutes despite Spain having delayed taking a free kick for at least ninety seconds. Oh well, sixty years of hurt at least then.

Meanwhile, a young goalkeeper has signed for the club. 19-year-old Crawley lad Jasper Sheik has joined on an initial one-year deal and, reading between the lines, is one for the future as loans are already being talked about to give him much needed experience. Ryan Sandford is also with us for another year and now gets his chance to vie for the number one shirt with JoJo Wollacott, who has just signed a two-year deal from Hibernian.

The first two friendlies have seen us win two nil at The Dripping Pan with different elevens taking the pitch for the two halves, Darcy and T.Riallist scoring the goals, and win by the same score at East Grinstead with Jay Williams and a different T,Riallist providing the goals.

Having watched the East Grinstead game, I was impressed with how quickly and accurately we moved the ball around the pitch and must agree with Scott that we just need to be more clinical in front of goal. We went in one nil to the good at half time thanks to a Jay Williams blast from the edge of the box when really it should have been three or four. JoJo in goal had hardly any goalkeeping to do, but showed, like Corey before him, he was comfortable and capable of playing it out from the back. The only disappointing aspect of the first half being an injury to new signing Scott Malone, which I hope will not be as serious as it initially looked.

The second half was more of the same but with nine different players coming onto the pitch, including a triallist goalkeeper and a triallist Number 9, who scored our second and last goal. The fact that the number nine shirt was worn by a triallist shows, I believe, that Scott and the Club realise we need someone to play alongside Rushian Hepburn-Murphy up front. Roll on the 10th.

24th July 2024
Wealdstone 1 Crawley Town 0

A game, against stronger, more robust competition in Weladstone, saw Crawley lose one nil, the goal coming in the

75th minute just after Scott Lindsey had made nine changes featuring six triallists. Scott seemed pleased with the effort put in but once again mentioned that we need to be more clinical in the final third. Sonny Fish is yet to start a game as is Muhammadu Faal, who has recently signed on a short-term six-month contract, presumably to prove himself and earn himself a longer one. Another newcomer, who was seen at Wealdstone but did not feature, is Max Anderson, who has signed from Dundee.

Creative midfielders seem to be the flavour of the month as far as we are concerned, with Armando Junior Quitirna joining us on a two year contract for an undisclosed fee from Fleetwood. As with all our new players, welcome and good luck and let's hope that Muhammadu, Rushian and Sonny make the most of the chances our creative midfield will put on a plate for them.

28th July 2024

Moving on to the game against Crystal Palace, it was good to see that Armando, Max and Muhammadu all got their first taste of the Broadfield Stadium, with the first two starting and Faal coming on as a substitute. The game started at an electric pace, at least as far as Palace were concerned. And before the 5,002 spectators could settle, we were two down in the first three minutes, three down in the first eleven and at half time went in losing by four goals. All of the goals, I believe, showed a little bit of naivety from Crawley, in that we tried to play it around as per last season but had forgotten that Crystal Palace are in fact a Premier League club and not in League 1 or 2. Playing first team squad players throughout, including one just signed from Barcelona and another from Lazio, it was always going to be both a stern test and a very good lesson for Crawley. After half time we scored, without doubt, the goal of the game when Rushian scored with a tremendous shot, after cutting in from the left and with a lot of spectators imploring him to pass it, and for a while the game was back on.

Crystal Palace then showed that they too are only human when their Andersen, not our Anderson, slipped over the ball and presented Rushian with a simple tap in to score his second of the game, but alas Palace scored their fifth soon after, before Ronan Darcy capitalised on yet another defensive error, this time by

Palace veteran, Ward, to wiggle his way into the box to lay on Crawley's third goal with a pass to substitute Jack Roles, who duly slotted it home. For a moment I was almost tempted to start the "we're going to win six five" song but unfortunately another defensive error from Crawley allowed Schlupp to score a sixth for the Eagles, and that was that.

Down hearted? No, Optimistic? Without a doubt, and if the rumours are true about a certain ex Doncaster Rovers player, then I think we are in for an exciting season back in League 1.

All I have seen of our last three friendly matches are the "extended" highlights of the Aldershot and Ebbsfleet games. Scott talked about a behind closed doors game against a Premier League club, the day before the Ebbsfleet match, which only goes to show that friendly games mean different things to different people. For a portion of fans, who are only satisfied with convincing victories during pre-season, they probably will not be satisfied with what we have shown thus far. For me, however, I will make my judgement after our first ten competitive games and will always seek to support the players in red, grey/white or blue, rather than make hasty judgements about players I have hardly seen play yet. Also, it has often been said that you don't learn much from a run of "meaningless" pre-season victories, and I am sure by the time we kick off against Blackpool that we will be ready to compete at League 1 level. I do think we need another forward to play alongside Rushian, and possibly another keeper to provide competition to JoJo, but whoever we start with next week I hope we all get behind them for the full 90 minutes.

I missed the Aldershot and Ebbsfleet games as I was on holiday with my sons in the Lake District, and on the way there we popped into Old Trafford to relive the magic memories of 2011. Whilst in the Superstore, I noticed a red tee shirt, which I almost bought but decided, in the end, just to steal the words from it to show how I would like all who support the real Red Devils to feel about their club.

It's not just a stadium   It's our home
It's not just a kit   It's our skin
We are not just eleven   We are thousands
We are not just a crowd   We are family
It's not just 90 minutes   It's a lifetime
It's not just a passion   It's an emotion
It's not just a game   It's our life

    I changed one word as I don't think we can claim millions of fans just yet. But in the future, who knows?

    I hope to have got to both the open training session and Fans Forum held on the 5th August, and I also hope that if you are currently having worries, fears or concerns about our ability to compete in League 1, that you too will have taken the opportunity to express them to Preston Johnson and Ben Levin in a considered manner.

    By the time the Blackpool game kicks off at 530pm next Saturday, I will have started my 69th year of watching Crawley Town, and having seen six promotions in the first 68 years I don't want it to end here. So, get behind Scott and the lads as they seek to prove the bookmakers wrong once again.

Game Day 1
10th August 2024 EFL1
Crawley Town 2 Blackpool 1
CTFC scorers Quitirna (16) Hepburn-Murphy (33)
Blackpool scorer Fletcher (74)
Rivals' results EFL2
AFC Wimbledon 4 Colchester 2, MK Dons 1 Bradford City 2

    A great start from Crawley Town, at a kickoff time which had nothing to do with Sky, honestly, well that's what Richard Keys promised back in the day. Seriously though, the whole of the team showed real spirit and endeavour to play the Scott Lindsey way, and the 4000 odd Crawley supporters present clearly found their voices as they cheered the Red Devils on to a result which PaddyPower, William Hill and bet365 will probably ignore for a while. The goals from Rushian and Armando in the first half must have had the most pessimistic fans wondering what they were worrying about and even when we gifted the visitors a way back with a typical Crawley gift, there was no doubt in my mind that we deserved the win. Blackpool, remember, had finished their first season back in League 1, after their relegation from the Championship, in 8th position just two places and three points off the playoffs. So, a good result against one of the better sides in the division, coupled with the addition of Eddie Beach (goalkeeper) on the bench and the return of Panutche Camara in the second half to rapturous applause sent the majority of the spectators home with a warm feeling in their hearts.

As Scott has said though, this season will not be easy, and by the time you will have the chance to have read this article we will hopefully have faced, and overcome another tough challenge in the League Cup first round against League 2 opposition in Swindon Town. We know they have strengthened their team in tempting Will Wright to join them, and they managed a draw at returnees Chesterfield thanks to a Wright special in the second half. The connections between us and Swindon will only seek to make Tuesday's (last night's) game even more important for both sides, but I feel it is one we must win, not only to put us through to the next round but also to put us in the right frame of mind to face another of the bookies favourites for the drop, in Cambridge United.

For those of you who like their recent history, and yes, I too would have liked some of the players who have left us to have remained, here is a short record of how they all did yesterday.

In League 1, Klaudi Lolos came on for Bolton Wanderers in the 75th minute, just after they had scored their winning goal against Leyton Orient.

Danilo Orsi, played the full ninety odd minutes at home against Lincoln City, but could not prevent an away victory for the Imps.

Corey Addai, played in goal for Stockport County and had half an assist for their first goal scored by Louie Barry, but also produced a Corey moment when playing out from the back, which had the County fans holding their breaths.

In League 2, three of our departees failed to make their squads. Nick Tsaroulla and Kellan Gordon for Notts County and Laurence Maguire for MK Dons. Notts County drew nil nil at

Tranmere and MK Dons two one at home to champions elect (in their eyes at least) Bradford City.

And lastly, Adam Campbell was credited with an assist in Hartlepool's one nil victory away at Yeovil, in the National League.

Thank you, lads for all you did for us, here at the Broadfield Stadium, but now we must make new heroes of those who don the Red Devils shirts.

13th August 2024
EFL Cup
Crawley Town 4 Swindon Town 2
CTFC scorers Adeyemo (34) Roles (56,88), Khaleel (89)
Swindon scorers Ofobah (60), Smith (66)
Rivals' results
Bromley 1 AFC Wimbledon 2, Watford 5 MK Dons 0

After Blackpool went home from their longest away trip of this current season in League 1 with their tails between their legs, Crawley went on, with a team that showed a number of changes, from that opening day win to defeat Swindon by four goals to two in the League Cup. Using players outside the normal starting eleven clearly showed that the system, or the style of play, will win Crawley matches this season.

At the beginning of last season many Crawley fans were asking who Joy Mukena is. Last Tuesday, Joy was our captain, leading from the front, or should it be the back, urging players around him to follow the Lindsey system. Jack Roles, who came to the club prior to Scott's arrival at the club, once again showed his worth with two stunning goals and Ade Adeyemo and Rafiq Khaleel added the others in a hard-fought four two victory over Swindon Town. Will Wright, one of last year's heroes for the Red Devils, appeared to have taken last year's green kit with him and must have been having strange thoughts when he stepped up to take a penalty against JoJo Woolacott, who last season was playing for Swindon, especially when he saw his kick saved and put out for a corner. However, with memories of Yusuf Mersin at the Amex, in the Sussex Senior Cup final, it seemed inevitable that we would concede from the corner and that is exactly what happened when Harry Smith nodded in at the far post from Will's exquisite delivery. A couple of years ago we would have gone on to lose, but not this team, under this manager.

The reward? Well, what better than a chance to avenge the 1992 five nil FA Cup defeat at the hands of Brighton and Hove Albion? We have played their U23 team since then, and will have played their youngsters once more, before we meet them in the week commencing the 26th August, and this time I do not foresee a repetition of that humbling way back when. I know they won three nil at Everton whilst we were beating Cambridge, but we are Crawley Town, yes, we are Crawley Town. Seriously, I am sure the lads will try their best and hardest against the Seagulls, cheered on by a large contingent from West Sussex, which we all know is the best part of the County. In that 1992 game, the kick-off was delayed by fifteen minutes or so to accommodate the numbers following the Red Devils, and led to us being in the cup fifteen minutes longer than Arsenal, who lost at the Racecourse ground to a pre-Hollywood Wrexham. The defeat at The Goldstone did not reflect the effort put in by Crawley, and was brought about, I believe, by Brian Sparrow, our manager at the time, leaving out ex Seagull winger Tony Towner in favour of Mark Searle.

17th August 2024
EFL 1
Cambridge United 0 Crawley Town 1
CTFC scorer Adeyemo (86)

Rivals' results EFL2
Bromley 2 AFC Wimbledon 0, Colchester 2 MK Dons 1

Back to League football, my family and I travelled, along with almost 500 more Red Devils, including Preston Johnson, to see us beat Cambridge United with a late winner by Ade Adeyemo who, after appearing to go too wide as he rounded their keeper, steered the ball into the net from what seemed an almost impossible angle. The crowd went wild and by the time the referee blew the final whistle we had risen to third in the table. I realise, and I know most of you will too, that it is far too early to get carried away, especially as we travel to Wigan next week who at the moment are in the bottom three, with zero points. If that is still the position at five pm next Saturday, that is all we should be concentrating on at the moment.

One last point, I don't know who is most put out. Steve Herbert for having his name printed alongside the photograph of an old man, or me for having Steve's name printed above my article?

Another week gone in the life and lives of Crawley Town, and everyone associated with it, manager, coaching staff, players and supporters, with mixed results and a fall to eighth in the league.

20th August 2024
EFL Trophy Crawley Town 2 Brighton and Hove Albion 2
CTFC scorers Barker (13), Papadopolous (55)
Brighton scorers Peupion (10), Duffus (84)
Penalties as per following write up
Rivals' results
AFC Wimbledon 1 Wycombe Wanderers 0

First though, let's look back at last Tuesday and our bonus point "victory" in the Bristol Street Motors Trophy. Back in the day, when I was just a lad, a Brighton U21 or U23 side would have consisted mainly of promising youngsters from around the beautiful county of Sussex. Now, however, it includes a player signed from Gothenburg for six million pounds, at least three internationals at U23 or U16 levels, and that is just in the five who took part in the penalty shoot-out.

In the Crawley team, including eight changes from the side that had won at Cambridge, the player I was most anxious to assess was Eddie Beach, the goalkeeper on loan from Chelsea. He didn't disappoint me and was not, in my opinion, to blame for either of the Seagull's goals, the first coming from a bad chest down by Mullarkey, which left Beach in no man's land and Peupion scoring for the Albion and the equaliser, coming in the 88th minute, which was, again a gift from our defence, scored by Dufus.

The penalty shoot-out, played in front of the home terrace, got off to a great start as far as Crawley were concerned, with Jensen

Weir, bought from Wigan for 500K, hitting Eddie Beach's right-hand post. From then on Cameron Bragg, Jack Roles, Junior Quirtina and Josh Flint all scored for Crawley, whilst Harry Howell, Imari Samuels and Cameron Peupion did the same for Brighton. This meant that the Six Million Pound man, Malick Yalcouye, had to score to make us take our fifth kick. He hit the ball to Eddie's left, who made the save and earned us the second point which puts us in second place in our group, behind AFC Wimbledon who had beaten Wycombe Wanderers in their first match.

24th August 2024 EFL 1
Wigan Athletic 1 Crawley Town 0
Wigan scorer Mukena (30,OG)
Rival results EFL 2
Cheltenham 0 AFC Wimbledon 1, MK Dons 3 Carlisle United 0

Yesterday, I travelled by train to take in the game at Wigan and was pleased that over 200 Red Devils had also made the effort. We were rewarded with a display that deserved at least a point but saw us come away with nothing. We bossed every statistic except the one that counts and lost one nil. However, the most pleasing aspect of the day was to appreciate the number of people wearing the red of our team who travelled to Wigan from Heathrow, Doncaster, Darlington, Liverpool, Leeds and York. Some had Crawley links, others had adopted us as their team. All were welcome. A big shout out to Dan, Alf, Malc, Lloyd, Luke, Miles and family, Alex and Danny. Thanks especially to Miles' two little children, who gave up a car ride to the stadium so that a silver-haired old duffer didn't have to walk. I must also mention, before I get on to the game, that will have already happened if you're reading this in print, Danny, who used to live in Crawley but now lives oop north. He was very proud to tell us that he has been free from his addiction for four years. Long may that continue.

Last night, against a team who are currently ranked at the top of the English Football Pyramid, Crawley Town, backed by thousands of Red Devils, w.......... See next week's edition for the rest of the story.

27th August 2024 EFL Cup
Brighton and Hove Albion 4 Crawley Town 0
Brighton scorers
Adinga (31), Sarmiento (45), Webster (84), O'Mahony (86)
Rivals' results 28th August 2024 EFL Cup
AFC Wimbledon 2 Ipswich 2, (AFC win by 4 penalties to 2)

31st August 2024 EFL 1
Crawley Town 0 Barnsley 3
Barnsley scorers Pines (13), Phillips (23, 45)
Rivals' results EFL 2
AFC Wimbledon 1 Fleetwood 0, Salford City MK Dons 1 (2/9/24)

 That was the week that was, a week of no goals for, as opposed to seven against, out of the League Cup and losing three nil at home in the League. Anything to be happy about, I hear you say? Well, after a considerable amount of reflection and critical thinking, I actually think there is.
 First of all, if you were at the Amex last Tuesday you were one of the 3,000 plus fans who supported their team throughout the match despite us going down by four goals to nil. Yes, it could have been worse, if Jay Williams had been cautioned for "that" tackle early on, or even worse sent off, but in my opinion, it could have and should have been so much better. Everybody in red ran themselves into the ground and for long periods of the game you would not have thought there were two divisions between the clubs.
 The show of support throughout and at the end of the game showed how much we have all come together over the last couple of years and clearly was a cut above the Seagulls' show of support. I must say also that, although the stadium is a good place to watch football, the public transport to and from leaves a lot to be desired. My family travelled by train from Three Bridges to Brighton and in passable comfort. However, changing at Brighton to go to Falmer was an experience that I would rather not repeat. Crowded together like cattle going off to the abattoir whilst waiting to board a four-coach train inevitably meant that

there would be an accident, and yes it featured me tripping on a curb stone which I couldn't see because of the crowd and cutting knee, elbow and nose in the process. To add insult to injury we missed the train and had to wait another twenty minutes before we finally got under way. The train we travelled on was staffed by a young man wearing a CTFC hat, and after he finished his commentary on where it was going, he ended it with a resounding "Come on you Reds".

We have to talk about Jay's tackle, which probably should have been punished more severely, I do think that the reaction to it across online media, the press and the Brighton fan base was way over the top, and as I sat in Redz four days later watching the Arsenal v Brighton game before our defeat to Barnsley, I wondered if there would be a similar reaction to some of the tackles made by their own players. No would be the answer you're looking for.

So, a four-nil defeat which, on another day, really could have seen a much different result was followed by a three-nil defeat at home to Barnsley which probably should have been much worse. Max Watters should have put them one up in the opening minutes but was soon replaced when he picked up an early injury. This didn't stop the Tykes going in three nil to the good at half time and try as much as Crawley did to change the outcome, that is how it stayed. We now sit in twelfth place, still in the top half and in a position most fans would have been happy with before the season had kicked off. If we had won both home games and lost the away games that would have been a good start to our season, 1.5 points per game would see us end the season safe in League 1 or even challenging for the playoffs. I know it could get worse, especially as we have Stockport County up next, but Scott, thanks to Burton Albion having some international players in their ranks, now has a full two weeks on the training ground to further integrate the players into the Crawley style of play.

Welcome, first of all, to Will Swan, who has already made his debut for the Red Devils, coming on as a substitute against Barnsley in the three nil home defeat last Saturday. On top of that we have also signed Nigerian International centre back, Benjamin Tanimu from Tanzanian side, Singida Black Stars on an initial two-year deal and Bradley Ibrahim from Hertha BSC on a season long loan. Bradley, a former Gunner, plays in midfield and replaces the unfortunate Michael Dacosta Gonzalez, who has returned to parent club Bournemouth after suffering an unfortunate injury. I am sure that the incoming players will help get us back on form when they play after the international break.

Talking international breaks, a couple of weeks ago it seemed like it was just our Burton Albion away fixture that had been called off due to call ups, but there were only four games played in our division last Saturday and they were Barnsley v Bristol Rovers, Charlton v Rotherham and Wrexham v Shrewsbury.

The most therefore we could drop in the league would be to 14th, and that would depend upon Rotherham beating 6th placed Charlton at the Valley and Shrewsbury winning at the Racecourse ground against second placed Deadpool, Wrexham. The Barnsley and Bristol Rovers result would only serve to give us a game in hand on both, with the winner being four points in front of Crawley and the loser just one ahead, or with both being just two points ahead. And at 5pm on Saturday 7th of September Rotherham had scraped a draw at Charlton, Barnsley had beaten Bristol Rovers whilst Wrexham went top of the table with their three-nil win over the Shrews. This means that without playing we have successfully stayed in 12th place.

Our next opponents on the 14th of September are of course, second in the table, Stockport County, who have won three games and drawn one, sitting on ten points with a goal difference of seven, having scored eight and let in just one. Their goalkeeper needs no introduction to us here in Crawley. He is of course Corey Addai. Hopefully, he will have an off day, and we will gain a valuable three points which will put us just one point behind them. You never know.

My Dad always used to tell me, back in the days of the League ladders available in many a comic, that you shouldn't look at the tables until everyone has played ten games. Our second set of five, after Stockport County, features Wrexham away, Bolton and Mansfield at home, Wycombe away and the Shrews at home. Looks and sounds frightening but only one of those teams are above us at the moment, so on that basis I am predicting we will gain ten points from those battles which will be a fantastic achievement in its own right.

Let's get behind the lads from Stockport County on Saturday, through those next five games and beyond and see what we can all achieve by the end of this season.

In closing, last week it was my great pleasure to hand over signed 2024/2025 shirts to the winners of the CTFC Exhibition Design a Shirt competition, Faith Gibbons, Harlow and Macey Gibbons. Well deserved, and your designs will go on display in the CTFC Museum which should be open before Christmas.

7th September 2024 EFL 2
Rivals' results MK Dons 1 Walsall 0

14th September 2024 EFL 1
Crawley Town 1 Stockport County 1
CTFC scorer Quirtina (69P)
Stockport scorer Barrie (5)
Rival results EFL 2 AFC Wimbledon 3 MK Dons 0

17th September 2024 EFL Trophy
Rivals' results Colchester United 2 MK Dons 1

In last week's article I set Crawley Town, us, a target of ten points from the upcoming games against Wrexham (A), Bolton and Mansfield (H) Wycombe (A) and Shrewsbury (H), and, after Saturday's performance against Stockport, I see no reason to amend that target. In every aspect, on Saturday, we matched County and fully deserved the point we won against them.

Seven points from the first five games represents, in my opinion, a better-than-expected start to the season for our Red Devils. Our defence on Saturday was resolute for all the game bar the time at the beginning of the game when Louie Barry was allowed to skip across the entire penalty area before slamming the ball past Jo Jo Wollacott unchallenged. In front of a crowd in excess of 4600, with 800 plus fans from Stockport, Crawley played really attractive football throughout the whole team, and it would have been an injustice if Stockport had been allowed to take all three points back with them up the motorways to their part of Greater Manchester.

As it was, an inspired triple substitution by Super Scotty Lindsey on 66 minutes resulted in Crawley getting the point they so fully deserved. Off came Jay Williams for new signing Bradley Ibrahim, probably to save Jay from picking up a second yellow card, and Ade Adeyemo and Junior Quitirna replaced Will Swan and Rushian Hepburn Murphy up front. Within three minutes the change had provided what was required with Junior, in particular, having a dramatic effect. His first touch of the ball was a free kick on the edge of the box which just failed to get the desired result, but it was soon followed by him being shoved to the floor as he made a run into the area, and for once the Referee made the correct decision, pointing to the penalty spot. Junior claimed the ball himself and Ex Red Devil, Corey Addai, who seemed bigger than last year, set himself in goal to try and stop the shot.

Last year, we found out how good Corey can be in goal, and we all waited in hope that he wouldn't reproduce the Playoff semifinal save. Junior sent him the wrong way as he rolled the ball into the net and the point was won. Personally, I was delighted with the point earned. Yes, it could have been more, but it so easily could have been less as both teams strove to the end to win, what was, an exciting game.

Wrexham next. Predictions anyone?

In closing, I would like to quash a rumour that may be circulating that my time supporting the Red Devils may be coming to an end. I am not intending to go to the Pearly gates just yet, and please ignore any petitions seeking to rename where I sand as The Steve Leake Corner. It is, and should be forever, known as Torres Corner. Note to Ivan Noel, please ensure your partner in crime, RH, lays off the beer !!

21st September 2024 EFL 1
Wrexham 2 Crawley Town 1
Wrexham scorers Lee (24), Cleworth (79)
CTFC scorer Quitirna (54)
Rivals' results EFL 2
Bradford City 0 AFC Wimbledon 0, MK Dons 1 Doncaster 1

Six games gone, two won, one drawn and three lost. Seven points from six games, we currently sit in seventeenth place, one point above Rotherham in twenty first place, who we have a game in hand over. The other teams in the relegation spots are Danilo Orsi's Burton Albion, four points from six games, Shrewsbury, three from seven and Cambridge United on one point from six games. This might seem a tad depressing, considering our two-match winning start to the season, but let's look at who we have played shall we?

Blackpool in 13th eight points from six games, Cambridge one from six, Wigan seven from six in 14th place, Barnsley in 3rd place with thirteen from seven, Stockport eleven from six in 7th place and yesterday's opposition Wrecsam (for those amongst you who speak Welsh) who are currently top with sixteen points from seven games.

All things considered I believe that from our games we have had one below par performance, against Barnsley, and that with more luck or drive in front of goal we could have been sitting on eleven points ourselves. Three more goals scored or indeed three less conceded against Wigan, Stockport and Wrexham would have seen us in touch with the playoff places. What if eh?

Before I am accused of being too optimistic, the next three games against Bolton Wanderers, Mansfield Town and Wycombe Wanderers now become crucial if my forecast of ten points from the 5th to 10th games is to be realised. They all won on Saturday, so that is where we, as fans of the real Red Devils, come in, especially as the first two are at home and the third is only just over sixty miles away and is easily accessible by road or rail. Let's drown out both Bolton and Mansfield at home for the entirety of the games and aim to take between four and five hundred to Wycombe. Let's make it so the players respond to our efforts and not the other way round.

Before we play Bolton on Saturday, let me share with you what I did yesterday while Crawley were losing valiantly in the Welsh border country. I listened to Gary Smith and Sam Gadsdon describing our positive display against the Deadpool variants (look it up) whilst doing what I thought only women could do. Double tasking. Alright, I wasn't cooking dinner whilst washing the floor or feeding the kids, but please believe me, listening to your team losing whilst watching England capitulating to the Aussies was just as exhausting. That is of course a joke. Some of my best friends are Welsh (well, one is anyway) and I believe I have at least a teaspoon of their blood pulsing through my arteries and veins, but to suffer two defeats in one day to two nations who like to beat us takes a real effort.

Off the field, I will be ordering furniture for the opening of the CTFC Museum in the next few weeks, so watch this space for details of the opening date. Thanks to the club for providing the portacabin and the CTSA and the Rollover members for providing the money to hopefully turn this venture into a reality within the next month or so. Any contributions, whether that be in time, money or memorabilia would be gratefully received.

28th September 2024 EFL 1
Crawley Town 0 Bolton Wanderers 2
Bolton scorers Dempsey (5), McAtee (78)
Rival results EFL 2
AFC Wimbledon P Accrington Stanley P Collapsed pitch due to the River Wandle overflowing, oh dear, never mind eh!
Bromley 1 Scott Lindsey's MK Dons 1

The King has abdicated, for more money I assume, and all I can say is "Long Live the King" albeit we haven't got a new one yet. Whoever he may be, I hope that he is an ex-forward who can teach our lads when to shoot. You will notice that I didn't say how to, as I believe they know how to, but it seems, at the moment that they all want to give the kudos to a teammate, rather than take the glory for themselves. If you don't buy a ticket (have a shot), you can't win the prize (score a goal).

Before I talk about my inept forecasting of results, it's only right to look at the Lindsey period of service at Crawley Town. Scott took over at Crawley Town on January 11th, 2023, with Crawley lying in 20th place in League 2 just above the relegation places. Up until then, under Betty, Young and Etherington (in turn not together, and not a music hall act featuring the amazing Betty Young and her talking dog Etherington) we had only won 22 points out of a possible 72 (30%). He didn't take charge of a game until the 28th of January, and it was a win in his first game that started the ubiquitous fist pumping towards the fans. We then went 8 games without a win slipping to 23rd in the League, but two runs of games without losing, of five and four respectively, eventually secured our place in the EFL. His record, with players he hadn't signed, saw Crawley collect 24 points out of a possible 66, which represented a rise of 6% in terms of points won. The gate in his first game was 2600 and over 4000 in the last home game against Walsall. The memories of our fight for survival, especially the win away at Hartlepool, will forever stay with me as long as I am able to watch the Red Devils.

Thanks to Scott, aided and assisted by our owners, last season saw our attendances rise because of the style of play that he brought to the club and because of the players that he was able to sign within the analytical model that the club employed. There were people (Crawley fans) at the time that imitated Alan Hansen, with comments like "We'll never win anything with these players" but we all know how last season turned out and I believe the sale of Humble pies increased as a result. For the record, the points won figure increased to just under 50% and the numbers of people who now identify as Crawley Town supporters has significantly increased.

This season, after just seven games in which we have won two, drawn won and lost four, the points figure has dropped to 33%, which is still higher than at the beginning of 2022/2023. Scott's legacy then must be, in my opinion, the style of football employed and the realisation for people in Crawley that it's good to support your hometown club, through then thin (2022/2023) and the thick (2023/2024) but, as with everything in football, there are lessons to be learnt.

Lesson 1 It is right and proper for people to be upset when popular figures, be they players or managers, leave the club they support.

Lesson 2 It is also right to put your support behind the incoming players and management team, for without that support they will have an even bigger fight on their hands.

Lesson 3 Don't set silly forecasts but enjoy every game in its own right. (NB Steve Leake)

Lesson 4 Every new manager or player will touch the badge and fist pump when things are going well, but it does not mean the same as when a supporter does it.

As far as the game against Bolton is concerned, we lost by two goals to nil, not because we were poor or because the referee was appalling (even though he was) but because of the fact that we failed to cut out the ball for their first and then because we gave the ball away on half way for the second. They attacked with pace and shot on target, whereas we bossed possession but failed to take advantage of it where it matters most.

Am I downhearted? A little bit, but whoever takes over the manager's position, shortly I hope, has a decent group of players to work with and more time to put things right than Scott had.

Onwards and upwards and just to cheer everyone up, we are currently in 20th place, above the relegation spots, and face fifth placed Mansfield on Tuesday (last night) and sixth placed Wycombe on Saturday.

COYR

Robbie Elliot, ex Charlton Athletic and Newcastle United goalkeeper and Gateshead United Manager has been appointed the person to take over the mantle of Crawley Town manager following Scott Lindsey's departure to MK Dons.

1st October 2024 EFL 1
Crawley Town 0 Mansfield Town 2
Mansfield scorers Gregory (12), Warne (90+2)
Rivals' results EFL 2
AFC Wimbledon P Crewe Alexandra P, Harrogate 1 MK Dons 5
EFL Cup Newcastle United 1 AFC Wimbledon 0

Another appalling display by the Referee and officials, but once again it was not the reason for last Tuesday's defeat against fifth placed Mansfield, managed by the man who will never have to come to Crawley again, Nigel Clough. With Ben Gladwin in charge for his second and last game and new manager, Robbie

Elliott watching from the stands, Crawley produced a carbon copy of the game against Bolton, conceding an early goal and, despite playing well throughout, conceded a second on 92 minutes to seal our fate.

The first goal, scored after just twelve minutes should have been prevented by us defending the corner properly, I know. However, the whole of Torres Corner exploded in protest as the ball was nowhere near overlapping the quadrant's white line as Lewis, the Stags number 8, swung the ball into the area. What made it worse was that the referee, perhaps realising his error, made sure that Lewis didn't repeat the trick when taking later corners. It should not have mattered, we should have defended the corner better, but rules are rules and with the Assistant referee at the other end of the pitch, it must be down to the Referee to make sure they are obeyed. The second goal, in our present run of results, seemed sadly inevitable but I still think that the only really below par performance this season was the game against Barnsley.

There were changes made by Ben Gladwin to the starting line up from the Bolton game, with Ibrahim, Forster and Adeyemo in for Bragg, Kelly and Camara and substitutions were made in the second half seeing Kelly, Anderson, Roles and Hepburn-Murphy replacing Forster, Ibrahim, Adeyemo and Swan. Hopefully, this will have given Robbie Elliott a chance to see the majority of the squad in action, However, there are so many questions that need to be answered about other players in our squad, that I wish would be asked by the professional media. For instance, why is there no goalkeeping substitute? Why is the club website showing players who, I believe, are no longer with us? Where is Sonny Fish, Showunmi and our Nigerian centre back??

5th October 2024 EFL 1
Wycombe Wanderers 1 Crawley Town 0
Wycombe scorer Onyedinma (29)
Rivals' results EFL 2
Salford City 1 AFC Wimbledon 0, MK Dons 1 Tranmere Rovers 1

And, as if by magic, Showumni is on the bench for the Wycombe game, so that's one of the questions answered. Panutche back in the squad, Kelly off the bench into the team and the afternoon's match gets underway, the first game of the Robbie Elliott era. Ifollow with no sound for the first nineteen minutes didn't augur well and when it did come on Ibrahim was denied a penalty and was booked for his protestations. Four minutes later Onyedinma scores for the home side, and it looks like we're in for another long afternoon.

At half time the scores from Burton (one nil up thanks to a certain D. Orsi), from Bolton, two down against Shrewsbury and from St James' Park where Cambridge United are losing yet again, sees Crawley Town down to 23rd and I'm clutching at straws. Yes, we might have had a penalty, and Harry Forster did hit the bar at the end of a good move, but we do need to stop giving goals away and start scoring some for ourselves. We have played six teams in the top half of the league, but when you have only scored five goals in eight and a half games and are the division's lowest scorers, it is no surprise we are struggling at the moment.

In the end, despite Crawley not having won in seven games and Wycombe not having lost in seven, Crawley just managed to hang on to 21st place as only Shrewsbury, out of the bottom seven, could gain a point from their draw at Bolton. Next week, Crawley at home to the Shrews now becomes vital in our attempt to climb away from the drop zone, Noli Cedere.

Robbie Elliott's thoughts about the game, along with that of Ronan Darcy, seem to be saying "Don't panic!!!". We are that close to getting a positive result and, according to Ronan "the white Pele" Darcy, from being an unbelievable side. There was talk from both after the game of different tactics having to be assimilated by the players and after just one game, almost achieving a positive result against a side in the playoff places, they are still in a positive frame of mind.

AFC Wimbledon in the Bristol Street Motors Trophy on Tuesday will give players a chance to show the new manager what they can offer. However, the website on Monday 7th October has issued the latest bit of news which could put the next two games out of our reach as far as wins are concerned.

"Crawley Town Football Club can confirm that goalkeeper Joe Wollacott and defender Benjamin Tanimu have been called up to their respective nations, and as a result, will miss Crawley's next two matches.

Joe has been called up by the Ghana National Team and Benjamin by the Nigerian National Team.

The club would like to congratulate Joe and Benjamin for their call-ups and wish them the best for their respective fixtures."

No mention of whether Beach is fit to take Jo Jo's place, or will we recall Sheikh from his loan at Whitehawk??? How come Benjamin can't get into our match day squad but is deemed good enough to be called up by Nigeria. Perhaps the media boys could think about adding those questions to the list I used earlier.

8th October 2024
EFL Trophy Group Match 2
Crawley Town 3 AFC Wimbledon 4
CTFC scorers Darcy (71P), Hepburn-Murphy (80), Flint (87)
AFC scorers Maycock (44), Stevens (55), Tilley (57), Pigott (90+6)
Rivals' results MK Dons 2 Arsenal U21 2
MK win by 3 penalties to 1

I should have known it was going to be a strange night when a steward asked me if I knew where I was going. We didn't concede early and looked as if we could go on and cement our place in the knockout rounds, but then, just as the first half was coming to a close, we left Maycock unmarked at the far post and, despite having most of the first half possession, went in one goal down. Playing in goal was emergency loan keeper, Connal Truman from Millwall, who played really well throughout and was not at fault for any of the goals. He will be with us for the Shrewsbury game before going back to his parent club next week.

Unbelievably, within twelve minutes of the second half starting, we found ourselves three goals down, again through unnecessary defensive errors, with the goals coming from Stevens and James (you may have heard of him) Tilley. It seemed as though we were in for a terrible evening and an embarrassing result but then we hit a purple patch of our own between the 71st and 87th minutes when Darcy scored via a penalty after Quitirna was pushed to the ground, followed by a header from Hepburn-Murphy and a shot from Josh Flint which brought us level. Indeed, Rushian had already had one header ruled out for offside and just as we were thinking about which end the penalties would be taken, Joe Piggott hit the winner for AFC in the 96th minute. A gutting result against one of our closest rivals but with nine changes being made from the team that narrowly lost at Wycombe there were definitely positive aspects to be appreciated by the crowd of just under 1500 (400 odd, making their way south from Kingston, I mean Merton.

Positives: not conceding early in the first half plus the effort put in by the team to comeback from three down. The positive attitude and respect shown by the supporters to the team throughout the game and, amazingly, at the final whistle. We really are creating something special at the Broadfield.

12th October 2024 EFL1
Crawley Town 3 Shrewsbury Town 5
CTFC scorers Swan (55), Quitirna (62), Kelly (90+5), Flint (Y, R 56)
Shrewsbury scorers Marquis (26, 76P) Nsiala (72) Lloyd (86, 90+2)
RIVALS RESULTS EFL2
AFC Wimbledon 4 Carlisle Utd 0, MK Dons 0 Port Vale 1

And then there was Saturday!! More sloppy goals conceded or should that be saloppy, but once again three goals scored at home. The question has to be asked, how do you score six goals at home over two games and not gain any points? I don't believe that Connal Truman was in any way to blame for the two defeats and neither do I think it was really down to a lack of effort from the players on the pitch. I watched Robbie's after match interview and most of it I agreed with, but either the question wasn't asked, or it was edited out. Why did we make the substitutions when we did and why remove the most effective players? Removing Junior and Darcy just after we had taken the lead for the first time seemed to revitalise the away side more than us and must have left Junior wondering "Why me?" after having scored and celebrated in the way he did. I am not the manager, and neither are the other spectators who shared my point of view and then we made another three substitutions eight minutes later when facing a corner which we duly conceded from. Perhaps an admission in the post-match interview that Robbie himself had made a mistake would have done him more credit than simply applauding the fans who were there to the very end. That brings me to my final point, how does it help the team for the "twelfth man" to leave the action with 15 minutes to go?

Think on people, and let's get behind the Devils at Reading on Saturday

19th October 2024 EFL1
Reading 4 Crawley Town 1
Reading scorers Mbengue (29), Wing (40), Savage (65), Smith (73)
CTFC scorer Forster (30)
Rivals Results EFL2
Morecambe 1 MK Dons 3, Notts Co 1 AFC Wimbledon 0

All the statistics were, once again, in our favour., bar the one that really counts.

More possession, more shots in general, more on target, more off target, less fouls committed but. rather strangely, more yellow cards gained. I have absolutely no problem with the commitment shown by our players, as when Harry Forster equalised I was quite confident we would get a good result. Even when Reading retook the lead just before half time, I wasn't unduly worried that we couldn't get back into the game and get at least a draw. This was backed up by the play being constantly in the Royals' half up until they scored their third in the 65th minute. From then on, although we had more chances, whatever we tried was unsuccessful and the game was finally killed off when they scored their fourth in the 73rd minute.

I know you only win a game when the ultimate statistic is in your favour, i.e. you score more goals than your opponents but if we look at the number of saves made by each keeper it clearly shows that we could have and should have drawn the match at least.

I think there is definitely a psychological problem with some of our players which hopefully will go away when we fluke a win when we might not deserve it by scoring off someone's back side or through an own goal.

The support at Reading was, once again, superb in terms of numbers and, up until their third goal, also in volume. Even some of our most stalwart supporters were taking their flags down with five minutes to go and left the stadium before the six minutes added on time was announced. The rest of us stayed until the final whistle, applauded the players for their efforts and told them to keep their heads up for future battles, which will only go our way if we stick at it; Town, Team Together.

What we must remember is that we were without Jay Williams and, in my opinion, our best defender Josh Flint because of suspensions and numerous other players who our media team hopefully will tell us about, as to their availability. Openness prevents damaging rumours circulating. On the plus side though, Benjamin Tanimu came on late on in Saturday's defeat and will hopefully strengthen our defence, and former Arsenal youngster Tyreece John-Jules, who hopefully will add to our goal scoring ability. He has joined us on a year's contract and although he will be mainly wearing Red in his time with us, I can say he is not a Dwarf.

And so, to Tuesday. Crawley Town 22nd in the League versus Lincoln City 7th in the Division having scored almost double our tally of goals in one less game and conceded half the number we have.

All I know is, a Devil must be considered stronger than an Imp, surely? Be there and help cheer the Red Devils to a good performance and a wonderful home victory.

Banker home win anyone? You never know.

22nd October 2024 EFL1
Crawley Town 3 Lincoln City 0
CTFC scorers Swan (46), Darcy (73), Hepburn-Murphy (90+5)
Rivals' results   EFL2

AFC Wimbledon 3 Morecambe 0, MK Dons 2 Accrington Stanley 1

Well, I was right about Tuesday, wasn't I? A devil does outtrump an imp!!
Three goals scored in the second half proved too much for 7th placed Lincoln City. The first scored by Will Swan, described by a Crawley fan on Facebook as "a tap in", which prompts me to enquire where the fan was sitting to describe it in such a way, set us on our way almost from the kickoff after the halftime restart. In the 73rd minute the player who everyone at the Broadfield sings this song about, "I saw my mate the other day! He said to me he saw the White Pele! So, I asked, who is he?! He goes by the name of Ronan Darcy!" added a delicious second, deceiving the goalkeeper by slotting his shot in by the near post whilst a far post shot looked more likely. The third goal should have been scored in the 83rd minute when Rushian Hepburn-Murphy saw his right-footed shot from the right side of the box miss to the left of the goal, when probably he should have slipped the ball to an unmarked Panutche Camará, following a fast break. As it was, the pair of them repeated the move in the 95th minute and this time RH-M finished with aplomb, sending the Crawley faithful home happy and looking forward to the away trip to Northampton, where we had high hopes of winning back-to-back matches for the second time this season, and in so doing overtaking the Cobblers in the league placings before the FA Cup game away to Maidenhead next week.

26th October 2024 EFL1
Northampton Town 3 Crawley Town 0
Northampton scorers Fosu (16), Williams (29 OG), Pinnock (55)
Rivals' results EFL2
Grimsby Town 1 MK Dons 3, PortVale 3 AFC Wimbledon 2

Now, we know that didn't happen; despite having 21% more possession than against Lincoln, despite having three times as many touches in the box than on Tuesday and despite having eight corners when on Tuesday we had none. Please don't read into this that I thought we were unlucky, because in my opinion we were not. The referee was consistently poor throughout, but was not biased, and did not affect the result in anyway. The most disappointing aspect for me was that if we had won, we would have been out of the bottom four. As it stands at the moment, we are five points behind them and the opportunity that had presented itself to us, of starting to climb the table, was sadly missed.

We were missing Armando Quitirno, who came off against Lincoln with an injury that could sideline him for a few weeks and unfortunately, we could also be missing Josh Flint for a few weeks, who went down yesterday with what appeared to be another serious injury.

I am not sure of the numbers who travelled to Sixfields, but it was a sizeable number who, once again showed how much they support the team with their vocal support throughout and almost to the last man, woman and child stayed behind to applaud their heroes off at the end. I hope that we travel in numbers to Maidenhead next Saturday, and that some of us will also be able to get to the Pirelli the following Tuesday for the rearranged fixture from earlier in the season. The National league side, Maidenhead, are 19th in level 5, but must not be underestimated, and the same goes for Burton Albion, who are currently bottom of League One, with no wins and having lost their last six games. After all, they do have a certain Danilo Orsi in their side.

Cutting through the doom and gloom, we should take heart from Cambridge United winning three in a week. If they can do it, why not us?

Noli Cedere

29th October 2024
Rivals' results
EFL Trophy AFC Wimbledon 0   Brighton & Hove Albion 3

2nd November 2024 FA Cup Round 1
Maidenhead United 1 Crawley Town 2
Maidenhead scorer McCoulsky (54)
CTFC scorers Mullarkey (90+5), Showumni (116)

3rd November 2025
Rivals' results FA Cup Round 1
Mk Dons 0 AFC Wimbledon 2
(Oh dear, never mind eh?)

The FA Cup, a glorious distraction or the start of another money-making adventure? After beating Maidenhead United by two goals to one on Saturday and drawing Chesham or Lincoln City at home in the 2nd Round only time will tell.

The game itself saw Robbie Elliott make numerous changes from the starting eleven that played against Northampton, with only three players, Wollacott, Mullarkey and Kelly, keeping their places after that three-nil defeat at Sixfields. Just how many of those changes were forced upon him will become clear on Tuesday, when we face Burton Albion at the Pirelli stadium.

Injury wise, Quitirna, Conroy, Flint are definitely injured, and Darcy is also rumoured to be suffering from a groin strain, whilst Wollacott was substituted on Saturday after a coming together with a goal post and a Maidenhead forward. By the time you read this in print, we will have played and hopefully beaten Burton Albion and there will be some clarity as regards who is injured and who was rested.

Back to the cup match, it was hard fought by both sides, but, with eight changes to the Crawley side, it was inevitable, I feel, that we would need time to settle down and get on top of a much more integrated unit. Our back three was Mukena, Mullarkey and Tanimu with Kelly, Bragg, Camara, Hepburn –Murphy, Roles, Showumni and Holohan playing in front of them with their roles seemingly pretty open to interpretation.

Up until the 64th minute, when Maidenhead's McCoulsky captitalised on a rare error by Joy Mukena to put the Magpies into the lead, I believed it was only a matter of time before we scored and took control but, after going behind, we suffered another injury blow which made our eventual victory even more amazing to say the least. This was of course the injury to Wollacott in the 72nd minute which led to 19-year-old Jasper Sheikh coming on for his debut. He was nervous to start, almost gifting a chance to ex Red Devil, Nathan Ferguson, but soon settled down and produced a capable performance with one top class save which contributed as much to our eventual victory as did the 95th minute Tony Mullarkey equaliser and the 116th minute winner from Tola Showumni.

The 600 or so Crawley Town fans who made the journey to Maidenhead went home with a mixture of feelings, I'm sure. Without doubt elated with the result but worried about the mounting injury situation and wondering whether we would seek to get another emergency loan goalkeeper in, either to take Jo-Jo's spot or to back up Jasper on the bench. One fan also went home with a shirt!! Bradley Ibrahim, on for Benjamin Tanimu in the 72nd minute, belted the ball off the pitch to stop an attack which caught an unsuspecting Crawley fan straight in the face from about five yards. Bradley immediately showed his concern for him and at the end of the game stripped off his shirt and handed it over to his happy "victim".

Yes, it was a struggle, but we did something that Huddersfield and Northampton couldn't do, beat a non-league side.

To round off my weekend perfectly, I spent half an hour talking to David Simmonds and his family at Crawley Museum. David played for our reserves back in 1954, and at the age of 92 it looks like he still might be able to play in goal if required. He has so many memories of local football and has loaned me some photographs for when we get the CTFC museum up and running.

COYR

After writing the above for the Crawley Observer I thought also about a conversation I had with Crawley Town Away Travel Guru, Alain Harper at Maidenhead. We both had to agree that Maidenhead was not a ground either of us had ever visited during our combined 120 plus years of watching the Red Devils. The only time we had played them before was in the first of the six promotion years either of us had witnessed, 1968/1969. Both of us, I think, were probably at evening classes and, as the match was in the Premier Midweek Floodlit League, we had to give the game a miss.

However, for those who love to reminisce, on the 25th of November 1968 we beat them at Town Mead by an Eddie McMullen goal to nil in front of 964 intrepid fans and completed the double over them on the 3rd of April 1969 away by a Dave Haining and Colin Blaber combination of goals, in front of just

347 spectators and their dog. Not only are we undefeated at Wembley Stadium, but also against the Magpies from Maidenhead. (Look up Maidenhead in the dictionary, I dare you.)

5th November 2024 EFL1
Burton Albion 0 Crawley Town 0

9th November 2024 EFL1
Crawley Town 2 Huddersfield Town 2
CTFC scorers Hepburn-Murphy (42), Anderson (65)
Rivals' results EFL 2
AFC Wimbledon 0 Grimsby Town 1, MK Dons 3 Swindon Town 1

After the excitement of the FA Cup, came an unusual week for me, a week when I was not able to see my beloved Crawley Town play in the flesh, so to speak. The first game against Danilo Orsi and Burton Albion, thanks to Sky Sports Plus, I was able to watch in the comfort of my own home and I was glad to see the Red Devils gain a much-deserved away point, even if it was against a team below us in the table with no wins to their credit. A great deal of credit has to go to the die-hard supporters who made it to this rearranged fixture and also to Connal Trueman, back in goal for an injured Wollacott who, after letting in nine goals in his previous two games for us, kept a most valuable clean sheet.

Whether it was the excitement of that well-earned point, or simply something I ate, is open to conjecture, but Wednesday saw me being taken to East Surrey by three paramedics who insisted I wear something "Crawley" for the ride up the road. Lee, one of the three, on seeing my living room bedecked as it is with Red Devil paraphernalia, shared with me that one of his friends used to play for Crawley. That player being Alex Malins, a product of our now defunct academy when I worked for them back in 2011 through to 2013. The chat about him playing against Sheffield United at Brammall lane helped get me to the hospital where I was superbly treated by the best team in this country, the wonderful NHS.

Still recovering from "food poisoning" on Saturday morning I decided that the residents of Torres corner would be better off without me for the game against Huddersfield Town, and it was then that I realised that no longer would I be able to count on my fingers and toes the number of home games I have missed in sixty-eight years of watching Crawley Town.

Anyway, enough about me, the radio commentary described perfectly the effort put in by those wearing the trident adorned red shirts, whether on the pitch or in the stands. Goals by Rushian Hepburn-Murphy and Max Anderson, both made by someone once described as the white Pele, Ronan Darcy, deserved more than the one point gained against the Terriers, but that said, we are now undefeated in three games and must continue this form and determination into the next two league games against Bristol Rovers and Steve Evans' Rotherham. Even if Wollacott is recovered for next Saturday he might be missing because of the international break along with Ben Tanimu. Squad players are showing their worth and it was good to see that Sonny Fish has made the match day squad. Hopefully, Tuesday's Bristol Street Motors game against high flying Wycombe Wanderers will see the likes of Ade Adeyemo, Jack Roles, Sonny Fish and Tyreece John –Jules stake their claims for the first team squad and with only a win after ninety minutes allowing us to progress one can only hope that it is a truly memorable night against League One's top team.

Even with our unprecedented average home gate of just under 4000 only Burton Albion sits below us in that respect. Long may that continue, as well as in the League table, and whatever the result Tuesday (last night) let's hope for our second league away win of the season against the Gas next Saturday, whoever is playing in goal. Noli Cedere.

12th November 2024 EFL Trophy
Wycombe Wanderers 2 Crawley Town 1
Wycombe scorers Hanlan (4), Leahy (30)
CTFC scorer Showunmi (14)
Rivals' results EFL Trophy
MK Dons 1 Orient 3, and that means Scott Lindsey will have to take MK to the League 2 play off final if he is to pay a visit to

Wembley this year. Crawley Town have two avenues to get there whilst AFC still have three.

16th November 2024 EFL 1
Bristol Rovers 0 Crawley Town 0
Rivals' results EFL2
Barrow 1 AFC Wimbledon 3, MK Dons 3 Cheltenham Town 2 (Lindsey in stands, naughty boy. Maguire (remember him) scores 86th minute winner as Lindsey says their performance was "not very good" despite them being 5th in League 2.)

Firstly, let's deal with our exit from the EFL Trophy at the hands of the high-flying Wycombe Wanderers. In the competition that gives us the best chance to pay another visit to the twin towers, so sorry, showing my age, the arch of Wembley stadium we bowed out gracefully by two goals to one. Yes, we could, and should in my opinion, have gone two one up if Jeremy Kelly had passed the ball into the net rather than trying to get it over the keeper, but that said, I thought a team showing eight changes from the previous game displayed enough capability to ensure we climb up the league in the coming weeks. Our team would also be strengthened by the return of at least some of our injured players in the coming weeks, but only if we, Town and Team all stick together.

I wanted desperately to go to Bristol for today's game but, still recovering from my bout of labyrinthitis (the correct diagnosis this time) I am making do with watching it on television. As I sit here in Oak Road, the team news shows a strengthening from Tuesday night's cup game and shows our intent with Swan and Hepburn-Murphy in the starting lineup, although it appears that Harry Forster must have joined those on the treatment table as he is omitted from the match day squad altogether as is Gavan Holohan.

At the end of the first half, despite having more possession than the Gas, we were lucky to not to be at least one goal down and if it wasn't for the metalwork and Connall Trueman, starring in goal, we most certainly would have been. We created some chances near the end of the half and with a little more grit could have snatched the lead against the run of play. We had to wait until the 44th minute for our first corner, and as the commentator wittily remarked, "just like a London bus, when one comes along another one comes just after it", but alas we did not take advantage of the opportunity offered.

With Connall Trueman being the likely winner of the man of the match award in the first half alone we, Crawley Town, needed an improvement in the second half if we were to get anything from the trip west, and that is exactly what happened. Even with Chris Martin in their side and Scott Sinclair coming on in the second half for his Rovers' return in the end it looked like the Reds just might end up ruling the world, in this match anyway.

As it was, the game ended nil nil for our second clean sheet in the last three games and valuable game time was given to John-Jules, Showunmi, Adeyemo and Roles with Jack almost scoring with his first touch. At the other end, Joy Mukena made a match saving tackle just when it was needed, and the loyal travelling Red Devils must surely have gone home well satisfied with the effort put in by their heroes in Red. Small in number, our support may have been, but they certainly out sung the home support.

Now all we need is for some of our missing from action players, Conroy, Flint, Williams, Forster, Holohan and Quitirna to recover and we can start to turn those draws into wins, starting, I hope, with the visit of Rotherham who are managed by the charismatic Steve Evans who, before Craig Brewster in 2012 and Scott Lindsey in 2024, was the manager who oversaw the important promotion from non-league to the EFL. Welcome back Big Man, but I do hope your visit is pointless.

19th November 2024 EFL2
Rivals' results
AFC Wimbledon 2 Accrington Stanley 2
Ex- Red Devil James Tilley hits a scorcher in the 7th minute of time added on to equalise after Stanley had held a two-nil lead up to the 89th minute.

23rd November 2024 EFL1
Crawley Town 1 Rotherham United 0
CTFC scorer Swan (21)
Rivals' results EFL2
AFC Wimbledon 0 Walsall 1, Fleetwood v MK Dons postponed

    Having listened to the preview of the Crawley Town v Rotherham United preview on the Crawley website I decided to investigate the game between Gateshead and Stevenage which Robbie referred to. Robbie had joined the 'Heed in August 2022 as Technical Director alongside Mike Williamson who a year later would join MK Dons as their coach. The incestuous nature of football is clear for all to see in this game, with the manager who achieved our place in the EFL back in 2011, Steve Evans, managing that other New Town club, Stevenage and ex Red Devil, Jordan Roberts, scoring for the 'Boro and getting sent off, whilst a "yet to be" Red Devil, Adam Campbell, provided an assist for Conteh to bring Gateshead level after being two down at half time, only for Luke Norris (Lewis Young's brother-in-law) to score the winner in the 73rd minute. The game was played in front of 1,039 spectators, including 139 from Hertfordshire. Not saying anything!!!! Robbie was on the bench, which would have given him a great chance to see Steve and Paul in action. Having also listened to the Rotherham version of the game preview I anticipate that if we get the performance we want, our support will show our friends from Yorkshire what "Town, Team, Together" is all about, no matter whether we win lose or draw.
    And, if you were there on Saturday November 23rd, you will know that is how it turned out. Rotherham were made, in my opinion, to look second best against a Crawley Town squad lacking Conroy, Flint, Williams, Forster, Hepburn-Murphy, Quitirna, Fish, Bragg and Papadopolous. The first eight being either injured or sick, whilst Antony is on loan. Both Toby Mullarkey and Will Swan combined well for the only goal of the game, Toby putting an irresistible cross field pass into a space which only Will saw, sending the home crowd into raptures after just twenty minutes as he slid the ball into the net. Town used all their on-field substitutes in the second half, leaving just two

goalkeepers, in Sheikh and Beach, to watch a glorious victory unfold.

The weather did play a part in the game, but the strong wind was to the advantage of the visitors in the second half when they were chasing the game. Crawley, to a man, withheld the Rotherham onslaught and against the wind created numerous chances themselves and when the final whistle went, after six minutes of added time, the Red Devil faithful showed the away support what it means to back your team. Town, Team, Together. For the second time in three games the Millers were booed off the pitch at half time and judging from big Steve's preview of the game that will not go down well with Rotherham's management. The clue is in the word "support".

The win takes us out of the bottom four and with three teams just one point ahead of us to aim at. However, our climb up the table must be put aside for one week as next Saturday sees cup action return to the Broadfield as we seek to beat Lincoln City and earn not just the prize money for winning but also the chance of a trip to a Premier League club and to make history once again.

26th November 2024 EFL2
Rivals' results Tranmere Rovers 0 AFC Wimbledon 2

30th November 2024 FA Cup Round 2
Crawley Town 3 Lincoln City 4
Rivals' results AFC Wimbledon 1 Dagenham and Redbridge 2

No cup glory this year then, despite going two nil up in the first thirteen minutes, but when you look at where we are with squad strength and availability at the moment then perhaps it was inevitable we would lose to one of the better teams in League 1, Lincoln City.

Conroy, Bragg, Forster, Darcy, Camara, Quitirna, Williams and Flint all missing from the squad and JoJo Wollacott replaced in goal by Eddie Beach didn't seem to matter as Crawley took the game to Lincoln City and thanks to goals, from Jack Roles and Tola Showunmi, were two up early on and some of us, no doubt, were already looking forward to the draw for the third round.

However, within six minutes of gaining that two-goal advantage, a return to sloppy defending of old saw Lincoln reduce the arrears and then five minutes before half time they drew level, once again because of a mistake at the heart of Crawley's defence. In fact, if Beach hadn't made an incredible double save in the dying minutes of the first half, we could even have been behind at the interval. As it was, within three minutes of the second half beginning, Lincoln scored twice which seemed to put the game completely beyond Crawley Town. Three goals conceded in nine minutes and with plenty of time left for a Torquay style comeback where we fought back twice from two goals down to eventually win by six goals to five perhaps the 3rd round was still reachable. When Jeremy Kelly produced the goal of the match in the 82nd minute the chance of extra time increased but unfortunately only five extra minutes were added on by the officials at the end of the game and Crawley, try as they might, could not find the goal that would secure those extra time minutes.

So, disappointment all round and £50,000 lost, combined with a smaller than usual attendance figure of 2,831, needs to be quickly put behind us if we are to get anything out of our trip to the Valley the day before this article will appear in print. Hopefully we will have Ronan Darcy, Will Swann and JoJo Wollacott in contention for places in the team, but I understand that we will have to do without the services of Toby Mullarkey and Max Anderson, who will both be missing due to suspensions.

I will have been at the Valley, as I hope a lot of you will have been too and who knows, we might have witnessed a remarkable performance to help us gain an impressive result.

3rd December 2024 EFL1
Charlton Athletic 1 Crawley Town 2
Charlton scorers Kanu (68)
CTFC scorers Showunmi (33), Anderson (80)
Rivals' results EFL 2
AFC Wimbledon 2 Newport County 2, MK Dons 3 Chesterfield 0
Remarkable performance tick.
Impressive result tick.

All accompanied by fantastic away support in excess of 700 Red Devil supporters and an almost perfect afternoon and evening was had by all. The qualification will follow later, but here is what made December 3rd special for me at least. First of all there was the realisation that one of our travelling number was in fact a real-life ex Red Devil player. Now I have known this chap in passing for a few years as Barry, one of Stuart Frost's friends but not by surname and when I found out his surname was Tait, the memories came flooding back. Barry joined Crawley Town in the early 70s as a promising 15-year-old and made 21 full appearances in League and Cup and another 5 as substitute. He scored two cup goals for us under the first Mr. Crawley Town, Stan Markham and played alongside Dave "Rubber man" Haining and the likes of Dave Easton and Ali West.

I can't remember how many pubs we visited before we took the train to Charlton, and I wasn't drinking, but in the last one, The Shipwrights Arms, we met two Finnish chaps who were over in England to watch three games of football. Jaan Vakio and Riku Riihilahti had already seen two games, including the West Ham v Arsenal one, but had obviously decided to leave the best to last and were taking in our game at the Valley, before returning home. Unfortunately, their tickets were behind the dug outs in home fan territory or, as has now been renamed, the silent reading area of the Charlton Library.

Our 700 plus supporters showed their 10,000 how to support their team as even when Kanu equalised for the Addicks our support went up a few decibels and no doubt contributed to the great effort, put in by the team, to regain the lead with ten minutes to go and hold on to it for the extra six minutes as well. Both of our goals were class finishes and were fully appreciated by the travelling fans. Tola Showumni and Max Anderson (who wasn't suspended, as I had feared), take a bow.

The only disappointing part of the evening, for me, was the lack of consideration shown by some of the Red Devil faithful to the travelling public. Support the team by all means, but when it leads to young girls, probably travelling home from work, having to leave the train in tears then that must surely be the time to look critically at our own behaviour. Enough said and hopefully that sort of inconsiderate behaviour will reduce with less pre-match drinking time for the upcoming Posh and Orient away trips.

I have my tickets for both these games as, contrary to what some may have heard, trains are running to London Victoria on Boxing Day, which means that the Orient game is reachable by train, coach and car. The Peterborough game is also easily accessible by train, so if you have done your Christmas shopping why not make it a day out to remember.

Sitting here writing this on a Saturday morning which has been wrecked by a storm named Darragh. If anyone spots the East stand on its way to Oz, please let the club know so they can get it back in situ for the Birmingham home game on the 23rd December, when yours truly will be singing Christmas songs with Inspire Choir outside Redz, pre match.

7th December 2024 EFL2
Rivals' Results Harrogate Town 0 AFC Wimbledon 3
EFL Trophy
Rivals' results Colchester United 2 AFC Wimbledon 0

14th December 2024 EFL1
Peterborough United 4 Crawley Town 3
Peterborough scorers Jade-Jones (20), Hayes (23, 61), Kyprianou (47)
CTFC scorers Adeyemp (38), Swann (53), Showunmi (57)
Rivals' results EFL2
AFC Wimbledon 1 Doncaster Rovers 0, MK Dons 0 Gillingham 1

Deja Vu? Not quite, I Hope!!

The last time this fixture took place in the League was way back in April of 2015 and marked the beginning of the end of our stay in League One. We led twice, at one nil and three two but ultimately lost when Bostwick (ex-Red Devil) equalised with two minutes to go for the Posh and then Connor Washington scrambled the ball home with virtually the last kick of the game to leave us in the relegation places on goal difference. Marvin Elliott (no relation to our current manager), Matthias Pogba (brother to Paul) and Josh Simpson (ex-Posh) had scored the goals which, up to the last gasp winner from Washington, would have maintained our League One status for another year.

Saturday's game brought back memories of that day but this time I am confident it will not lead to the same eventual outcome. This game was a contest of defensive errors, on our part, and of an incredible fight back also from the players in red. Two goals down after twenty-eight minutes because of mistakes at the back it looked like we were in for a long afternoon and a humiliating defeat, but when Ade Adeyemo lashed home in the 38th minute the Crawley players and supporters had new hope of getting something from the game, Unfortunately, within two minutes of the beginning of the second half, Posh's Kyprianou had restored their two goal lead and you could have been forgiven for thinking negatively about the inevitability of the outcome. However, within eight minutes of the Cypriot having seemingly confirmed the result, Crawley were level with an exquisite goal from the much-maligned Will Swan and a poacher's goal from Tola Showunmi which was put on a plate for him by the awesome persistence of the White Pele, Ronan Darcy. Three goals all and there was only one team that was going to win, but that's where football is both beautiful and ugly depending on the colours you are wearing.

Rob Elliott substituted Swann, Showunmi and Darcy in the 66th minute for the fresh legs of Rushian Hepburn-Murphy, Tyreece John-Jules and Harry Forster and within two minutes we were behind yet again and despite the later additions of Jack Roles and Bradley Ibrahim for Camara and Anderson, that was how the score remained.

Two games, nine and three-quarter years apart, with the same score but because of the timing in the season hopefully not the same ultimate outcome.

There were some in the after-match comments and discussions, some alcohol fueled, some not, who thought that the substitutions came at the wrong time or should have been done differently. Personally, I think Rob was trying to win the game by putting fresh legs up front rather than by bolstering the midfield and for that he has my full support.

Anyway, that's history now and we have nine days on the training ground and in rest to prepare for the biggest game of the season so far, Birmingham City at home. After that, in the same space of time, 9 days, we have two away games against Orient and Exeter City and the New Year's Day clash against recently defeated Charlton Athletic. No points target from me, except to say I hope all Red Devils have a wonderful Christmas and a prosperous New Year.

21st December 2024 EFL2
Rivals' results
Chesterfield 1 AFC Wimbledon 0, Newport County 6 MK Dons 3

23rd December 2024 EFL1
Crawley Town 0 Birmingham City 1
Birmingham scorer Stansfield (79)

I listened to Luke White, representing the Red Devils on Tilton Talk, as I prepared for the biggest League match we have hosted for a while against Birmingham City. Their Away End podcast wasn't too condescending, but the general feeling was that we would lose but by how many was in question. As it turned out, in spite of the fantastic support from an almost capacity crowd, Birmingham secured a one nil victory thanks to a 79th minute Jay Stansfield goal. The team and the supporters did everything they could, in the true spirit of Town, Team, Together, to secure at least a point but it wasn't to be and everyone went home anticipating another good performance on Boxing Day against Orient.

26th December 2024 EFL1
Leyton Orient 3 Crawley Town 0
Orient scorers Kelman (33), Agyei (50), Beckles (55)
Rivals' Results EFL2
AFC Wimbledon 1 Swindon Town 1, MK Dons 0 Notts County 2

Unfortunately, that wasn't to happen as we underperformed in front of 419 travelling Red Devil fans. The great majority of the travelling support accepted the performance and result with good grace, applauding both players and Rob Elliott as they reciprocated in a manner which, to me, suggested they realised that they had not performed well. However, some of our travelling support, presumably the same people who had started the "We are "a four-letter word meaning excrement"" chant during the second half, started to abuse the players with foul and abusive language in front of the players families and friends. When I remonstrated with them all I got was a "we follow them up and down the country at great expense and that gives us the right to criticise them". Indeed, it does, but in a positive way such as "Come on lads, you're better than that. Chins up and make sure it doesn't happen again". I could even accept the use of a certain expletive before the words "better" and "doesn't". As for the negative chanting during the second half, how was that supposed to encourage the players to play better. I do appreciate that we are a self-deprecating lot, taking pride in being the underdog. I, myself, have even used "Tinpot and Proud" as the title of my third book but I would never dream of doing the opposition supporters job for them.

29th December 2024 EFL1
Exeter City 4 Crawley Town 4
Exeter scorers Alli (35), Harper (60), Woods (60), Mitchell (90+3) CTFC scorers Camara (15), Swan (37), Showunmi (42) Quitirna (45+1)
Rivals' Results EFL2 MK Dons 1 Crewe Alexandra 1

And so, to Sunday. Before the game I do believe we would have been pleased with a draw against the Grecians of Exeter City but when we took the lead through Panutche Camara after just 15 minutes a shock result was beginning to enter into my thoughts. Then, in twelve crazy minutes before half time we relinquished the lead and then put the game beyond the home side, or so it seemed at the time, through goals from Will Swann, Tola Showunmi and Armando Quitirna.

We held the four one score line until we made our first substitutions in the 59th minute, Quitirna making way for Joy Mukena and Tola Showunmi for John-Jules and within a minute Exeter had scored their second and were on their way back into the game. Gary Smith on Ifollow got a little carried away, saying the deficit had been halved, but that's just me trying to make light of the fact that squeaky bottom time was just about to start.

I personally think we should have gone looking for a fifth goal prior to making the first of our substitutions, and for me, listening to the game in my sick bed, it seemed inevitable that we would concede at least another goal, or two or maybe even three.

In the end it proved to be just two and we earned a point we weren't expecting before the game but was two less than we thought we might get at half time.

Will it be the point gained, or the two points lost, that define our season?

30th December 2024 EFL2
Rivals' Results AFC Wimbledon 1 Gillingham 0

1st January 2025 EFL 1
Crawley Town v Charlton Athletic, Postponed due to waterlogged pitch
Rivals' Results EFL2 Chesterfield 1 MK Dons 2

2nd January 2025
Rivals' Results EFL2 Newport County 1 AFC Wimbledon 2

4th January 2025 EFL 1
Barnsley 3 Crawley Town 0
Barnsley scorers Russell (11), Watters (51), Kellor-Dunn (54)
Rivals' Results EFL2
MK Dons 0 Salford City 1

The New Years Day "almost a derby match" was frustratingly called off at the very last minute because of a waterlogged pitch, though why the officials took so long to come to that conclusion will forever be a mystery. Following on from that we travelled to

Barnsley and came up against a team who put us to the sword by three goals to nil, as they did back in August of last year.

This time the goals came early in both halves, which unfortunately seems to be a common occurrence this season despite us being equal in nearly all the stats that, at the end of the day, don't really matter. I am hoping that the performance was of a fighting nature better than that witnessed in London on Boxing Day, with supporters accepting defeat against one of the better sides in our league so that the players appreciate that we will be behind them in two weeks' time when we face Burton Albion at the Broadfield.

Only in England could a football club be scheduled to play five games in twelve days, albeit because of the Charlton postponement we only played four, for us then to have to wait fourteen until we face Danilo Orsi and the Brewers.

Personally, I think the break should help Rob in his efforts to bed in any new players we might sign this week (Welcome to Ben Radcliffe, signed from Derby County) and to get the players in the right mindset for what looks like it might be a battle till the end of the season. The prime objective being to score more goals than the opposition and also to prevent Danilo from using his trademark celebration against us on January 18th. Having to watch the scores come through on the Sky "Teleprinter" (showing my age there) because of a problem with Ifollow, made me wonder how ex Red Devil Max Watters celebrated against us!! How we miss a player of his promise.

Over the Christmas period we have scored four goals in the four matches we have played and let in eleven. We obviously need to improve in defence, but I am a firm believer that it can be done by scoring more goals as well as by conceding fewer.

Fortunately, most of the teams above or below us in the bottom half of the table dropped points, with only Northampton and Bristol Rovers picking up maximum points against Burton and Cambridge (both below us) and Stevenage and Rotherham picking up a point a piece. To add to that, we have yet to play the three teams directly above us at the Broadfield Stadium, so how we perform as a fan base will be of vital importance as we seek to maintain our League 1 status.

Even more so, that support will be paramount throughout the rest of January and February as we face five of the top ten sides, three away in Stockport County, Mansfield Town and Bolton Wanderers and two at home in Wrexham and Wycombe Wanderers.

The phrase "The darkest hour comes before dawn" springs to mind here, but as with other non-football related uses of this phrase, hopefully the dawn will be golden tinged with a reddish hue.

5th January 2025
Rivals' Results
Fleetwood Town P AFC Wimbledon P

11th January 2025
Rivals' Results
AFC Wimbledon P Cheltenham P, Carlisle P MK Dons P

With no game this week, because of our defeat by four goals to three back on November 30th last year to Lincoln City in the second round of the FA Cup, I think it is probably best to look back over the past and forward to the future in order to properly assess where we currently are and what our prospects are for the rest of this season.

Let's go back to 2022/2023, the season of our survival prior to the season of ultimate triumph at Wembley. When Super Scottie Lindsey came to Crawley Town on the 11th of January 2023, with us lying in 20th place in league 2, and after sixteen league games, the same number that Robbie Elliott has been in charge of, we had dropped to 22nd place and had taken just sixteen of the forty-eight points available. In the remaining six games we won two and drew two which secured us a place in League 2, finishing just one place above the relegated Hartlepool and Rochdale.

Now, as everyone knows, if we drop to 22nd this year we will be relegated back to League 2, from which we were promoted last year.

In Robbie's first sixteen games we won one fewer than we did under Scott but sit one place higher in 21st place than we did when we escaped relegation but because it's four down from League 1, we find ourselves one place below safety.

We obviously need to improve if we are to stay in League 1 and I feel that with a few fresh faces in the next three weeks coupled with a much needed "reset", as asked for by Robbie himself, it is very much still in our own hands.

In this window we have transferred out Jay Williams to MK Dons and Scott Lindsey but have signed Ben Radcliffe from Derby County. In addition, Southampton have recalled Cameron Bragg, and we have brought Anthony Papadopolous back from Maidstone United, where he has scored five goals in fifteen appearances. Whether rumours about other departures actually become fact is pure conjecture at this time, but as long as we end up with a squad that want to play for the shirt and the fans there is every chance that we can stay up. That starts at home on the 18th of January at home to Burton Albion, but before then both Burton and Cambridge United faced tough away games against Stevenage and Blackpool, that is until the weather intervened, postponing those matches and leaving the bottom of the table frozen, as it were, at least until next weekend. The one game played in EFL 1 on Saturday saw Steve Evans' Rotherham United defeat Bolton Wanderers 3 – 1 taking them to 13th place and safely away from the dog fight in which we are involved.

I understand there are some more incoming players likely to arrive before our next match against Burton Albion and hopefully no more outgoings of key players. Away from this year's concerns fourteen years ago on Monday 10th January saw non-league Crawley Town defeat Robbie Savage and Derby County by two goals to one. On the Saturday before the game Gareth (now Sir) Southgate returned to Crawley, where he was brought up, to do a vox pop in the Town Centre, whilst Robbie Savage attempted to interview our manager and players at the Stadium. He was at the time a member the Derby first team squad and thus was, politely, refused entry. We went on to win by two goals to one, through goals from Craig McAllister and Sergio Torrrrresssssss. Happy memories, of which I'm sure there will be many more.

Tuesday January 14th 2025

It is rumoured that we are in the process of signing a midfielder from Gateshead, Robbie's former club, and a centre back from Milton Keynes as Scott seems intent on demolishing the club he fist-pumped for last year by putting in a bid of £500,000 for Rushian Hepburn-Murphy. All will be revealed soon I hope, but surely we can't afford to sell any more players at the moment, can we? Apparently, Football Manager has run a simulation which predicts this latest raid by MK, and if it becomes reality will make it four ex red devils on their playing staff, in Maguire, Kelly, Williams and Hepburn-Murphy. The rumoured midfielder from the 'Heed is Regan Booty, whilst the defender from MK is Jack Tucker, who joined MK Dons from Gillingham in 2022. So far, he has made 81 appearances for the League Two side, but he hasn't featured since MK's 1-0 loss to Port Vale, back in October 2024. In the 2024/25 campaign he has made just nine first team appearances. Nice to see though that the MK author of this rumour sees it as a step up for Jack.

Thursday 16th January 2025

For the first time in my life, I settled down to support a Welsh team against an English one. The teams being Wrexham and Shrewsbury Town. Why? In the vain hope that the Hollywood superstar team would prevent the Shrews from leapfrogging above us in the league. In the end it wasn't to be, and the English side went above us on goals scored thanks to a two one win. One of the "stars" of Deadpool and Wolverine, ex Red Devil Ollie Palmer wasn't in the Wrexham squad, and the other one, Paul Mullin, only came on as a second half substitute with little effect. That is definitely the last time I will commit an act of treason in order to try and gain an advantage for the club I love. From now on, it is what we do on the pitch and the terraces and seats in the stands that will decide our fate.

18th January 2025 EFL1
Crawley Town 1 Burton Albion 1
CTFC scorer Showunmi (72)
Burton scorer Burrell (25)
Rivals' Results
AFC Wimbledon 2 v 0 Tranmere Rovers, Walsall 4 v 2 MK Dons

That brings me to the game against Burton Albion which was being labeled as a must win game by a lot of our supporters. I did not feel that was the case at the beginning of the game but at half time, with Crawley trailing by a disputed goal to nil, I was happy to concede it had certainly become a must not lose contest. Happy to say that we managed a draw, thanks to a wonder of a strike by Tola Showunmi, and that we should really have gained the win with a little more accuracy and confidence in front of goal.

As far as the transfer rumours go, Rushian came on as a substitute in the second half so that one has hopefully been laid to rest, but there was still no sign of the white Pele in the playing squad so that might go on until the window has closed at the end of the month. Rob tells us that Ronan has a problem with his legs at the moment and isn't far off a return to action. I really hope that is the case and that his return to playing is for us at Crawley Town rather than for anyone else.

Although it may appear that the bottom four are beginning to drop off the pace needed for safety, a couple of wins on the road against Stockport County and Mansfield, currently in sixth and tenth places respectively, could be the start of the Great Escape music starting to be heard around the Broadfield stadium once again.

21st January 2025 EFL2
Rivals' results Fleetwood Town 2 MK Dons 1

25th January 2025 EFL1
Stockport County 2 Crawley Town 0
Come on Steve McQueen, please start revving up the motorbike!!!!
Rivals Results MK Dons 0 AFC Wimbledon 0

When I submitted last week's article to the Crawley Observer, I was not aware of the situation as regards longtime supporter Carol Bates, and that is the only reason I did not refer to it. Here are my views on the situation and of course you are absolutely entitled to agree or disagree with some or all of my points. Firstly, the survey, I believe, was aimed at all supporters regardless of their age, sex, creed, colour or mental capacity. There were, I think, two questions in the whole survey which caused this whole situation to get out of hand. The one about the dish and the other about the animal.

If the one about the dish had been worded slightly differently e.g. What would you like to see served at the stadium, then I am sure it would have been a useful piece of information for the club and its' caterers to have.

The one about the animal seems to have raised people's concerns about Reggie the Red, whereas perhaps it was meant as a way to introduce another mascot, with closer links to Crawley, to accompany Reggie on match days and in the wider community. I suggested having a Crow, and if you don't know why, may I suggest a visit to Crawley Museum at The Tree, 103 Hight street, where you might just learn something about where you live.

As for how Carol was treated, this can be looked at in two ways, I believe. Carol, as a "face" of Crawley Town perhaps should have mentioned her concerns to the club before posting them on "X" and the Football club should have taken her service for the club into consideration when dealing with the situation. I don't believe the reaction from the CTSA in issuing their own survey helps the situation, especially at a time when we should all be focusing on our league position.

Meanwhile, the football continues and with Burton Albion winning during the week it seems to me, even more so than ever, that Town Team Together is what is needed now.

A feeling that became even more paramount even before we kicked off at 3pm on Saturday. Cambridge United having gone three up against Mansfield Town were seemingly going to jump above us on goal difference but two late goals from the Stags were to deny them that opportunity.

Starting line up trying to gain some points from Stockport; Wollacott, Hepburn-Murphy, Barker, Conroy, Radcliffe, Adeyemo, Kelly, Ibrahim, Camara, Swan, Showunmi with Sheik, Anderson, Forster, Darcy, Roles, Tanimu and John-Jules on the bench.

At 3pm on Saturday 25th January three points covered the bottom four with Crawley lying in 21st place and with games in hand on all around us. At half time, sadly, we had sunk to the bottom, conceding two goals in the 25th and 34th minutes. I am Mr. Optimistic but even I felt a little despondent, especially having heard rumours about the possible departure of Junior Quitirna.

With Harry Forster coming on at half time to replace Will Swann surely our fortunes could get no worse, or could they? The answer was no, but only because they couldn't. Despite bringing on Roles, John-Jules and Darcy in the second half, the score remained two nil and we sit in 24th place, bottom of League 1. However, despite all that, Bristol Rovers and Peterborough both lost and Northampton drew at Wycombe which means that no club in the bottom seven can count themselves safe and with Crawley still to play five of them, four at home all is not lost, Admitted, we do have to grasp any opportunity that comes along, including getting some new blood in, to turn the ebbing tide but being bottom has its advantage. THE ONLY WAY IS UP!!!

Just as I submitted last week's article to Sussex World, the last five words needed modifying, thanks to a 96th minute winner for Charlton Athletic from Thiery Small which meant that Shrewsbury were bottom. Somewhat cheered that we weren't actually bottom it made me hopeful of a Mansfield away style performance circa 2024 on Tuesday night and, apart from not winning four one, that's exactly what we got!!

28th January 2025 EFL1
Mansfield Town 0 Crawley Town 1
CTFC scorer Adeyemo (81)
Rivals' results Crewe 1 AFC Wimbledon 1, MK Dons 2 Harrogate 1.

On Tuesday I was sitting waiting for the game against Mansfield having just read about our new loan signing from Tesco, I mean Brighton and Hove Albion. Welcome to Kamari Doyle, a midfielder who played for Southampton before joining the Seagulls and has been on loan at Exeter City this season scoring four goals in the process. He played against us for Exeter City in the four all draw over the Christmas period, although he was substituted prior to the Grecians comeback.

An hour before the Mansfield game kicked off and two more players had joined the club, goalkeeper Matthew Cox on loan from Premier League Brentford who went on to make his debut against the Stags and defender Rory Feeley from Barrow on a one-year contract. Feeley didn't make the squad for the game, but Kamari Doyle made the bench. Notable absentees from the squad that played Nigel Clough's side were Ronan Darcy, Junior Quitirna and Jeremy Kelly. I made a mental note to ask Preston on Thursday later in the week as to whether it was their fitness or possible departures from the club that was keeping them out of the squad. Jo Jo Wollacott was also missing from the squad with Jasper Sheikh sitting on the bench.

What an incredible game it was, not only because of the good performance and result, but also because of the unusually generous and gracious remarks from the Mansfield boss, Nigel Clough. Mansfield, having been humbled by Cambridge United (relegation zone) in their last match had me worrying that they might react to the ignominy of that defeat by taking it out on the Red Devils but that proved not to be the case as Crawley matched them in every department and thoroughly deserved the victory. Watching it on the television was, I believe, more stressful than watching the game live albeit a lot cheaper. The supporters who were at Field Mill were a credit to Crawley and hopefully they will thoroughly enjoy the promised "pie and pint" courtesy of the players. I'm sure that the travelling fans and those who were watching from home would have enjoyed the combination of excellent performance and result.

Next up were Wrexham, who themselves had won only once since the beginning of 2025, and had lost three times including a defeat to relegation threatened Shrewsbury Town.

1st February 2025 EFL1
Crawley Town 1 Wrexham 2
CTFC scorer Ibrahim (90)
Wrexham scorers James (2), Lee (90+5)
Rivals' results EFL2
AFC Wimbledon 1 (Tilley) Bradford City 0, Doncaster 2 MK Dons 1

What we needed to do was go for them like we did against Mansfield, which is what we did.....after going a goal down in the second minute.

The squad did not include Ronan Darcy, who had departed earlier in the week to Wigan Athletic but Jeremy Kelly was on the bench, although Quitirna and Wollacott were not. News concerning their status as Red Devils and news about other incoming players will be known before you read this article in print, as the transfer window will have shut at 11pm on Monday 3rd February.

In my opinion we were dreadfully unlucky to have lost in the 95th minute of the game, especially as the highlights clearly show Kelly being fouled in the build up to their winner. Our equaliser, just five minutes earlier was a stunner from Bradley Ibrahim, but unfortunately it didn't bring us the rewards we so rightly deserved. Play like that against the other sides in the relegation mix and we could yet see a wonderful end to the season.

The saga regarding Armando Quitirna seemed to be over on Monday 3rd February, as at midday the club issued the following statement;

Crawley Town Football Club would like to issue the following statement regarding the transfer speculation which concerns the Reds' attacking midfielder Armando.

Despite various online reports, a deal between Crawley Town Football Club and Club Atlético Talleres was never reached. Therefore, further reports which state that the deal fell through due to an issue with the paperwork are also false.

The club had received an initial approach from Club Atlético Talleres, and therefore Armando was not available for selection while the two clubs were in communication, which is standard transfer practice. The club wanted Armando to remain as a

Crawley player and are pleased that the 24-year-old will spend the rest of the 2024/25 campaign with the Red Devils.

Both the club and Armando remain committed to helping Crawley survive in League One this season, and we look forward to seeing him back in a Crawley shirt soon.

I hope so, as I also hope that our fan base welcome him back with open arms and ecstatic voices.

7th February 2025

Before the trip to Bolton and the hilariously named Tough Sheet stadium there were several things that arose, either on social media or in the press that, for the less discerning of our fans would no doubt have caused concern. The recent fans forum held just two days after the Mansfield victory gave worried and unworried fans their chance to air their views and question Chairman Preston Johnson and Vice Chairman Ben Levin on all aspects of the club. The vast majority of fans conducted themselves well, no matter what their opinions were, and showed respect for those with different standpoints. Unfortunately, not all knew how to conduct themselves properly and after the evening had finished there were reports of antisemitic behaviour from at least one person, presumably aimed at the vice chair. Writing this, whether you read it in the Crawley Observer, online at Sussex World or in this book, the day after attending a play about Corrie Ten Boom, a Christian lady from Holland who helped save numerous Jewish people in the last war, makes me wonder why this kind of bigotry is still in the air today. Look Corrie up online or read her life story The Hiding Place by herself and Elizabeth and John Sherill.

Also, in the last week I read the following about our club and thought to myself, well I won't write what I thought in fear of prejudging the outcome.

A professional football club has been accused of breaking the Modern Slavery Act by a former employee who was asked to work excessive hours. According to a report in The Guardian, London South employment tribunal is set to hear an unfair dismissal and age discrimination claim by a former kitman of Crawley Town FC

Suffice it to say that the word Slavery is highly immotive.

The last bit of news that concerned me in the week before the Bolton Wanderers game was the news of a last day of the window signing by Crawley Town. The player concerned is midfielder Liam Fraser, a Canadian midfielder who has played for his country 19 times. The fact that he hasn't, apparently, played for six months does make me wonder why we have signed him on a six-month contract as that would seemingly say that he is fit to play now and help in the fight against relegation. However, that concern doesn't make me tweet or X about it and as far as I am concerned, he should be made welcome around the club whether he proves to be a short-term signing or one for the future after he has achieved full fitness. Never write off anyone wearing the shirt, at least not until they deserve to be.

Players out in the window include Rafiq Khaleel, Dagenham and Redbridge bound to play under ex Red Devil Lewis Young and Jack Roles who is going out on loan till the end of the season at Robbie Elliot's old club, Gateshead. Good luck to them both and thanks for being a Devil.

8th February 2025 EFL1
Bolton Wanderers 4 Crawley Town 3
Bolton scorers Osei-Tulu (52), Murphy (68), Sheehan (85), BarkerOG (90+9)
CTFC scorers Hepburn-Murphy (50,62), Swan (54)
Rivals' Results EFL2
MK Dons 0 Bromley 1, Accrington Stanley 0 AFC Wimbledon 0

And so, to the game against Bolton Wanderers, in front of the largest league attendance we as a club have experienced. Just over 20,000 fans, including 258 Red Devils, watched an incredible match where at one point we were three one up, whilst having less possession than Bolton, but succumbed late on when Charlie Barker, unfortunately, sliced the ball into the net past Cox in our goal and we eventually lost four three. I would have loved to have stayed to show my appreciation of the effort put in by the lads but our train, which ironically turned up late, beckoned and an inexplicable 12 minutes of added on time in the second half alone made that impossible. We sunk a couple of places in the table but if we play like we did at Horwich against the teams around us in the league, then I think we might be alright.

11th February 2025 EFL1
Crawley Town 3 Stevenage 1
CTFC scorers Forster (50), Quitirna (87), Doyle (90+4)
Stevenage scorer Hanlan (53)
Rivals' results
Barrow 2 MK Dons 1, AFC Wimbledon 3 Crewe 0

What a difference two games make, just three little hours. Four points gained; four goals scored with all of them fantastic strikes, and several of the concerns involving players answered.

First of all, the New Town Derby against Stevenage produced a much-needed victory by three goals to one with Harry Forster opening the scoring on 50 minutes and Armando Quitirna seemingly scoring the winner in the 87th minute following a run and shot from Rushian Hepburn-Murphy, which the goalkeeper could only push in to the path of Armando. There were no signs of him not wanting to be at Crawley as he joyfully celebrated with the home fans, but for me the best was yet to come when Kamari Doyle scored the goal of the game four minutes into added on time, running forward from the halfway line before lashing the ball into the net left footed from just inside the penalty area. A wonderful victory which in a small way went to erasing the injustice of the last-minute defeats against Wrexham and Bolton Wanderers. The only downside of the win against the other New Towners was conceding the equaliser just three minutes after Forster had shot us into the lead.

We beat Stevenage when they were 12th in League One, so in my opinion this was a marker for how we must fear no team that we come up against in the fight to maintain our League One status and that is how we approached the game against second placed Wycombe Wanderers.

15th February 2025 EFL1
Crawley Town 1 Wycombe Wanderers 1
CTFC scorer Swan (5)
Wycombe scorer Udoh (20)
Rivals' results EFL 2
Tranmere Rovers 1 MK Dons 1*, AFC Wimbledon 1 Salford City 0

    Having lost to them twice already this season, one nil in the away League game in October and by two goals to one in the EFL Trophy in November we knew it would be a tough game, and it needed a stunning goal from Will Swan in the 5th minute to earn us a share of the spoils as Udoh equalised for the Chairboys in the 20th minute. There is no denying that this was a vastly different kind of performance than that shown against Stevenage, as we had to defend resolutely throughout against a team worthy of their second in the league status, but in my opinion, it was a point won rather than two lost.

    The crowd was 4330 with about 3000 of them being Red Devils and following a second half played by Liam Fraser, our new Canadian signing rumoured to be unfit and some more valuable minutes played by Armando, seemingly not Argentina bound as yet, a good friend of mine gave me the following idea. It is meant as a lighthearted look at our owners, their supporters and objectors.

    A fly on the wall report from the latest meeting of the People's Front for the Liberation of Crawley Town FC.

Anti: And what have WAGMI ever given us ?!
Fan: Promotion to League 1?
Anti: What?
Fan: And our first day out at Wembley
Anti: Oh, Yeah, yeah, they did give us that. Uh, that's true. Yeah.
Fan 2: Good training facilities.
Fan 3: Oh yeah, remember the 3G at Horsham and the dog poo at Bewbush?
Anti: Yeah. All right. I'll grant you the promotion and the training facilities are two things that Wagmi have done.
Fan 4: And the improved food outlets

Anti: Well yeah. Obviously the food outlets, I mean, the food outlets go without saying, don't they? But apart from the promotion, the training facilities, and the food outlets
Fan 5: Better fan interaction.
Fan 6: A record-breaking play off scoreline
Anti and friends: Huh? Heh? Huh...
Fan 7: Self-serve beer pumps.
Anti's friends: Ohhh
Anti: Yeah, yeah. All right. Fair enough.
Fan 8: Bigger attendances and cheap tickets.
Anti's friends: Oh, yes. Yeah...
Fan 9: Yeah. Yeah, that's something we'd really miss, Anti, if Wagmi left. Huh.
Anti: All right, but apart from promotion, a day out at Wembley, training facilities, improved food outlets, good fan interaction, a record-breaking playoff scoreline, self-serve beer pumps, bigger attendances and cheap tickets, what have Wagmi ever done for us?

Tongue in cheek, yes, but worth thinking about. Thanks to Ivan Noel and his mate Monty.

*Danilo Orsi scored his first goal for MK Dons whilst on loan from Burton Albion, wearing an all-red strip and celebrating in the usual Orsi way. Some fans are calling their team the Crawley Dons, since the addition of Orsi to Maguire, Kelly and Williams to their ranks and Danilo had this to say to Toby Lock of the MK Citizen after the game at Tranmere.

"There are a few of us here now, and a few people on Twitter (Or is it X?) are calling us the Crawley Dons, but we're not looking at it like that. We're at MK Dons now, it's a big club and we all want to get it back to where we think it belongs...... Last year is done, it's about right here, right now. People can say what they want but it's all about MK Dons now. Coming into a club where you know a few players and the manager as well helps massively because you know the demands. That has helped me bed in a bit quicker than if I didn't know anyone. It's a massive club and we want to get back to where we belong."

Sorry Danilo, is it where you think they belong or where they actually belong? Clubs belong where they are based on points alone and not on their spending power or the whims of where their board think they should be. Anyway, Merton has its own set of Dons now, who, at the time of writing, are doing better than the Buckinghamshire version.

18th February 2025 EFL1
Crawley Town 1 Wigan Athletic 1
CTFC scorer Barker (42)
Wigan scorer Taylor (39)
Rivals' results EFL2
Fleetwood 0 AFC Wimbledon 0

    Another point towards whatever total we finish with against a side containing Ronan Darcy, ex Red Devil, the white Pele and, according to some Crawley fans, a legend. Don't get me wrong, I liked Ronan but he was with us for just 66 games scoring six goals, important though they were, but a legend? I'm not so sure. True, he laid the chance on a plate for Taylor to open the scoring for the Latics and he seemed to have been playing for them for a long time in the manner he marshalled their midfield, but he's gone now and the Pele song that was sang in his direction at the end of the game from the South Terrace should be the last time we acknowledge him as being once a Red Devil.

    We have new players now who may or may not reach some of the standards of the 2023/2024 team but all the time they play with guts and determination, as shown against Wycombe and Wigan they deserve the applause they rightly received at the end of the game against the Lancashire side. Having let in quick goals after having scored in numerous games this season, it was very pleasing to reverse that against Wigan and what a very special goal it was. Scored by Charlie Barker from out on the right, it rocketed into the net and will join goals by Ibrahim, Showunmi, Quitirna, Swann and Hepburn-Murphy in what will be the goal of the season competition to end all goal of the season competitions. Three home games, five points gained and, with only eight games left at Broadfield, we will need to ensure we at least equal that return from them if we are to achieve the great escape. From the home games alone, that would get us up to around 42 points needing at least eight points from seven away games involving trips to Blackpool, Lincoln, Huddersfield, Rotherham, Stevenage, Birmingham and Shrewsbury to achieve the 50-point target so often mentioned as being necessary to stay up. A tall order perhaps, but one that would be made easier if we turned the remaining eight home games, five of which are against the four teams directly above the drop zone, into home wins.

22nd February 2025 EFL1
Blackpool 3 Crawley Town 1
Blackpool scorers Ennis (10,18), Evans (80P)
CTFC scorer Doyle (30)
Rivals' results EFL2
Bradford City 2 MK Dons 0, Colchester United 1 AFC Wimbledon 1

As I settled down to listen to the Blackpool game whilst watching England play Australia in the cricket (who says men can't multitask?) Gary Smith commented that Blackpool hadn't won at home since September, and we hadn't won on a Saturday since beating Rotherham in November, I just knew something had to give, and when Ennis had put the tangerine clad Blackpool two up in the first eighteen minutes it seemed that it would be us on the wrong side of a mauling. Doyle pulled one back on the half hour though and when Blackpool's Fletcher was sent off just two minutes later, I rather foolishly thought we could win. However, it was not to be, and when Blackpool extended their lead with just ten minutes to go, even my red tinted specs couldn't see us coming back. This leaves us on 29 points with 32 games played and with Burton winning away at Lincoln and Cambridge beating Stockport at home we have seemingly lost all that we had gained in the last three matches. Deep breaths everyone, ten points cover the bottom nine clubs, and we have to play four of them at home as well as Cambridge United next Saturday and Shrewsbury away on the last day of the season.

To add insult to injury England lost to Australia and as I'm finishing this article England's Rugby Union team are losing to the auld enemy, albeit with the second half to come.

Back to the Red Devils, let's hope a week on the training ground will lead to a performance and result against Cambridge

United on St. David's Day that puts us in good stead for the game away to Lincoln on the 4th of March. Heads up, chests out, we can still do this!!!!!!!!

As far as our so-called rivals from the division below are concerned, AFC Wimbledon, with ex Red Devil James Tilley, stand in the last of the automatic promotion places just ahead of two other ex-Crawley Town players, Tsaroulla and Gordon, and Notts County on goal difference only. MK Dons, with the whole of last year's Red Devils' coaching staff and four players in Maguire, Kelly, Williams and Orsi, lie in 17th place on thirty-nine points. They are, however, equidistant in terms of points between the last play-off position and the relegation spots. In comparison, at this point last season after the same number of games, 32, Scott Lindsey's Red Devils were in 14th place and had accrued seven points more which this season would have had Crawley Town on the verge of the play-offs much earlier than we were.

Hope you all understood that? I did, at least when I wrote it.

Last week, my son, David, moved out of Crawley to live in Hove actually. At some point in helping him move I must have tweaked my back, and it was so bad Tuesday evening that I took myself to the UTC at Crawley Hospital. Just two hours after arriving, I had been triaged, seen by a doctor and sent on my way complete with the sort of pill you don't swallow and a prescription for heavy duty painkillers to pick up from my local pharmacy. Arriving back home I tried to watch some football, Stoke City v Middlesbrough, when I saw Northampton v Barnsley was also available to watch. The Cobblers, happily for us at Crawley, lost two one, not having quite enough to come back from two nil down despite the Tykes having a player sent off with three minutes of normal time and nine of added on time left. The "happily for us" comment is because the result just about keeps them in our sights. Northampton in 17th with 36 points from 33 games, and Crawley in 22nd with 29 from 32. Winning the game in hand and beating the Cobblers in our last home game of the season could take the fight for survival right to the last day against Shrewsbury, that is if we haven't secured our status before then. To do this we must, of course, also win more games before then but with four of our home games being against teams in 18th, 19th, 20th and 24th there should be no reason why we can't do it.

Saturday 1st March 2025 EFL1
Crawley Town 0 Cambridge United 2
Cambridge scorers DoyleOG (33), Digby 64)
CTFC Red card Hepburn- Murphy (60)
Cambridge Red card Gibbons (66)
Rivals' results EFL2
AFC Wimbledon 0 Bromley 1, MK Dons 0 Colchester United 1.*

And then came the Cambridge United game which was, it has to be said, played between two poor teams, officiated by an unbiased but poor referee and lost us the chance to take advantage of one of those games at home against a team below us. We lost, which I can accept, but to lose because we didn't get enough shots on target, one out of seventeen attempts and that coming in the last ten minutes. We bossed possession but didn't take advantage of that fact and as a result we are now in the depths of a real fight to maintain our League 1 status because of two sloppy goals given away and a lack of attacking endeavour.

Barnsley beat our opponents on Tuesday 4th of March, Lincoln City whilst Bristol Rovers lost at home to Rotherham United. Burton Albion drew with Mansfield Town, as did Exeter City and Northampton Town. The Posh beating Shrewsbury being the result that, thankfully for the time being, keeps Crawley from the nadir of the League 1 table.

With Crawley not fancied to get positive results against Lincoln City away, Reading FC at home and Huddersfield away in our next three games, it will need us to produce some incredible form in the remaining ten games, six of which are at home, if we are to stay up.

Now is not the time for division between the fans, the club and the team, as a concerted effort is needed from all in the remaining thirteen games of the season. Who knows? By the time you read this in print on Wednesday we may have secured an unlikely victory at Sincil Bank against the Imps, James Collins and all.

A draw or win at Lincoln would set us up with renewed appetite for next Saturday's game against the Royals of Reading and the only thing that I would suggest to Robbie Elliot is that people would rather us have two forwards on the pitch at home and go down, if we must, fighting to score goals rather than bossing possession and only getting one shot on target, as we did against Cambridge United.

*The defeat at home against Colchester United proved too much for Mk Dons, and as a result they have sacked head coach Scott Lindsey. The loss was MK's 11th in 16 League Two matches dating back to mid-December. While they managed two wins in January, MK had picked up just nine points from a possible 48 during that dire sequence, which had seen them slip to 17th in the table. Scott was in charge for just over five months since leaving us, dropping a division to take over a club with supposedly more potential. He led them to third in the table in December 2024 after overseeing six successive wins, but this was followed by a poor run since then that had seen them drop well out of the promotion race.

His departure was announced on the MK Dons website the day after their defeat at home to Colchester. Scott spoke defiantly after the game yesterday, the result which left them 16 points adrift of the play-off spots and only 13 points above the relegation places.

"It's really clear to me the players are really fighting and didn't deserve that today, We are really hurting in there at the moment because of the run of form, in terms of results. I don't want them to get down about it. Of course we are, it's natural, but we have a big game on Tuesday and we have to dust ourselves down. We can't feel sorry for ourselves. We have to stick together, work hard and stay focused. I'm pleased there is a game on Tuesday where we can put it right."

Despite that though, they must now travel to League Two strugglers Accrington Stanley without Scott in charge.

Meanwhile, back at Crawley Town nothing much has happened since our defeat against Cambridge United......except for our Supporters representative on the board resigning, rumours that Tobias Phoenix, our Director of Football, seemingly offering a supporter outside after the game and some supporters speculating on a return to the Broadfield for Scott Lindsey, following his departure from our supposed rivals, MK.

Dealing with each in turn, I can't see the point in resigning from representing the supporters on the board of directors at a time when that person is concerned about how the club is being run, unless there are personal issues involved, and, to be fair, there was.

The next matter re offering people outside depends on how the fans started the discussion with the "men in the posh seats" I suppose, as to whether or not the response was appropriate or whether it was meant as it was received. The response from the Club seems to insinuate that the invitation was for a chat and not, as suggested, a fight.

As for Scott Lindsey returning to Crawley Town, as the Crawley Observer's Mark Dunford has stated, there is no vacancy at the club for a manager. Now, we all know that can change but what would really be the point at this moment in time. Surely, we should be trying to settle the nerves of the only people who can get us to safety in League 1, the players and coaches.

Tuesday 4th March 2025

Sitting down to watch tonight's game on Sky, Posh are away to Blackpool, Cambridge at home to Stevenage, Mansfield home to Wigan, the Cobblers home to Stockport whilst Shrewsbury entertain Bristol Rovers, and the Brewers visit Wycombe. I know it's down to what we do against the Imps, but it would also help our cause if Blackpool, Stevenage, Stockport and Wycombe were to win, with the game between the Shrews and the Gas being the only one where any result might be acceptable.

EFL1
Lincoln City 4 Crawley Town 1
Lincoln scorers Collins (14), Makama (24), Jeffries (32), Gardner (88)
CTFC scorer Doyle (6)
Rivals' results EFL2
Accrington Stanley 2 Mk Dons 0, Morecambe 1 AFC Wimbledon 0

Well, after having taken the lead early on when Swan fed Barker and he in turn passed the ball into an empty space for Doyle to score, it all went downhill from then on. James Collins scored, showing why he is still a class forward at League 1 level, in the 13th minute and then unfortunately our heads seemed to drop and by half time it was all over. Having said that, if we had scored a second goal early after the break then perhaps, we might have found renewed spirit and made a contest out of the game. Looking behind the scenes as to team selection it is important to note that we were without Fraser, Ibrahim and Camara with new injuries, Mullarkey, Kelly and Flint with injuries we already knew about, and Harry Forster was on the bench. Surely, if he had been 100% fit, he would have been included in the starting eleven, wouldn't he? In addition to all that, Dion Conroy was substituted in the 64th minute with what looked like a groin injury. Away from injuries, we also had Rushian Hepburn-Murphy and Tola Showunmi starting the first of their three game suspensions due to a red card issued against Cambridge during the game and one issued after the game. When you're down, everything seems to go against you and that must be overcome on Saturday. The only slightly good news on Tuesday was that no other club in the bottom eight managed to win.

8th March 2025 EFL1
Crawley Town 1 Reading 1
CTFC scorer Camara (90)
Reading scorer Ehibhatiomhan (29)
Rivals' results EFL2
AFC Wimbledon 2 Notts County 0, with James Tilley scoring for the Dons and coming out on top over Nick Tsraoulla's Notts County.
MK Dons 2 Morecambe 1, with Orsi scoring the winner as Ben Gladwin provides the new, if only temporary, new coach bounce with four more ex Red Devils in their squad, Trueman, Maguire, Kelly and Williams.

Being one of the early kick off games on an unusually warm March Day, it was good to see Toby Mullarkey back in the side from the start, alongside Liam Fraser, with Camara and Ibrahim on the bench. Harry Forster however was not included in the squad but at least it looks like we are beginning to get back some players who could affect our results. Reading were well supported by a sellout away end and took the lead on 29 minutes when Harvey Knibbs fed Ehibhatiomhan and he stroked the ball in from close range and in a position which suspiciously looked offside. Crawley though were competing well, and it was hard to tell who the side fighting for their League 1 status were, as opposed to who were chasing a playoff position. Panutche Camara salvaged a point for the Red Devils in the last minute, scoring with a deft touch from close range after being fed by Doyle, but as per usual home fans were left in dismay when the referee, Charles Brakespeare, blew up for the end of four minutes added on time just as Will Swan smashed the ball into the net for what would have been a fantastic victory. Robbie Elliot was booked for dissent, because of his protestations, by the official, but really, he had every right to question the decision as Camara's goal came just after the additional time had been shown meaning there should have been at least five minutes added on instead of the four that was displayed.

In the games involving other teams in the relegation maelstrom, Cambridge United, Burton and Shrewsbury all lost but the chasm between the bottom four, including my beloved Crawley Town, and the safety of 20th, appears not to be getting any smaller. Hopefully, completing our first double of the season against Charlton will have kick started an unstoppable run of form, that will have us revving our motorbikes Steve McQueen style, by the time you read this in print.

11th March 2025
Having just watched the preview for the game against Charlton this evening I am encouraged that the injury crisis seems to be easing, and that Jeremy Kelly might feature in some capacity against the team from Southeast London.
EFL1
Crawley Town 0 Charlton Athletic 1
Charlton scorer Small(31)
Rivals' results EFL2
AFC Wimbledon 1 Cheltenham Town 2

After another encouraging performance against Charlton, but an ultimately disappointing result, we had to go to Huddersfield just four days later and try and get something out of the game in terms of points rather than just a feeling that we played well. The game against an improved Charlton Athletic team saw us perform well but with no reward and we paid the price for one slip in concentration in the first half. The encouraging part of the evening was being able to see nearly all our injured players taking part in the game, including Jeremy Kelly who has been sorely missed in recent times. Despite the result and Bristol Rovers and Exeter winning, Cambridge United lost as did Mansfield which leaves us needing wins urgently if we are to climb out of the drop zone.

Saturday 15th March 2025 EFL1
Huddersfield Town 5 Crawley Town 1
Huddersfield scorers
Taylor (3) Barker OG (8) Marshall (16) Pearson (29) Roosken (76)
CTFC scorers Adeyemo (90+6)
Rivals' results EFL2
Carlisle 1 AFC Wimbledon 2 (3rd place in automatic promotion spot) PortVale 3 MK Dons 0 (18th but 12 points above relegation)

The Stags, managed by our old "friend" Nigel "I'll never have to come back to Crawley again" Clough are without a win since January 4th and have lost nine times in that run of thirteen games including against each of the current bottom four. They are however, eleven points above Crawley at kick off time on Saturday and would have to lose another four whilst we have a run of four wins if we were to catch them. (Make that five and five as they won against Barnsley).

The Cambridge United versus Peterborough United game, which kicked off early at 1230, was nil-nil at half time and had seen us drop a place to 23rd, that was if points were awarded at half time. However, just as the Crawley Town starting lineup was announced at 2pm, Edun scored for the Posh with a delightfully placed free kick which is how the score was to remain, lifting Darren Ferguson's side up to 17th before everyone else, except for Bolton Wanderers and Stockport County, had kicked off. The Lolos versus Addai game ended in a one nil away win for County, consolidating their place in the play offs and giving a chance for our opponents, Huddersfield Town, to leapfrog the Wanderers into the last playoff place, if they were to beat us later in the afternoon.

The Crawley Town team included Jeremy Kelly and Tola Showunmi in the starting lineup and named Josh Flint as a substitute for the first time since his injury against the Cobblers back in October. Apparently, the Terriers hadn't scored at home since Boxing Day, but it only took them three minutes to breach our defences for the first time and just nine minutes to go two nil up. Sixteen minutes and the game had gone as the Terriers went three up, and even I am getting fearful, not only about today's result but also about any chance we had of escaping the drop. Twenty-nine minutes gone and a free header makes it four nil. One has to wonder how a team can succumb as easily as this, especially after two reasonable performances and if you thought it couldn't get any worse, we will have no goalkeeper next week because Woollacott will be on international duty with Ghana.

The second half saw Camara, Fraser, Swan and Kelly replaced by Adeyemo, Hepburn-Murphy, Armando and Flint, and although Huddersfield were limited to just one more goal this could well be a defining negative moment in our fight against relegation.......and then Adeyemo scores with the last kick of the game to rapturous applause from the travelling fans.

On the plus side, if there can be one or even two, we did draw the second half and Bristol Rovers lost by five against Lincoln City. Next game at the Broadfield? Bristol Rovers next Saturday.

Waking up on Sunday morning after a Saturday I would rather forget I am challenged to find a reason to believe that WE can find a way out of the situation we are in. I don't believe a change in owners or manager at this point would make any difference as to whether we stay up or go down. What is needed is a conscious effort by all who love our club to do their utmost to gain as many points as possible out of the remaining nine games.

I realise that these words will not be read until after the event but if you are a football fan you must surely realise that, as sure as the sun comes up every morning, times like we are going through at this moment will occur again.

Saturday 22nd March 2025 EFL1
Crawley Town 1 Bristol Rovers 0
Doyle (19)
Rivals' results
AFC Wimbledon 2 Barrow 2, Cheltenham 0 MK Dons 1
The Wombles still in 3rd despite conceding equaliser in 92nd minute and Mk Dons stop the rot.

You go away for a couple of days to attend a funeral of a friend's auntie and all hell breaks loose. The funeral was in Truro, and it was good to meet some football supporters (male relatives of the deceased) who knew about Crawley Town and wished us luck for the fight for survival. One of them was a Cardiff supporter with his own relegation worries but a couple were Truro City fans with worries of a different kind, as they are currently in second place in the National League South, just below Worthing. As far as Crawley Town are concerned, I heard of Robbie Elliott's departure just as we arrived in Truro on Wednesday evening and to be honest, I was not entirely surprised with the news, if a little about the timing of it. Having a day to think about it whilst in Truro, my thoughts went to how the interim head coach and his assistant would be feeling, and whether they could rally the players to perform an almost impossible escape act and then I get a message that Scott Lindsey is back in charge on a three year contract. My thoughts are mixed to say the least, but only because of the fact we are points behind, in terms of survival, and even Scott may find it hard to achieve the requisite number of wins in the nine games left. I accept that if we were relegated the prospect of having a whole season with him in charge would help keep supporters behind the club, but I hope the owners have ensured that his contract to June 2028 is watertight and that they will give him the resources to keep him loyal to Crawley Town. I am Mr. Optimistic and hopefully Scott's rejoining our great club will somehow revitalise the team and help eclipse last season's success at Wembley and then we can go for the League 1 playoffs next season.

And after having written that on the eve of the Bristol Rovers game and sitting down to write the first installment of what would truly be "The Greatest Escape" my optimism is growing by the minute. Not to the extent that I am 100% certain of staying in League 1, but whatever happens I am now confident that next season will be one that we can all look forward to whether we stay up and consolidate our place in League 1 or whether we take part in another promotion season in League 2.

The first half against the Gas should really have seen us go in at the break with more than the one goal lead. As it was, our single goal was one of pure beauty, created by Rushian Hepburn-Murphy and scored by Kamari Doyle after it looked like Rushian had taken on, and beaten, the whole of the Rovers side. The second half was more tense as we successfully held on to our lead and survived seven minutes of added on time and now sit in 22nd place still, but with the margin between us and safety down to nine points and goal difference. Northampton lost today while Cambridge United dropped two points when Barnsley equalised in the 92nd minute. Our remaining games are against two top half of the table teams in Birmingham (A) and Leyton Orient (H) six bottom half teams in Rotherham (A), Peterborough (H), Stevenage (A), Exeter and Northampton (H) and Shrewsbury (A). No predictions from me but next week's game against Steve Evans' Rotherham followed by the home game against the Posh could well define our season.

Come on you rip roaring Reds!!!!

Tuesday 25th March 2025 EFL2
Rivals' results Carlisle United 2 MK Dons 2
Saturday 29th March 2025 EFL1
Rotherham United 0 Crawley Town 4
CTFC scorers Doyle (23,52) Holohan (84) Camara (87)
Rivals' results EFL2 MK Dons 2 (1 goal for Danilo Orsi) Fleetwood 4, Walsall 1 AFC Wimbledon 1. (AFC in 5th place,

two points below 3rd and MK back in 17th, but 13 points above Morecambe in 23rd place.)

Two days after the great result against Bristol Rovers I heard of the passing of a wonderful lady who has been connected with Crawley Town since the 1960s after her and husband, Les, moved to the New Town with Edwards High Vacuum back in the late 40s /early 50s. I am of course referring to Audrey Turnbull. Audrey will be sorely missed, not just by her blood family but by the Crawley town family as well.

I wrote this on Sunday 30th March 2025 at 9am, or was it 10am, after a night of celebration with fellow Red Devil Bill Webber and his wife Jane, who were celebrating their Golden Wedding anniversary in Redz, and one of the talking points was how Crawley had showed they were up for the fight by demolishing Rotherham four nil. We talked about football and of growing up in Crawley and I met their daughter Sarah, who had been in my tutor group at ICC about 30 years ago. She herself is now a teacher and is on the verge of becoming a grandparent. That made me feel a little old, but I was overjoyed, upon leaving for home, when the team coach rolled into the stadium car park, and I was able to congratulate some of the players and management on a wonderful result. I may be a little kid at heart despite the advancing years.

To win against Bristol Rovers last Tuesday in Scott's first match in charge was vitally important but even I did not expect us to go to the New York stadium just four days later and demolish Steve Evans' Rotherham as completely as we did. Kamari Doyle is proving invaluable in our fight to maintain our League One status; his two goals being struck with deadly accuracy before Gavin Holahan and Panutche Camara wrapped the result up in the last few minutes. How Brighton must have wished for just one of his goals as they succumbed in the FA Cup against Nottingham Forest.

To make our result even more valuable, there were no other winners in the bottom ten clubs, with only Northampton Town, Cambridge United and Wigan Athletic picking up single points. There is a full fixture list on Tuesday 1st April which will see Burton at home to in-form Leyton Orient, Cambridge at home to

Wrexham, the Red Devils trying to win three in a row for the first time this season at home to the Posh, whilst the Shrews visit Wycombe Wanderers. If the results of those matches all go our way, we will still be in the relegation places, but in 21st place and looking up at the four or five teams just above us and with two of them, Northampton and Exeter City, still to visit the Broadfield.

The gap on Mothers Day between us and safety was down to just six points and hopefully by 10pm on Tuesday that will have been whittled down to just three points and the Great escape will really be on. One thing for sure is that if we fail in our efforts to escape, at least we will have gone down fighting till the end.

I am a season ticket holder so will be at the remaining four home games standing in Torres Corner with my family and friends and I will also be at Stevenage next Saturday, Birmingham on Good Friday and Shrewsbury on the last day of the season. I know that all of you who love Crawley Town will do your utmost to attend as many of these games as you can to cheer on the lads to what could be a wonderful end to the season.

Mick Fox and I will be staging an exhibition at Crawley Museum between Thursday 17th July and Saturday 16th August, which is tentatively titled "Great Escape 1,2 and 3?" and will tell the story of the last two- and a-bit seasons. I just hope that we can delete the question mark before it opens.

Tuesday 1st April 2025 EFL1
Crawley Town 3 Peterborough Utd 4
CTFC scorers Quitirna (12) Kelly(33), Hepburn-Murphy (49)
Peterborough scorers Odoh (22,29,42) Jade-Jones (90+7P)
Rivals' results EFL2 Swindon Town 2 AFC Wimbledon 1

Wednesday 2nd April 2025 EFL2
Rivals' results Notts County 3 MK Dons 0

Saturday 5th April 2025 EFL1
Stevenage 3 Crawley Town 1
Stevenage scorers White (20), Reed (89), Kemp (90+1)
CTFC scorer Ibrahim (70)
Rivals' results 5th placed AFC Wimbledon 1 Harrogate 0, 19th placed MK Dons 0 Barrow 3

After the tremendous result at Rotherham, Crawley succumbed to Peterborough in what was probably one of the best games ever seen at our level of football. We led once, came back twice and then lost out in added time on top of added time. Having recovered from the first defeat under Scott Lindsey in his return, I set off for Stevenage with my family and over 600 other Red Devils for the New Town Derby. I am not going to talk much about the football in this week's article as we all know, those who were there that is, that we did not perform with anywhere near the same intensity displayed against the Posh. Going into the ground we had been buoyed by the result from Wrexham which saw the Welsh side beat Burton Albion by three goals to nil, but it was soon apparent that Stevenage were not going to treat us lightly and went ahead with a free kick in the first half, and although we equalised in the second half when Jack Roles crossed for Bradley Ibrahim to score, we didn't see the game out and succumbed to two goals in the 89th and 91st minutes.

Are we relegated? Not yet. However, the task has got a lot harder now and realistically we will probably have to win all our remaining games, including away to Birmingham and Shrewsbury.

Can we do it? Well, we certainly won't if we start haranguing our players when things aren't going our way. "You're not fit to wear the shirt" chants would not encourage me to play any better, if in my wildest dreams I had been good enough to wear the shirt in the first place. What we can do, and Scott himself mentioned it in his after-match interview, is stay united and all pull in the same direction. The Orient are next at the Broadfield, followed by the trip to St. Andrews, two home games against Exeter and Northampton and the last day out at Shrewsbury, so let's stay up or go down, fighting till the end, all doing our best, whether it's in coaching, playing or supporting.

On Saturday, at Stevenage, I was disappointed in the result but what upset me even more was the lack of effective stewarding in allowing some of our supporters to stand in the aisles between the blocks of seats, thus blocking the view of many of their fellow supporters. What made this even worse was that the supporters should have shown more respect to their fellow fans, being that they were not youngsters and should be setting an example to those who they purport to represent. There were seats aplenty for all the 600 plus of our fans, so a little bit more consideration next time please.

Sad to say that wasn't the only part of the day that caused me grief, as on the train home a group of our supporters lowered the name and the reputation of our club and town by using offensive language (and I do mean very offensive) in a carriage containing both young and old people who were just part of the travelling public. Their behaviour got so bad that I felt compelled to quietly ask them to respect their fellow travelers and to accept our defeat quietly. They did not comply and for the first time in my life I was ashamed of people from my town.

To the person who wrote on my ticket envelope, "Make us dream", thank you, and to other Red Devils who were moved to mention the behaviour of some of our fans on Facebook, there are more fans who know how to support properly than those who don't and I'll see you on Saturday.

Saturday 12th April 2025 EFL1
Crawley Town 1 Leyton Orient 3
CTFC scorer Quitirna (49P)
Orient scorers Kelman (52, 53P) Donley (90+2)
Rivals' results EFL 2
Doncaster 1 AFC Wimbledon 1 (3 points below 3rd but 4 above 8th) Gillingham 1 MK Dons 0 (Gills safe in League 2, well done Joe Comper).

Well, that was a crazy four minutes, wasn't it? However, before I get to the game and the situation we find ourselves in, I must first of all mention the introduction of the latest tee shirts worn by the young ladies who serve in Redz. They bore the phrase "Achieve the unachievable" and up until about five past four yesterday I firmly believed we were going to do that. That was, of course, when Junior Quitirna expertly struck the penalty in the 49th minute which put us one nil up and, for three wonderful minutes, the Red Devils were staying up. However, in the 52nd and 53rd minutes Leyton Orient took full advantage of a defensive error and a penalty to turn the game around and go two one up. No matter what was tried in substitutions and an increase in effort, that was how it remained until the O's scored the third goal in added on time.

We are still just six points from safety, but our precarious position has us now looking over the precipice whilst having to hold on with our blood-stained fingertips to League 1 status. Cambridge United and Shrewsbury are still below us, having lost at home to Charlton and drawn away at Lincoln respectively. The two places above us, however, have changed with Burton's emphatic victory against Huddersfield taking them out of the bottom four at Bristol Rovers' expense. The Gas lost at home to Exeter City and, having a worse goal difference than Burton Albion, now occupy 21st place six points above us and with a six-goal superior goal difference.

To make things even worse, Burton have five games left to play, one more than Crawley Town and Bristol Rovers.

Theoretically, and without the aid of a super brain, AI or a fortune teller, no club from 15th position down is mathematically safe, but realistically three relegation places, assuming the Shrews are doomed, are still to be avoided by six clubs. We would have to win all four of our games to endanger either Mansfield or Northampton, both being on 47 points, one less than the maximum we can achieve.

Whilst it would be highly amusing to see Mansfield (sorry Nigel) take one of the three places we all want to avoid, the four clubs who are in most jeopardy are the Brewers (42 pts from 41 played), the Gas (42 from 42), the Red Devils (36 from 42) and Cambridge United (35 from 42).

On Good Friday, we are away to a team who will having nothing to play for except pride, in Birmingham City, whilst the other three are also away, but to teams who still need points for varying reasons, Exeter City, Wrexham and Huddersfield.

I'm going for Brum to be overhung from celebrating their Championship, which they achieved yesterday (Saturday) without having to kick a ball, and which I hope both our team and fans will acknowledge in the right way, before securing a much needed three points by being the only team to have won at St. Andrews. I hope all who travel to the game have a safe and fruitful journey and that all who can't make the trip can find a television to watch the game on. I will not be there for personal reasons.

We aren't down yet, no reason to tear up your season ticket (not much of a gesture anyway, with only two games to play) and no reason to boo or demean the players no matter the result.

Of course, after the Holy weekend we will be either deep in despair or looking forward to the Cobblers at home and Shrewsbury away.

Keep the faith

18th April 2025 EFL1
Birmingham City 0 Crawley Town 0
Rivals' results EFL2
MK Dons 0 Newport County 0, AFC Wimbledon 0 Chesterfield 0

21st April 2025 EFL1
Crawley Town 3 Exeter City 1
CTFC scorers Hepburn-Murphy (7, 23), Camara (9)
Exeter scorer Watts (25) Francis Red Card (89)
Rivals' results EFL2
Crewe Alexandra 0 MK Dons 1, Gillingham 1 AFC Wimbledon 0 (marking the Gills second victory over a "Dons" side in the last three games)

Are we going down? Maybe, even probably, but we aren't down yet, are we? I know one Crawley fan thinks we are, as he said there was more likelihood of him being able to dance naked with Kyle Minouge than there was of us staying up. (Editor, please don't correct my spelling of the antipodean, as I am not sure whether he meant Kylie Minogue or Kyle Minouge).

I watched the game from St. Andrews with my son in law and grandson and we were impressed with the commitment shown by the Red Devils, both on and off the pitch. Rushian will know he should have scored in the second half but that might have spurred City on, and they may have beaten us. We should not forget either the incredible goals he has scored from almost impossible positions. All the team came out with immense credit by gaining the point against the Champions, none more so than Toby Steward, our eighth goalkeeper of the season, making his full EFL debut and helping us achieve a clean sheet.

We aren't down yet and after the game against Exeter City, that is still how it stands. Three goals in the first twenty-three minutes for the Red Devils appeared to put the game beyond the Grecians but they struck back in the 25th minute which must have had fans remembering the game over Christmas at St Jame's Park where Exeter came back from four one down to take a point. Crawley's goals came from Rushian Hepburn-Smith and Panutche Camara and the people in the stands started to ask the question; Can we escape? As it stands after the trip to Birmingham and the win against Exeter we are not doomed, as Birmingham City found their shooting boots at the Pirelli (or whatever it's called now) to beat Burton, and that, combined with away wins for Stevenage and Orient against the Gas and Cambridge United respectively. has put us in with a real chance of performing the Great Escape

I took good heart and encouragement from the choice of exit music I heard at a funeral service last Thursday. Composed by Elmer Bernstein, it was of course the theme tune to The Great Escape, and it was good to hear it echoing around the stadium as we went into added time and awaited the final whistle.

The remaining games for Crawley are both against teams with nothing to play for but pride, Northampton at home on Saturday 26th April and Shrewsbury away on the 3rd of May, and if we were to win both that would put us on forty-six points. Cambridge United play Burton Albion this Saturday which provided we win ourselves would suit us to be a draw. Bristol Rovers are at home to Reading who are challenging for a play-off place.

Burton would then play their game in hand against Wigan on the 29th, leaving the final day of the season with us at already relegated Shrewsbury, Cambridge at home to the Champions, Bristol Rovers away to Blackpool and Burton away to Charlton Athletic. We would still need both the Gas and the Brewers to drop points, but hey, it's possible, isn't it?

Everything will be ok in the end, and if it isn't ok, then it's not the end!!

Go down or stay up, Crawley Town, my team, our team, will still be here next season as will I, but whether Kyle or Kylie will be dancing in the buff, remains to be seen.

26th April 2025 EFL1
Crawley Town 3 Northampton Town 0
CTFC scorers Hepburn-Smith (39), Kelly (66), Doyle (88)
Rivals' results EFL2
AFC Wimbledon 0 PortVale 2, MK Dons 0 Grimsby 0

I could go on forever about how it isn't over yet, but instead I am going to make the following statements.

I, Steve Leake, am an optimist.

I, Steve Leake, have supported Crawley Town since 1956.

Putting those two statements together, I am very optimistic about Crawley Town for the 2025/2026 season, regardless of which division we find ourselves in, and as a result I am looking forward to completing (God willing) my seventieth year of being a Red Devil supporter.

If you were one of the 5,105 spectators in the ground yesterday you would have joined in the salute to someone who won't be on the "terraces" next year, the one and only "Travel" Ken Blackmore. Ken, the whole CTFC family will miss you greatly, whether it's for your work around the club, your partnership with Gary Smith on away commentaries or just for being you.

After the tribute to a true Crawley Town stalwart, an unchanged side from the team that beat Exeter City on Easter Monday set about the job of keeping the club in League One. Whether they knew that Bristol Rovers had already lost to play-off chasing Reading, I don't know, but it was apparent from the start that they were up for the challenge and superb goals from Rushian Hepburn-Smith, Jeremy Kelly and Camari Doyle secured a victory for the Red Devils. The only thing that could spoil the day would be a win for the Brewers against fellow strugglers, Cambridge United. Just before half time, in their game at the Pirelli stadium, both sides had a player sent off in separate incidents, which meant their game would not finish at the same time as ours.

The Brewers took the lead in the 48th minute which, if that is how the game ended, would have meant that we couldn't catch them without a thirteen-goal swing in goal difference in our favour. Then in the space of about another eight minutes the situation changed twice. First of all, as our game ended in victory, Neil Harris's Cambridge United scored an equaliser which for a moment meant that we could catch the Albion, if we won at Shrewsbury and they dropped points in their remaining two games. Unfortunately, just as our players were starting their end of season lap of honour another score came through from Staffordshire, and unfortunately it was to be a winner for the Albion.

This now means that Burton would have to lose both their remaining games whilst we beat Shrewsbury and for there to be that thirteen-goal swing in goal difference previously mentioned. Something like Burton to lose by two at home to Wigan and by four at Charlton, whilst we record our highest ever EFL victory at Shrewsbury be seven goals.

I will be at Shrewsbury, whatever the situation we find ourselves in, as will be many others wishing to show their support and appreciation of the lads in Red and will be looking forward to the pre-season friendlies with an enthusiasm that hopefully will never wain.

Tuesday 29th April 2025
I saw my mate the other day, he said to me he saw the white Pele
So, I asked, who is he? He goes by the name of Ronan Darcy
Ronan Darcy, Ronan Darcy
He goes by the name of Ronan Darcy

I had nothing to do last Tuesday but ponder over whether Ronan could do us any favours by inspiring Wigan Athletic to a much-needed win over Burton Albion. Much needed by Crawley Town that is, and not by Wigan Athletic as they sat in no man's land on fifty-four points, eleven above the bottom four relegation spots and twenty-one points shy of the play offs. Nothing to play for but professional pride and being honest till the end. The game was on the tele that night and I recorded it to watch when I arrived home after my House group had finished. As it was, on the short walk home from my night out, the white Pele scored with a cross cum shot which evaded both the Wigan forwards and the Albion keeper to give a tantalising glimmer of hope but, as we all know now, time ran out and the Red Devils were relegated along with Bristol Rovers and Cambridge United along with Shrewsbury who already knew their fate for this season.

If only Ronan had come on earlier than the 66th minute.

If, if, if.

The next morning, I was asked if I would like to submit an online article about our season and where we had gone wrong, but I thought I would leave it until after the Shrewsbury game and I am glad I took that stance because Scott expressed my thoughts in his Shrewsbury preview when he said basically that we were relegated because over the season we just weren't consistent enough to stay up. Also, in that preview, he appeared to be quite confident about building on the foundations of the current squad, rather than starting afresh, and was hopeful of being able to keep all the players he wants to keep. Next week, according to Scott, we should know more about who wants to embark on the new season in League 2 and he seems optimistic that it will be an interesting ride.

Last Thursday, it was my privilege and honour to attend the funeral service and celebration of the life of Audrey Turnbull at the Surrey and Sussex Crematorium and the Executive Suite. I was lucky enough to meet ex-players Vic Bragg, Tony Vessey, Micky Turner and Ricky Fitzgerald and also John and Margaret Duly, Sheila Marley, Sarah Markham and Audrey's daughter Jackie and her family and the chance to talk to them all to remember the lives of Audrey, and Les her husband, was one not to be missed.

Saturday 3rd May 2025 EFL1
Shrewsbury Town 1 Crawley Town 2
Shrewsbury scorer Benning (87) Feeney RED CARD(49)
Crawley scorers (Hepburn-Murphy (50P), Anderson (60)
Rivals' results EFL2
Grimsby 0 AFC Wimbledon 1, Swindon 0 MK Dons 0
AFC now have to face Notts County (with Nick Tsaroulla and Kelan Gordon) in the League Two play off semi finals over the next two weeks, whilst MK Dons finished in 19th place.

On to last Saturday and a great day out in Shropshire where just about 300 plus Red Devils turned out to thank the "team" for their efforts this season. The Shrews didn't surrender but Crawley weren't in the mood to let them take the last League One points on offer for a while. Rushian and Max Anderson scored our goals in a two one win which, alongside Burton's three one defeat at Charlton, saw us finish just one point below safety. Max's goal earning itself a spot in the History of the Football League by being the 600,000th goal in its history

So, going back to that question "Where did it go wrong?" here is my attempt to answer it.

Firstly, it didn't go wrong because of one terrible refereeing decision as in the game at home against Wrexham as that would only have given us one point and we would then have missed out on goal difference. Did it go wrong because of individual player mistakes? I don't think so. It went "wrong" because over the season we didn't win enough games that we should have won and the most obvious of these were Exeter City away and Bolton Wanderers away where we let three and two goal leads disappear costing us two victories and five points. However, other teams will be saying the same sort of things about their seasons and, after all is said and done, that is the beauty or the ugliness of our game depending on your club's circumstances.

There will be some supporters who will point at the difference between the percentages of points gained by the team under the three different people in charge, and for those who feel that way here are the stats; Robbie Elliot 23 points from 90 available, Ben Gladwin 0 from 3 and Scott Lindsey 23 from 45 available. To bear in mind here though, we must remember Scott left us for his own reasons and is now thankfully back with us to help the club, it's owners and supporters achieve what we all want and that is success in the long term.

Over the next few weeks, it will become clearer what our prospects will be next season as we endeavour to sign existing players up for next season and new ones to strengthen the side for a real go at automatic promotion, and indeed what teams we will be up against. Already we know that Morecambe and Carlisle United will not be amongst them as they will be plying their trade in the National League. We won't be playing Doncaster Rovers (Champions of League 2), Port Vale or Bradford City either, as they secured automatic promotion even though Vale's promotion party was somewhat spoilt by Gillingham at Vale Park, when they lost by one goal to nil. The Gills, whose supporters mingled with the Reds fans at Oxford services, finished in 17th place thanks to a 12-match unbeaten run which saved them from slipping out of the EFL. As mentioned earlier, AFC Wombles must face Notts County in the Play off semi- finals, as Chesterfield take on Walsall in the other semi, with the final scheduled for Monday 26th May. Personally, and sorry to any Wombles reading this. I would like it to be a Walsall v Notts County final which would mean a revival of our rivalry with AFC, at least for another year. Here's hoping. Coming up from the National League will be champions Barnet on 102 points and one other club from York City, Forest Green Rovers, Rochdale, Oldham Athletic, Halifax Town, Southend United, Gateshead and Tamworth, although this list will be cut down today, May 5th, as they play their 46th and final game of the season before the play off places are confirmed.

PART 2
YEARS V YEARS
THE BEST YEAR EVER (OR WAS IT?)

Chapter 7
Back to the Future
and wherever that may lead us

Tuesday May 6th, 2025

As a result of yesterday's National League games both Gateshead and Tamworth are resigned to playing in the same league next season after the 'Heed could only draw at home to Southend United and the Lambs could only draw away to Altrincham. One has to wonder what might have happened if Jack Roles had not been brought back off loan from the Northeast.

Rochdale will now play Southend in a one match qualifier to see who will play against York City away in the first semifinal, whilst Oldham must face Halifax to see who will play in the land of the Vegans against Forest Green Rovers in the other semifinal, with the final due to be played on Sunday the 1st June.

Meanwhile, back at the Broadfield, Chairman Preston Johnson has issued the following message to the Crawley Town faithful

"As we reach the end of the season, I want to take a moment to reflect on the year and share our renewed commitment to the journey ahead following our relegation to Sky Bet League Two.

I returned to Crawley Town in the summer of 2024 fully aware of the challenges we would face in League One. My aim was to do everything in my power to keep us up and build on the momentum we carried into the season.

There are plenty of "what-ifs" from the past nine months. In some versions of this season, we stay up—but the reality is we didn't, and as Chairman, it's on me.

That said, my partners and I have an unwavering commitment to this Club. We expect nothing less than promotion back to League One next season and are excited for the future. It's my responsibility to deliver on that vision with the support of our team, staff, investors and most importantly each of you.

The recent improvement under Scott is no surprise. Our expected goals (xG) differential this season was nearly identical to last year, despite playing in a tougher league with an even bigger budgeting deficit relative to our opponents. We were hit hard by injuries—our projected starting back three never played a single minute together—and many young players were asked to step up, which they did admirably. I'm proud of the squad, and with Scott leading the team again, I'm confident in what we're building.

Behind the scenes, we've already started work on the retained list and will share updates with you as soon as possible.

Off the pitch, we're making meaningful progress that will support the long-term health of the club. There's much to be encouraged by, including record-breaking attendance this season. The energy at Broadfield Stadium has been incredible, and we're grateful for your continued support.

Our long-term vision extends beyond League One. We want to lay the foundation for Crawley Town to reach the Championship. This will take time, commitment, and significant work both on and off the pitch—but we believe in it. Ownership is fully behind a multi-year plan, and we'll be sharing more in the coming months.

To grow the club sustainably, we're focused on several key initiatives:

Enhancing our retail experience both in-store and online, including renovating an expanded, bigger and better club shop

Increasing club-operated food and beverage options, including an additional Fan Zone

Expanding our commercial department to attract more local and regional sponsorships

Investing in content and matchday experience to deepen fan engagement

We're also thrilled about the new kit—we'll reveal the design to supporters soon.

Pre-season plans are nearly complete, and we're excited to host two home fixtures against Premier League and Championship sides.

Season ticket information will be released on May 5th.

We have a lot to do, and we're ready to get to work. Let's take on the challenge together—and prove the doubters wrong once again.

Thank you for standing with Crawley Town."

Preston Johnson, Chairman

10th May 2025
Rivals' Results
League 2 Play off semifinal first leg
Notts County (without Tsaroulla or Gordon in the squad) 0
AFC Wimbledon 1 (with James Tilley in starting eleven)

As of last Tuesday, the 6th of May, the season ticket prices have been announced and whilst they show an increase of 15% for the West Stand and 10% for all other parts of the stadium, they are still lower than they were in 2021. Personally, if the extra income raised helps our playing budget and improves our squad, I'm all for it.

I know some people have expressed concern that children under 14 will now have to pay £4 a game but, with the cost of a season ticket at £23 for that age group, that reduces to just £1 a game.

With over 100,000 people watching the team at home during 2024/2025 and nearly 2000 season ticket holders we will need the extra income because the attendances at the Broadfield will inevitably decrease because League 2 will not have the size of away support that we have become used to this year in League 1.

Barnet are coming into the EFL which will mean another relatively easy pair of games to get to, and I would dearly love Southend United to be successful in the National League playoffs rather than away trips to York, FGR, Halifax, Oldham or Rochdale. All will become clear over the next couple of weeks, but it looks like AFC Wimbledon, who won one nil against Notts County on Saturday, are trying their hardest to avoid having to play us next season. Having said that, there is still the second leg to come of that semifinal so let's hope Messrs. Tsaroulla and Gordon can get a win at Plough Lane.

As far as we at Crawley Town are concerned, the announcement of a retained list will hopefully have materialised by the time you read this in print, and even more hopefully, in my opinion at least, it will include the majority of the players we already have. There are definitely some players in our squad who will have attracted interest from other clubs, but hopefully Scott and the owners will do their utmost to persuade them that their value will increase even more if they stay with us, stay injury free and contribute to a season that will hopefully bring us automatic promotion.

There are some players we could afford to lose but equally there are others we can't. We will all have our own thoughts on this I'm sure and it is vitally important that we replace players that leave, for whatever reason, with players of a higher quality if we are to seriously challenge for honours. Without naming names, I believe we must solve the goalkeeping situation this coming year as, even if JoJo Wollacott remains as our first choice, we need to have confidence for whoever goes between the sticks whilst he is on international duty or is injured. Our main priorities, I believe, are to strengthen our squad from back to front, including a goalkeeper, a defender who can also be good in the opposition box at corners and set pieces, a ball winning midfielder and a goal scoring centre forward who will not only score goals but unlock the potential of those playing alongside him.

Having spoken to Preston in the last week I know he is optimistic about next season, and I wouldn't be surprised if we signed more players from the States, hopefully in the same mould as Jeremy Kelly and Liam Fraser, and elsewhere as we did with Bradley Ibrahim and Josh Flint.

I know there are fans out there who will not feel as positive as I do about the future under our current owners, but let's see if we can all pull together in the same direction to ensure we bounce back up to League 1 at the earliest opportunity.

One person who won't now fulfill his lifelong dream of playing for the Red Devils is me. Last Friday, the 9th of May, I tried to resurrect my Walking Football "career" at the Crawley

Town Community Foundation Hub and ended up grazing my knee and bruising several of my ribs. On top of all that have just been told I have severe Osteo Arthritis in my left knee (the grazed one) and my right shoulder. Replacement knee and shoulder now on order, but I have put an end to my playing the beautiful game.

The retained list is now out as of the beginning of this week and the players who have been released are Sonny Fish, Jasper Sheikh and Tyreece John-Jules, whilst the loanees, all key players in my opinion, Kamri Doyle, Bradley Ibrahim and Toby Steward have all returned to their parent clubs. There are another eighteen players; Wollacott, Feely, Barker, Anderson, Holohan, Swan, Roles, Camara, Hepburn-Murphy, Tanimu, Quitirna, Adeyemo, Mullarkey, Papadopolous, Flint, Showunmi, Radcliffe and Watson who are all under contract, but that doesn't necessarily mean they will still be here come the start of the 2025/2026 season. I would expect other clubs to make offers for at least three of that number and on top of those players we have six who are under negotiations at the moment in Conroy, Forster, Fraser, Sandford, Kelly and Mukena. Let's hope we retain the best of them and strengthen across the pitch as suggested earlier.

The make-up of both League 1 and 2 for the upcoming 2025/2026 season has become a bit clearer this last week with playoff matches taking place in both the EFL divisions and the National League. The interesting aspect of these matches, for me anyway, are the number of ex Red Devils taking part. Sonny Bradley, playing for Wycombe Wanderers, will have to console himself about missing out on a trip to Wembley, as the chairboys lost to Charlton Athletic setting up an all London League 1 playoff final with Leyton Orient.

Lucky Leyton Orient saw off Stockport County on penalties in the second game and Corey Addai, in goal for the northern side, will no doubt feel aggrieved at one of Orient's goals being allowed in the first game when Orient's leading scorer, Kelman, put the O's ahead from a blatantly obvious offside position. He was about as far offside as James Tilley's shot was over the Orient goal line a few years back. I wonder if the referee apologised for the mistake, which cost the Hatters promotion?

The League Two playoff final will be between Matt Sadler and Darren Byfield's Walsall and AFC Wimbledon, complete with ex Red Devil James Tilley, in their side. Personally, I would love Walsall to win the final because it would mean a renewal of our rivalry with the Plough Lane Phoenix club and a shorter away trip.

In the National League the playoffs are a little more complicated. The Champions (including Dom Telford) are automatically promoted, with the second and third teams, York City and Forest Green Rovers receiving byes to the playoff semifinals. Fourth placed Rochdale (complete with ex Red Devil and Tanzanian international Tarryn Allarakhia in their side) lost to seventh placed Southend United at home by four goals to three after having led three one, whilst Oldham Athletic won a battle of the roses encounter by four goals to nil against Halifax. This means that the dream of having another "localish" match with Southend United lives on until June 1st at least.

One club we won't be playing next season is Bradford City, who I have always thought of as a club who look down on the rest of us, thinking that they deserve to be in a higher league by some divine right. However, my opinions have been mellowed this week because I watched the "Unforgotten - The Bradford City Fire" documentary on BBC. If you haven't watched it yet, I urge you to do so. In it you will recognise, I hope, that every club is made up of the same variety of characters and that there is more that unites us than divides us. I pray that we may never experience what they did, forty years ago, but I know that if we did, we would come through it as they did, stronger than before.

17th May 2025
Rivals' results EFL2 Playoff
AFC Wimbledon 1 Notts County 0

A lot can happen in between weekly issues of the Crawley Observer and the last week hasn't been an exception. Whilst there doesn't appear to be much coming out of the Broadfield Stadium at the moment, some of the matches that will define the make-up of League 2 for the 2025/2026 season have been taking place and whilst the composition of the division will not be finalised until June1st, the day of the National League Play off final, the final combatants for both the League 2 and National league Play Offs have been determined.

Firstly, our "rivals" AFC Wimbledon have booked their place by beating Notts County two nil on aggregate and will have played Matt Sadler's Saddlers Walsall by the time this article is in print. James Tilley, former Red Devil, plays for AFC but I'm sorry James, I hope Matt's team can do it as this will renew the rivalry between our clubs, whilst also providing a closer away trip.

In the National League, York City, who had been waiting patiently for their home ground semifinal, crashed out by three goals to nil against Oldham Athletic, whilst the vegans from the West Country lost to Southend United at home on penalties. This means that the possibility of getting another southern club into League Two is still on, although that will be the last piece in the puzzle on June 1st.

I watched Tottenham Hotspur v Manchester United in the Europa League Final whilst Southend were beating FGR, courtesy of Preston Johnson, in the Executive Suite. I tried to remain neutral between my Spurs loving daughter and son in law and my Manchester United loving sons, but the game itself, doing nothing for the environment by being played in Bilbao also failed to excite and was not the best advert for English football, but then it was between two of this season's most unsuccessful teams. It was decided by a goal that looked like a Luke Shaw own goal but was credited to Spurs' Brendan Johnson. In the end I didn't have to sit between my sons and my daughter, as neither of the boys made it to the stadium. The scores coming through from the National League Play off semifinal were of more interest to me. Southend took the lead and relinquished it before going behind after four minutes of extra time. Then, with just four minutes left the Shrimpers equalised through a Jack Bridge goal which took the tie to penalties, duly won by Southend by four goals to two, setting up the final with Oldham Athletic.

Oldham Athletic, in my opinion, must be favourites having scored seven goals in their play-off games with Rochdale and York City.

However, I am backing the shrimpers as they snuck into the last playoff place and appear to have the momentum with them bringing into question the National League play-off system, which had runners up York and third placed FGR sitting on their back sides while the other sides kept on playing.

26 May 2025
Rivals' Results (and the last one of the 2024/2025 season)
EFL LEAGUE 2 PLAY OFF FINAL
Walsall 0 AFC (I repeat AFC) Wimbledon 1

You might sense that I am not happy with the result from League 2's showpiece game, but, when all is said and done, AFC deserved their win against Walsall in a game that did not come anywhere near the standard of last year's game. There were just over 50,000 spectators there with apparently 33,000 of them supporting the Kingston team which makes me wonder why they didn't support them in those numbers pre the AFC being inserted in front of their name. AFC deserved their victory and thus the rivalry between them and us and MK Dons has only temporarily, I'm sure, come to an end.

The thing that really got to me was the continual references to the 1988 FA Cup victory over Liverpool accompanied by shots of Dave Beasant and Dave Bassett watching from the stands. That was a different club, a different time and whilst the move and renaming of the original club to MK Dons should never have been allowed to happen, or even be sanctioned by the Football League, it is now history and surely AFC would be better playing on the "we've come from nowhere" ticket.

Am I being unfair? Crawley FC folded before the Second World War in 1935, only to reform three year later by merging with two other clubs, namely Crawley Athletic and Crawley Rangers. The name of Crawley FC lived on, mainly because the officials of the new club were largely from the original Crawley FC. Something to think about perhaps?

Since the League 2 play off final decided there would be no league trip to Plough Lane this year, the National League Play off final took place and once again the result was not to my liking. Southend, despite being two one up after just one minute of extra time, sadly surrendered the lead in the 100th minute before losing the game to a third Oldham Athletic goal in the 112th minute.

This means that the make-up of League 2 is as follows

Accrington Stanley, Barnet, Barrow, Bristol Rovers, Bromley, Cambridge United, Cheltenham Town, Chesterfield, Colchester United, Crawley Town, Crewe Alexandra, Fleetwood Town, Gillingham, Grimsby Town, Harrogate Town, Milton Keynes Dons, Newport County, Notts County, Oldham Athletic, Salford City, Shrewsbury Town, Swindon Town, Tranmere Rovers and Walsall.

Alphabetically 10th in the table, 12th according to one bookmaker and not the smallest club in the division. There are in fact five clubs with smaller capacities than us and ten that claim bigger capacities than 10,000. I think, and it is only my opinion I know, that there are no real favourites for the upcoming season and I am confident that, provided we keep certain players and sign some good level replacements for those who might leave, we have every right to believe that the coming season will be a good one.

We have already signed midfielder, Reece Brown, and forward Harry McKirdy, both of whom who speak highly of Scott Lindsey, having played for him at Forest Green Rovers and Swindon Town respectively.

Perhaps the next week will see more players being signed or renewing existing contracts as it is only a matter of just over three weeks before the team jet off to Spain where they will train and play a 4th of July friendly against Scottish Premiership side Heart of Midlothian at the Pinatar Arena. This is not the first time that Crawley have faced Hearts, as Crawley made the long trip to the Tynecastle Stadium in July 2022 for a friendly fixture which ended in a 2-2 draw courtesy of two second-half goals from Dom Telford, who, incidentally, did not sign until June 24th that year.

I am hoping that Crawley Town will be able to organise some travel packages for fans and sponsors to watch the Red Devils play in Europe as some of us need to enjoy that experience before it is too late.

I want to share with you a family anecdote that truly shows how small our world is. I have just got back from a visit to the Mumbles near Swansea in South Wales, and whilst there I and my travelling companion met up with my cousin and his wife. They have lived in another part of Swansea called Cockett for about 40 years, whilst my partner owns a holiday home in Limeslade bay about six miles away from their house in a street called Lon Coedbran. I knew Lon was Welsh for Lane and asked my cousin if he knew what Coedbran meant in English. To my astonishment he said that "Coed" was wood and that "bran" was crows, or as google confirmed with its Welsh to English translation app, "CRAWLEY".

11th June 2025

Rushian Hepburn-Murphy has departed Crawley Town on a transfer for an undisclosed fee to, of all people, MK Dons. Thanks for the goals you scored for the Red Devils, just a pity you didn't make the most of your opportunity, in front of an open goal, at St Andrews. I am a bit narked and I am really hoping this isn't the start of an exodus.

And then another departs in Toby Mullarkey to Fleetwood. His undisclosed fee rumoured to be in bitcoins has everyone shouting, "What a load of Mullarkey". Seriously though, can we please have some good news?

It has been announced that the 2025 FA Cup winners are coming to the Broadfield on Friday July25th. Last year's fixture against Crystal Palace saw Crawley score three goals against Premier League opposition for only the second time in our history, coming back from four nil down at half time through two goals from, the now departed, Rushian Hepburn-Murphy and one from Jack Roles, to eventually lose by six goals to three.

Whilst waiting to hear about the latest signings and possible travel packages to the friendly against Hearts at the Pinatar complex, I thought I would bring everyone up to date with the proposal for the CTFC Museum soon, he writes hopefully, to become a reality at the Broadfield Stadium. Naturally the priority for the Club is to utilise space available at the stadium to generate income to feed the playing budget. The original portacabin that was proposed to be used for the museum will now be used for another purpose which means that we have been offered the portacabin that has been used for buying and collecting tickets. The club feel that the new ticketing system, brought in last season, negates the use of the cabin for that purpose. Whilst the cabin is smaller than the original proposition, both Mick Fox and I feel that it offers enough space to house rolling exhibitions perhaps covering different eras in the club's history which will also mean that people's interest will be refreshed on a monthly or so cycle. Watch this space!!!

So, two players in and two players out and also news of Herta Berlin transferring Bradley Ibrahim to League 1 Plymouth Argyle whilst there appears to be a signing inward bound in the shape of a National League South player, who might or might not be Danny Cashman, once of this parish when we had an academy, and who has played for Coventry, Rochdale and Worthing.

19th June 2025

If there is anyone reading this who played for Crawley Traders back in the day, when men were men and women weren't really allowed to talk about, let alone play, football, today is my father-in-law's birthday. His name was Les King, and he managed the Crawley Traders team with his son, Richard, as one of his players. Sadly, gone but not forgotten, as is also a good friend of mine, Steve Preest, who passed away earlier this week. Steve was a supporter of the Red Devils and one of the long-standing members, along with his wife Yvonne, of the Crawley Town Community Foundation Extra time hub. Steve played for Upjohn in his younger days and was a member of the team, coached by Stan (Mr Crawley Town) Markham, who won the European Championship back in 1975. That was of course the Upjohn European Championship, and not to be confused with competitions of a similar, but less prestigious, nature such as the Champions League, Conference League and Conference Trophy. Up until about eighteen months ago he still ran out on a Friday lunch time for Walking football at the Hub, but I guess that should have said walked out. He enjoyed home and away matches watching the Red Devils from his East stand seat and introduced his grandson to the pleasure of watching real football and learning how to accept victories and defeats with the same good grace and humour. Steve, you will be sadly missed.

Danny Cashman has signed for the Red Devils and is keen to get started. He actually started his football career with Crawley Town when we had an Academy back in 2010 through 2012, but following the closing of our academy went to Brighton and Hove Albion. He then went on to sign for Coventry City, before being loaned out to Rochdale prior to his successful period at Worthing FC in National League South. However, not many people will know that he starred in a short educational film, produced by Southern Water, entitled Water Matters. He was about twelve at the time and appeared alongside a young girl, roughly of the same age, who was the film producer's daughter, and basically followed the water that our players need to keep hydrated, from Hardham to Broadfield stadium.

Meanwhile, as Danny joins Harry McKirdy and Reece Brown as players coming into our squad, Armando Quitirna has sadly, for us, departed on a permanent transfer to League 1 Wycombe Wanderers. What is needed now is for there either to be some really good, experienced signings and/or for there to be no more of our existing players leaving. Kelly and Fraser hopefully will be encouraged to stay, and I understand that, according to the Liverpool Echo, we are close to acquiring the services of goalkeeper, Harvey Davies, on a long-term loan deal, and that Portsmouth are also looking to put Toby Steward back out on loan as well. Toby was our eighth goalkeeper, and probably the best, last season and I, for one, would have him back at the Broadfield like a shot. Back to Armando, I wish him luck and do not resent him signing for a League 1 side. Shortly after that piece of news was issued, we also found out that Panutche Camara had also been transferred to Dundee United because of a clause in his contract allowing him to leave if we were relegated. Perhaps he will feature in the Dandy as desperate Pan. I have to say I'm not sure where I stand on that as he was a member of the team that was relegated. Good job the majority of supporters don't have that clause attached to their season ticket renewal.

Unfortunately, the planned packages for sponsors and supporters to travel to Spain to watch the team play Heart of Midlothian, will not now happen as, according to James Ball and Tobias Phoenix, there was not enough time to organise them. Just hoping my time doesn't run out before we play in Europe again.

I also read this in last week's Crawley Observer, about Matt Turner, who has just been awarded an MBE in the King's birthday honours.

Is the following true ?

"When you look at the calibre of Matt's work and what he has achieved in 20 years, it's astonishing. From buying 50% of Crawley Town Football Club........"

Fixture release day coming soon.

25th June 2025

Well, the fixtures are out, but first the comings and goings in terms of players, to and from the club. Sadly, Jeremy Kelly has decided to return to the USA and has signed for Charleston Battery in the USL. The club website does not mention the club, or any fee involved, but the Reddit site unbelievably claims it was a free transfer. Surely not.

Rory Feeley has also left the club to go to Irish side, Cork City, for, according to the CTFC website, an undisclosed fee. As with all players who have left us there will be differences in opinion as to their supposed value, but I know who I would value the most out of Jeremy and Rory and I don't think there would be many Red Devils who would disagree.

We have signed both Harry Forster and Joy Mukena on for another year, and Ryan Sandford on for an initial 6-month extension. Harry and Joy just need to stay fit and not succumb to injury, as both, I believe, show promise if they can be injury free. Ryan, as we all know, is a goalkeeper who was signed a six-month contract. Harry is probably the closest to making a first team start as both Joy and Ryan are yet to resume training with the first team after both of them sustained bad knee injuries last season. Owner, Preston Johnson had this to say about them. "We wanted to make sure that both Joy and Ryan were looked after in the appropriate manner after they suffered unfortunate injuries last season. We continue to make big strides in looking after both players and staff at Crawley Town Football Club, and releasing the pair with the injuries that they faced would not have been right or fair. That, paired with the fact that we believe both of them can make worthwhile contributions to the team, made this a very easy decision." Well done CTFC.

We have also signed Harvey Davies on a season-long loan deal from Premier League champions Liverpool. He is a highly rated goalkeeper who signed his first professional contract with Liverpool in 2021, after having been with their academy since he was eight.

Whilst he has been praised for his calm presence in between the sticks, he is also known for his ability to play out with the ball at his feet and is also said to have exceptional shot-stopping capabilities.

He spent last season on loan at Crewe Alexandra, making 32 appearances in all competitions and appears to be really happy to be here and, according to Scott Lindsey, will be played as first choice keeper.

On the subject of new players, Scott feels we are still short of the squad he would like to start the season with but stresses that more signings are imminent.

Oh yes, the fixtures are out as well and in August alone we face three matches away, with Grimsby on the opening day, Crewe Alexandra on the 16th of August and Chesterfield on the 30th interspersed with home matches on the 9th, 19th and the 23rd against Newport County, MK Dons and Tranmere Rovers respectively. On last season's results the hardest fixture would appear to be the Spireites way, as they only suffered three home defeats last year, finished in the last play-off place, but failed to make a Wembley appearance, going out to Matt Sadler's Walsall in the semi-finals. Grimsby away conjures up memories of that famous three two victory at the start of our promotion season but hopefully we won't go two down this time before we start playing. The other four league opponents we face in August had poor seasons by their previous standards with Newport (22nd) and Tranmere (20th) only gaining three and four away wins each. Crewe failed to repeat their performances of the previous season finishing in 13th place and MK Dons (who?) ended in 18th place, but this game will probably be our toughest as they appear to be signing forwards galore, including of course, a certain Rushian Hepburn-Murphy.

As well as the six league games, we also face a tough away Carabao Cup tie in Wales against Swansea City, the week commencing the 11th of August and hopefully a second-round game in between the Tranmere and Chesterfield league matches.

On top of all that we have been drawn to play Aston Villa U21s, Peterborough and Orient in the group stage of, what is now, the Vertu EFL Trophy. Deja Vu, me thinks.

STOP PRESS: JAY WILLIAMS IS BACK

28 June 2025

Yes, Jay Williams is back. Let's hope that his words about "coming home" and "Our fans are the best that I have ever played in front of, so I can't wait to see them again." ring truer than what he was alleged to have said when he left for the land of the concrete cows. Seriously, He could be a really good signing for Crawley, especially if he can reduce the number of cautions he gets and plays more games as a result.

30th June 2025

Rumours are rife about two other promotion winning stars returning to Crawley, but I guess we'll just have to wait and see. I am now going to close this tome after the first league game against Grimsby Town as hopefully, by then we will have a much better idea of our prospects for 2025/2026, but who knows, I might even decide to include up to and including the MK Dons home game which will also allow me to include the visit to Swansea in the Carabao Cup.

Away from Crawley Town, the England U21 team won the Euro Championships on the 28th June against Germany, having surrendered a two-goal lead courtesy of goals from Harvey Elliot (5) and Omari Hutchinson (24) to Nelson Weiper's bullet header in first half stoppage time and Paul Nubel's 61st minute equaliser. Just when it looked like both sides had settled for extra time, Nubel almost broke the three lions' collective heart but could only find the bar with Beadle in the England goal beaten.

With both sides using iced towels at full time, because of the heat in Bratislava, it was England who grabbed, what was to be the winner, when Jonathan Rowe, with almost his first touch since coming on as a substitute, twisted in mid-air to head the three lions into the lead once more, this time from an exquisite cross from Tyler Morton.

The score remained at three two until the end of the game, but it could have gone to penalties when a little bit of magic from Germany's Merlin Rohl, hit the England bar with almost the last kick of the game.

Tom Fellows, who was on loan at Crawley Town in 2022/2023 and made 38 appearances, played for the last 27 minutes of the group game defeat against Germany and is now playing regularly for West Bromwich Albion.

Those of you who know me will appreciate I am also very keen on cricket, but to be honest it could be ludo or snakes and ladders if one of the competitors was wearing a three lions or red rose adorned piece of kit, and I did spend a lot of time last week watching an intriguing Test match between England and India. India got themselves in to positions where they should have gone on to put the game well beyond the host nation, but in both innings failed to capitalise on good starts and in the end succumbed to excellent bowling and batting from a side demonstrating the never say die attitude that so many of our sporting heroes possess.

Yesterday, Sunday 29th June, I ventured, after church to Jubilee field the home of Three Bridges FC, to watch Beth, my granddaughter, play for Sutton United against Three Bridges, who were once AFC Crawley (her old club). The game, played in sweltering heat and in four twenty-two and a half minute quarters, ended one all and probably should not have been played because of the heat. Played on a 4G pitch, and I do appreciate why lower league clubs use them, was played for the most at an understandably slow pace with clouds of black particles jumping into the air every time the ball bounced. Oh, and there were no refreshments on offer either.

Back in the slightly less hot confines of my flat, later that afternoon I watched England Lionesses beat a Jamaican side, but with no one actually born in Jamaica in it, by seven goals to nil. The goals coming from Toone (2), Bronze, Stanway, Russo, Beever-Jones and Mead. I enjoy watching girls play football for various reasons, none of which are dubious, I hasten to add, and one of them is they are not afraid to talk about their relationships, whether heterosexual or not. There will be girls playing in the Euros against teams that their partners play for and they will be open about it, which, I don't think would happen in the male version of the sport. What a funny world we live in.

Back at Broadfield, the players of Crawley Town will no doubt be getting ready to depart for their Spanish training camp and the first friendly against Heart of Midlothian, and perhaps the appearance of some quality triallists on show.

Rumours still persist about two other promotion winning stars returning to Crawley, but I guess we'll just have to wait and see. Perhaps the rumours might now dissipate as we have signed forward Kabongo Tshimanga on a two-year contract following his release from League One side Peterborough United, winger Dion Pereira, following his release from Luton Town earlier in the summer and former Chelsea and Brighton & Hove Albion striker Louis Flower. Indeed, Flower opened his Red Devils account by scoring against Hearts in the friendly in Spain and Benjamin Tanimu has been transferred to a club in Morocco whilst Jamie Day is back at Crawley to assist Scott. The game against Scottish Premier Division Hearts ended in a three one defeat, but I do feel the club let us, the supporters, down by not communicating well enough how the game could be watched.

During the close season, although football doesn't seem to have stopped at all, Crawley Town have gained more players, with Kyle Scott arriving from Orange County being the latest arrival and have also lost players, with Canadian Liam Fraser joining Reading and staying in League 1.

Our friendlies have seen us beat the teams we should beat, Three Bridges five nil, East Grinstead and Dagenham and Redbridge, both by five goals to one, and lose against the teams above us in the Football Pyramid, one nil away to Portsmouth (in a game hastily played behind closed doors on Pompey's training ground due to a waterlogged pitch at the Broadfield Stadium), two one away to Southampton U21s and by three goals to nil, in the only game played at the Broadfield Stadium, against FA Cup holders, Premier League Crystal Palace. I missed that final game as I was on holiday in Wales but have heard and read good reports of our performance from friends and the media. All in all, I have to say that Mr. Optimistic (what some of my old friends call me) is generally happy with what he has seen so far. I have seen all the players, new to the team, fit into our style of play really well except for Kyle Scott, but only because I haven't seen him play, and now it is time for Super Scotty and his coaching staff to try and work out the best starting eleven and bench for the game that is really important, the opening day away trip to Grimsby. The last time we played there, two players, now sadly at pastures new, scored the goals that got us back into the game after having gone two down with one of the Grimsby goals having been scored by a present Red Devil Gavan Holohan. The match ending after ex Grimsby player Danilo Orsi scored the winner almost with the last kick of the game. It was a fantastic victory and hopefully one that we will repeat once again on the 2nd of August. I won't be there this time, in body that is, but you can take it for granted that Ifollow will be in use that day.

I must mention the Pompey game which should have been played at the Broadfield Stadium but was, as mentioned earlier, transferred to Pompey's training ground. I checked the club website before setting off at 1220pm but could see no mention of a postponement, unless of course it was on twitter or whatever it's called these days. The match was actually called off just before midday, but I would hazard a guess that quite a few of our fans don't use the method of communication used by the club, so perhaps that's something the club should consider for the future.

I, along with other disappointed home fans made the most of the trip and purchased a home shirt, mine to go with my away shirt that had just been given to me as an early birthday gift. Both designs, I think, show a realisation of what our club should be about, community and history, and the club should be applauded for them. Whilst leaving to catch the bus back into town I met a dad and his young son, proudly wearing their Pompey kit. We had a chat, wished each other good luck for the coming season but the dad wanted to know if he could claim their trip to Crawley as a valid entry in their quest to attend the 92 grounds of the Premier and Football League. Thoughts anyone????

On the first day of my holiday in Wales I received a telephone call from the BBC asking me to comment about Preston Johnson's decision to step down as Chairman of Crawley Town, stating that other members of the Wagmi group were pushing for a change in direction with regards to our recruitment policy. Having just heard about Preston's decision I said that, speaking on my own and not for the CTSA or any other faction of our fan base, in my opinion he will be missed and that I always found him open to constructive criticism and very approachable. Earlier in this book I mentioned the setting up of the Crawley Town Museum but now, with Preston's departure it seems that may have to be postponed yet again, as the promised Portacabin has now been moved and is still being used for ticket sales. Perhaps the directors Daniel Khalili, Ryan Gilbert and Maxwell Strowman, as mentioned in the July 23rd issue of the Crawley Observer, might be able to help in this matter.

Extracts from Preston' statement from Mark Dunford's piece in the Observer quotes him as saying "WAGMI United is in the process of transitioning to new lead investors who will guide the club forward – and they have a different vision for its future. As a result, this summer's player recruitment has gone in a different direction than the data-driven approach that has powered our success over the past few years. I do not believe this shift represents the best path forward for the club, which is why I have made the difficult decision to step back and make space for the new leadership to pursue their vision without my involvement".

In response, the club made the following statement, but without indicating who wrote it.

"Crawley Town Football Club thanks Preston Johnson for his service as Chairman and CEO. We are grateful for his innovation, leadership and commitment over the past few years.

Recruitment at Crawley Town is, and will remain, a balanced process, one that draws on data, experience and instinct. While we acknowledge Preston's recent statement, we believe that multiple perspectives contribute to a successful footballing strategy. Data will continue to play a key role in our decision making, alongside other critical considerations. We are excited by the calibre of players who have joined us in recent weeks, many of whom have already made a strong impression during pre-season.

The Crawley Town community can look forward to the start of a promising new era. An official update regarding ownership and personnel will be shared at the earliest opportunity."

I, personally, can see a slight change in direction as regards recruitment could be good for us, but I will miss Preston's involvement and hope that he will still be in the background as we approach our 130th birthday. One thing is for sure; I hope that the title of this book is not a harbinger of doom.

I was privileged to attend the funeral of close friend, Steve Preest, on the 28th of July and was pleased to witness supporters of our club exhibiting what it means to them to be part of our footballing family. I hope that our new directors will also see the importance of us remaining a united body of people who appreciate the individuals that make us what we are. In my opinion the naming of the media centre after the stalwart that was Ken Blackmore isn't a bad start.

Having a granddaughter who is a semi-professional footballer herself it would be remiss of me not to mention the supreme efforts made by the Lionesses in retaining the Euro Championship this year. After having lost their first group game against France, they then beat Holland and Wales to enter the knockout stages and played extra time in all three matches; defeating Sweden in the Quarter final, after having come back from two down to force extra time and penalties and finally winning by three spot kicks to two in what must have been one of the poorest quality penalty shoot outs in history, then beating Italy by two goals to one after coming back from only one down this time after extra time and then finally winning the final against Spain, again after going behind and taking it to extra time and penalties by three penalties to one.

The Spanish captain was not amused and said the best team hadn't won. I might agree that they had better, more skillful players on the pitch but I do believe that "OUR" girls were the better team as they exhibited a never say die, noli semper cedere spirit throughout the whole tournament and thoroughly deserved their final victory.

Back to Crawley Town, as of today, the 1st of August 2025, we are now under new ownership. The new owners are KB Sports and Leisure, and the new chairman is Raphael Khalili, but before I write about them, I would like to share with you about my attempts to watch the Barnet versus Newport County Carabao Cup Preliminary Round game earlier in the week. I recorded the game on Sky, as I was otherwise occupied when the game was played. On returning home from my engagement I settled down to watch, primarily because we face Newport at home in our first game at the Broadfield and wanted to see what they were like. They went two up in the first half with two stunning strikes but were pegged back when Barnet scored twice in added on time. The game ended two all, and if it had gone to extra time, I couldn't see any other winner but the North London club. However, as we all know there is no extra time in the Carabao anymore and so it went to penalties. I paused the recording so I could get myself a cup of tea and settled down to watch the spot kicks. On pressing "play" however all I got was the talk amongst the players prior to the kicks and then the programme ended. Newport won four two in the end and will have to be taken seriously when we play them on the 9th of August.

In other news, Danilo Orsi has signed for AFC Wimbledon, and I beg you to see Ivan Noel's reaction to this news which is included in the photographs in the pages just before the appendix.

Klaudi Lolos, once of this parish, has left Bolton Wanderers and signed for Peterborough United, and could well feature against Crawley Town in our final Vertu Trophy game on the 11th of November. Shouldn't be too hard to remember, should it?

Rivals' Results
EFL 1
1st August 2025
Luton Town 1 AFC Wimbledon 0
Danilo on after 70 minutes but AFC concede in the 85th minute through Johnson heading it back over his own keeper. The commentator on Sky, when Mick Harford briefly appeared on screen next to David Pleat said that he had played in the 1988 FA Cup semifinal between these two clubs. Oh dear, someone tell him, please!! The result, by the way, puts one of our rivals at the bottom of EFL 1, at least until five pm tomorrow, the 2nd of August.

2nd August 2025
EFL2
Grimsby Town 3   Crawley Town   0
Grimsby scorers Kabla (10P), McJannet (30), Khouri (64)
Rivals' results MK Dons 0 Oldham Athletic 0
GRIM BY NAME, GRIM BY NATURE!!

    Let's get it out of the way quickly. just as Scott did in his post-match interview, we were rubbish and no amount of moaning about the penalty decision will change that. We didn't compete and the data shows that dramatically. Grimsby, on the other hand, did compete and thoroughly deserved their opening day victory. However, it is only the first game of the season and, as was pointed out by Scott, we lost six nil away to Swindon in 2023 and ended up being promoted. We also lost to Grimsby in the first game of the season back in 2010 and ended up being champions with what was then a record points total.

    I couldn't make the game away yesterday (Saturday) but because of there being no Championship matches until next week was able to watch it on the television with about twenty other fans in the Downsman public house on Southgate parade. Before the game the younger members of the audience were up for it and very optimistic about this season, whereas the more senior, in terms of age, of us were a little more restrained. As the match wore on and it clearly wasn't going to be our day the youngsters' barometer moved to stormy, whilst mine and that of the older people watching seemed to accept it wasn't going to be our day and you could hear all the cliches being said such as "It's a marathon not a sprint" and "we lost at Morecambe six nil and Swindon six nil and went on to win promotion in both of those seasons".

    The first goal, the penalty, should never have been, but to use that as an excuse for the defeat would be totally incorrect and Scott, to his credit, didn't. In fact, if I heard him right, he appears not to be able to comment on the performance of officials this season because of directives handed down from above. The EFL presumably. I am not bound by those restrictions, so here goes. Davies clearly plays the ball, and the penalty should not have been given in my opinion. The referee awarded the penalty, as it appears, because the assistant referee put his flag across his chest and I think the fact that our keeper wasn't booked or sent off shows there was some doubt in the referee's mind. If there had been VAR, as in the Playoff final, it would have been probably overturned, and the game would still have been nil nil. We would still have lost because of our lack of effort and commitment, or would we? Anyway, match over, and on to next week when perhaps some of the players missing from the starting squad will be included. Danny Cashman, Pereira not in yesterday's squad, would be nice to know why, and no goalkeeper on the bench also something that needs to be addressed.

I hope you had time on Thursday, Friday or Saturday from the 17th July to pay a visit to Crawley Museum to see "The Great Escape?" exhibition which tells the story of the last three seasons in the life of Crawley Town FC. Please let me or Mick Fox know what you thought of it. The club kindly donated three family tickets to a League 2 match in the 2025/2026 season, for prizes in the Museum trail competition. You might even have had the chance to see some players there, but I guess, that after the result and performance at Grimsby, Scott might think they need to get things sorted before we play two Welsh clubs in the space of four days. If you hadn't been to the revamped club shop and seen the three new first team shirts, they, thanks to Tom Allman, they were on display in the exhibition at Crawley Museum.

9th August 2025
EFL 2
Crawley Town 1   Newport County   2
Crawley Town scorer Anderson (96)
Newport County scorers Smith (67), Baker (70)
Rivals' results Barrow 0 MK Dons 2
EFL 1 AFC Wimbledon 2 Lincoln City 0

I have my tickets, both train and match ones, for both games coming up this week, away to Swansea City in the League cup and away to Crewe Alexandra in the League. I know what you're thinking, that I had bought them before the two defeats against Grimsby and Newport County, but that would only be true about the Swansea game. I watched the Newport game in incredulity, wondering how we hadn't gone into the half time break at least two goals ahead and then saw us commit two terrible defensive errors in the space of two minutes to put us two goals down and out of the game. We did pull a goal back in the 6th minute of added on time through Max Anderson, on as a late substitute, but in the slightly off the mark words of Scott Lindsey, in his after-match interview, "You can't win the lottery if you haven't bought a ticket". Off the mark only because, in my opinion, we bought plenty of tickets but then proceeded to throw them straight in the bin because of our poor finishing. Every statistic, bar the one that really matters, was in our favour and Scott clearly knows things need addressing and quickly.

Forster, Perreira, Cashman and Radcliffe are all out injured and, according to Scott, will not make the squad this Tuesday for our visit to Swansea, but I do feel that Anderson, Roles, Flower, Watson etc need to have been given a chance in this game to show what they can do. On top of those players, one of Wollacott, Sandford or newly signed Will Heater should be in the match day squad (if fit) as if Davies was to get injured the only course of action open to us would be to put an outfield player between the sticks.

Anyway, that's Mr. Optimistic giving his opinion and hoping that by the time you read this in print we will have beaten Swansea City and will be looking for our first league points of the season at Crewe Alexandra. Swansea went down by one goal to nil on Saturday away at Middlesbrough but will no doubt provide a stern test for us. They narrowly beat us back in 2012 by three goals to two, when they were in the Premier League and we were in League 1. Spanish international, Michu, opened the scoring for them at the Broadfield but goals from Josh Simpson and Hope Akpan had us dreaming of reaching the 4th round of the league cup, until Danny Graham equalised for them and Gary Monk scored an undeserved winner in 90th minute. Hopefully a good performance against the Swans will regenerate our confidence before we take on top of the table, Crewe Alexandra, on August 16th and 6th in the table MK Dons on August 19th at the Broadfield Stadium. Just in case you may have forgotten what happened the last time we faced these two clubs, back in May 2024, why not pay a visit to Crawley Museum on

Wednesday 13th August through Friday 15th August where you can relive the events of a wonderful time in the history of our club. (The actual exhibition ends on Saturday 16th August, but hey, you'll all be in Crewe watching us gain our first league win of the season.)

12th August 2025
EFL CUP 1st ROUND
SWANSEA CITY   3   CRAWLEY TOWN   1
Crawley Scorer Tshimanga (75), Holohan Red Card (84)
Swansea Scorers Ronald (4), Wales (67), Galbraith (90+4)
Rivals' results Gillingham 1 AFC Wimbledon 1 AFC win 4-2 on penalties. Bristol City 2 MK Dons 0.

    Before I share with you all what I thought of the game against Swansea City I have just watched the second-round draw, if we had won last night, we would have had Ball 11, been first out of the bowl and been drawn at home to Bristol City, whom we beat in the third round of the FA Cup in 2011/2012 at the Broadfield Stadium. They had David James in goal, but he couldn't stop Matt Tubbs scoring his 17th goal of the season which sent us on to the fourth round away to Hull City. Alas, we did not beat Swansea City last night, but if we had not had Gavin Holohan sent off in the 83rd minute I am convinced that we could have taken the game to penalties. It wasn't to be, and they scored again in added on time to make the score 3-1.

    Before all that however, the day started well with travelling Red Devil supporters gathering in the Cross Keys Pub from half three on, until they all made the short trek to what is a beautiful stadium just north of the city centre. Crawley fans such as Lloyd and Lauren from Leeds, Alf and Scouse Dan from Liverpool, Darryl from somewhere in darkest Wales all together with those who had made the journey from West Sussex united in supporting the team and club they all love. Were they expecting a win? Probably not, but they were expecting a performance to be proud of, and for the most part that is what they got. All the statistics went in the championship sides favour, including alas the only one that matters, but for me there were signs of the team starting to gel together, despite Conroy and Scott not being in the match day squad. Will Heater, the 18-year-old goalkeeper, who recently signed after being in the Foundation team, was rewarded with a place on the bench and Jack Roles and Max Anderson started the game as did Joy Mukena. In my opinion, we displayed the Noli Cedere spirit throughout, both on the pitch and in the stands for the most part. However, we do have an element of younger impatient fans who need to look up the definition of support. Tinpot and proud we may be, but some of the chanting and abuse levelled by some at the team and/or individual players does go beyond the limit. Super Scottie Lindsey said, in his after-match interview words to the same effect, so it's not just a supporter, starting his 70th year watching the Red Devils, who thinks there is a right and proper way to support the team. I joined in the singing of the National Anthem and was somewhat taken aback at the home fans retaliating by booing but I didn't join in the one about how they feel about their farm animals as I knew, from trips to Wrexham, that the home fans would join in as they delight in their reputation of being animal lovers, even if it is somewhat exaggerated. Last moan from me must be that there are over 200,000 words in the English vocabulary other than those that begin with F and C.

Several away fans stopped us after the game to wish my son and I good luck for the rest of the season and we reciprocated as all real sports fans should. Game over, we live on to play another day, not in the Carabao cup 2025/2026, but most certainly in the League.

16th August 2025
EFL 2
Crewe Alexandra   1   Crawley Town   0
Crewe scorer O'Reilly (24)
Rivals' results MK Dons 5 Cheltenham Town 0 (Rushian Hepburn-Murphy with their fourth goal against the other CTFC)
EFL 1 Reading 1 AFC Wimbledon 2

Onto Crewe and another example of grit and determination almost gaining a point against the club at the top of the table. The only statistic that didn't go in our favour was the only one that really counts. A one nil defeat which would have seen us go bottom of the premature table if it hadn't been for the five-nil thrashing of the other CTFC at MK Dons. The performance only lacked a goal in the Alex net and was much appreciated by the travelling fans, many of whom had attended the Swansea game earlier in the week. Three people who weren't there on Tuesday, was a young lad Harry Ball and his Mum and Dad. Harry lives in Crewe, supports Port Vale but plays as Crawley Town on his computer. Good on you Harry, perhaps one day you can make it to the Broadfield. The other Harry, McKirdy that is, has a chant now and we have a very exciting player in Kaheim Dixon, on loan from Charlton Athletic plus Danny Cashman in the running for a starting place. Keep the faith and Noli Cedere.

19th August 2025
Now, if I end the book here that would be a sign of losing faith in the Red Devils, which I have not done, so ....
EFL 2
Crawley Town 1 MK Dons 1
Crawley Town scorer Adeyemo (45+7)
MK Dons scorer Offord (71)
Rivals' results
EFL 1   AFC Wimbledon 0   Cardiff City 1

    Before the game I looked at who we have played against this season and where they are currently in the league. We have played first placed Crewe Alexandra, fourth placed Grimsby Town and fourteenth placed Newport County, whilst MK Dons have played teams in 16th, 17th and 24th positions. I know you can read into this what you like, so I will not get carried away and think things will improve without the whole of Crawley Town putting in a very considerable effort. Listening to Scott previewing the game as I write this, he seems to be up for the job at hand and has nothing but possible comments about the new owners and their efforts to strengthen the team in this window, possibly with one player coming in for the visit of Tranmere on Saturday 23rd August. I shared my theory with David, my son, and he immediately saw a possible flaw, in that the teams we have lost to are above us exactly for that reason and the teams that are below MK because they have beaten them. However, if you take three points from Grimsby, Newport and Crewe they would still be in the top half of the table because of their other results. Both Grimsby and Crewe won again whilst we were playing MK Dons,

Before the game, it was clear Scott Lindsey wanted an all-out performance by his team selection. Cashman, Watson and Dixon in as was Dion Conroy and his plan almost gained us our first victory of the season. Almost, but not quite. Ade Adeyemo tied their left back up in knots with his sorties down the wing and everyone in red played to the limit of their ability and beyond in keeping MK restricted to break away moves. The breakthrough came seven minutes into added on time when Ade latched on to a loose ball in their box and drove his shot past the keeper into the franchise's net. Liam Kelly and Rushian Hepburn-Murphy were playing for the Dons, but it wasn't until he was substituted late in the game that most around me realised RHM had been on the pitch. Liam Kelly though was at the core of everything that MK did, and he rightly earned some applause from the home crowd in Torres corner when he came over to take their corners. For all their money though, they did not look that special to me and those around me and even when they snatched their equaliser in the 71st minute, in my opinion, we were the most likely to win the game. Off the mark, out of the relegation spots on goal difference, if only for a day as second from bottom Shrewsbury play tonight (20th August 2025). The result of which you will have to look up for yourselves as, apart from noting that once again we had no keeper on the bench and that Pereira and Forster were not back from injury, but that Tola Showunmi was, coming on in the second half, I would like to quote Porky Pig , who is famous for saying on numerous occasions , "That's all Folks", at least that is after you've read the Epilogue and looked at the Photo Gallery and the Appendix of this book.

Thanks for reading this my fourth book, and if you have any ideas for the fifth, please keep them to yourselves, at least until we are pushing for the play offs and beyond.

NOLI CEDERE, NOLI SEMPER CEDERE
STAGNI OLLAM ET SUPERBUS
MELIUS DIABOLUM
TOWN, TEAM, TOGETHER

PART THREE

EPILOGUE

Having read this book please talk the seasons over with your friends and family, who are also red at heart, and see if you can agree on your choice of seasons that out rivals the others in your hearts and minds. If you aren't a Red Devil and perhaps a supporter of AFC or MK, please accept this book for what it is, an attempt to look at football at our current level and realise that rivalry should only really be about the individual games played and just for the 90 plus minutes they last for.

When I was much, much younger I didn't always feel that way but now I am older and wiser I enjoy talking to opposition fans before and after games. There is more that unites us than divides us and when it boils down to it, the one thing we should all admit to is our love of football and the realisation that we all belong to the wider football family regardless of our gender, ethnic background, political persuasion or religious loyalty.

PART FOUR

APPENDIX

They played for both (whether it be for CTFC and one of Wimbledon, AFC Wimbledon or MK Dons)

CRAWLEY TOWN	WIMBLEDON	AFC WIMBLEDON	MK DONS
Charlie Ademeno		Charlie Ademeno	
Gary Alexander		Gary Alexander	
Kwesi Appiah		Kwesi Appiah	
Chris Arthur		Chris Arthur	
Jason Banton			Jason Banton
Tyrone Barnett		Tyrone Barnett	
Ashley Bayes		Ashley Bayes	
Andre Blackman		Andre Blackman	
Jeff Bryant	Jeff Bryant		
Dannie Bulman		Dannie Bulman	
Mustapha Carayol			Mustapha Carayol
Darius Charles		Darius Charles	
W Cummings		W Cummings	
Kieran Djilali		Kieran Djilali	

CRAWLEY TOWN	WIMBLE DON	AFC WIMBLE DON	MK DONS
Peter Fear	Peter Fear		
Paul Fishenden	Paul Fishenden		
George Francomb		George Francomb	
Gareth Graham		Gareth Graham	
Mitch Hancox			Mitch Hancox
Martin Hayes	Martin Hayes		
Neil Jenkins	Neil Jenkins		
Ben Judge		Ben Judge	
Andy Little		Andy Little	
C MacDonald			C MacDonald
Kyle McFadzean			K McFadzean
Izale McLeod			Izale McLeod
Filipe Morais			Filipe Morais
Dean Morgan			Dean Morgan
Rhys Murphy		Rhys Murphy	
Bondz N'Gala			Bondz N'Gala
Ollie Palmer		Ollie Palmer	
Dominic Poleon		Dominic Poleon	
Daniel Powell			Daniel Powell
Ryan Sandford		Ryan Sandford	

CRAWLEY TOWN	WIMBLEDON	AFC WIMBLEDON	MK DONS
Brian Sparrow	Brian Sparrow		
F Sutherland		F Sutherland	
James Tilley		James Tilley	
Matt Tubbs		Matt Tubbs	
A Wordsworth		A Wordsworth	
Kelly Youga		Kelly Youga	
Moved between clubs since June 2024			
L Maguire			L Maguire
R. Hepburn-Murphy			R. Hepburn-Murphy
Danilo Orsi		Danilo Orsi	Danilo Orsi
Kabi Tshimanga			Kabi Tshimanga
Liam Kelly			Liam Kelly

CRAWLEY TOWN GOALSCORERS VS WIMBLEDON FC
1 goal
Ernie Healer, Roy Jennings, Bobby Finch, Dave Hannam, Brian Knight, Dave Haining

CRAWLEY TOWN CLEAN SHEETS VS WIMBLEDON FC
John Maggs 3, one in 1964/65 and two in 1969/70

MOST SUCCESSFUL CRAWLEY TOWN MANAGERS VS WIMBLEDON FC
Fred Cook 2 wins (1x Southern League, 1x Premier Midweek Floodlit League

CRAWLEY TOWN GOALSCORERS VS AFC WIMBLEDON
4 goals
Matt Tubbs
2 goals
Dannie Bulman, Ashley Nadesan, Jefferson Louis, Danny Forrest
1 goal
Ronan Dracy, Rushian Hepburn-Murphy, Josh Flint, Danilo Orsi, Will Wright, Jack Powell, Max Watters, Gwion Edwards, Gary Alexander, Claude Davis, Hope Akpan, Sergio Torres, Kyle McFadzean, James Dance, Charles Ademeno

CRAWLEY TOWN CLEAN SHEETS VS AFC WIMBLEDON
Only Corey Addai has been able to keep a clean sheet against AFC, in fact he kept two in successive league away matches.

MOST SUCCESSFUL CRAWLEY TOWN MANAGERS VS AFC WIMBLEDON
Steve Evans, 3 wins League (2x Conference National/1x League 2 the latter remained as CTFC's biggest away win since promotion to the Football League until Newport away in 2023/24 and a certain playoff semifinal in the same year. It was also the first time the sides had met in the Football League)
1 win League Cup
Scott Lindsey 2 wins League 2
John Yems

1 win FA Cup (this match signified AFCs' first-ever defeat at their new ground.)
Robbie Elliott 1 loss EFL Trophy

CRAWLEY TOWN GOALSCORERS VS MK DONS
4 goals
Danilo Orsi
2 goals
Billy Clark, Izale McLeod, Jay Williams
1 goal
Ronan Darcy, Andy Drury, Mike Jones, Liam Kelly, Jack Roles, Nick Tsaroulla, Ade Adeyemo

CRAWLEY TOWN CLEAN SHEETS VS MK DONS
Paul Jones had three in 2012/2013 (2) and 2013/2014(1) and Corey Addai had one in the home leg of the 2023/24 League 2 Playoff semifinal.

MOST SUCCESSFUL CRAWLEY TOWN MANAGERS VS MK DONS
Scott Lindsey, 3 wins including one in League and two in 2023/24 play offs featuring Crawley Town's biggest away win as a Football League club, one draw and one loss

Richie Barker	1 win and 1 draw
John Gregory	1 win and 2 losses
Dean Saunders	1 draw
Gaby Cioffi	2 losses

PART FIVE
PHOTO GALLERY

The 1968-69 Promotion winning team. Back row: Tony Goodgame, John Leedham, Derek Leck, John Maggs, Colin Blaber, Dave Cockell, Eddie McMullen, Stan March. Front row: Phil Basey, Dave Haining, Vic Bragg, John Standing, Derek Tharme.

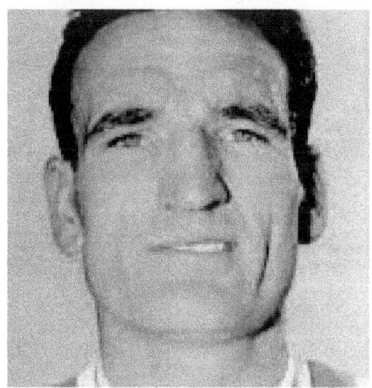

ROY JENNINGS, in his Tesco Shopping bag shirt, before becoming the best penalty taker I have ever seen and managing Crawley Town to promotion in 1968/69.

Stan Markham, exhibiting his knack with the mower on the wonderfully pristine Town Mead pitch

The 1983/84 promotion winning team

Can you name them?

The 1983/84 team, can you name the ground?

FRANCIS VINES
Manager of the 2003/2004 Championship winning team

The 2003/2004 triple winning team
Southern League Champions, Southern League Cup winners
and Southern League Trophy winners

Steve "Marmite" Evans (I like Marmite!)
The manager who took Crawley Town into the Football League

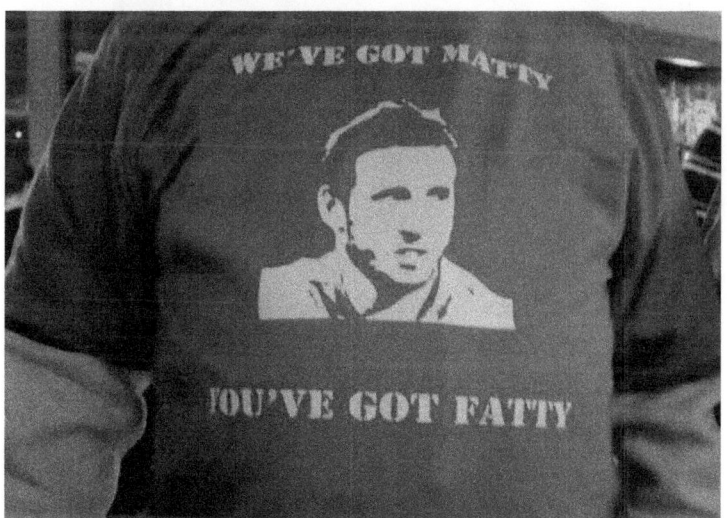

AFC making the most of Danny Kedwell's bad decision making and Crawley fans seeing the other side of the story.

Promotion celebrations as Conference champions at Tamworth

SCOTT NEILSON SEALS PROMOTION
TO LEAGUE 1, 2012

LEGENDS AND FRIENDS WEARING THE WRONG COLOURED SHIRTS

IN SCOTT WE TRUST!!!

ONE TO TELL THE GREAT GRAND KIDS ABOUT

Rob Elliott, at the start of his reign, hence the smile!!

IN SCOTT WE TRUST, PART TWO

"Another of our Jedi lured to the Dark Side" credit Ivan Noel

"I remember Obi Wan Kenobi referencing Plough Lane in one of the original movies" credit Ivan Noel

Imagination needed here. It was hoped to have a picture of Obi Wan Kenobi talking to Luke Skywalker saying the immortal words:
"You will never find a more wretched hive of scum and villainy" as he warns him of going to the Borough of Merton.

Alas, I don't want to have another pending court case because of a possible copyright infringement, so you will have to watch the film.

THE END